D1474089

Market Making and the Changing Structure of the Securities Industry

**Lexington Books/Salomon Brothers Center
Series on Financial Institutions and Markets**

The Deregulation of the Banking and Securities Industry
Edited by Lawrence G. Goldberg and Lawrence J. White

Exchange Risk and Exposure
Edited by Richard M. Levich and Clas G. Wihlborg

Securities Activities of Commercial Banks
Edited by Arnold W. Sametz

Mergers and Acquisitions
Edited by Michael Keenan and Lawrence J. White

Crises in the Economic and Financial Structure
Edited by Paul Wachtel

Option Pricing
Edited by Menachem Brenner

Financing and Investing in Hi-Tech
Edited by Fred B. Renwick

The Emerging Financial Industry
Edited by Arnold W. Sametz

**Market Making and the Changing Structure
of the Securities Industry**
Edited by Yakov Amihud, Thomas S.Y. Ho,
and Robert A. Schwartz

Market Making and the Changing Structure of the Securities Industry

Yakov Amihud
New York University and
Tel Aviv University

Thomas S.Y. Ho
New York University

Robert A. Schwartz
New York University

Lexington Books
D.C. Heath and Company/Lexington, Massachusetts/Toronto

Library of Congress Cataloging in Publication Data

Main entry under title:

Market making and the changing structure of the securities industry.

    Includes index.
      1. Stock-exchange—United States—Addresses, essays, lectures. 2. Stock-exchange—Law
and legislation—United States—Addresses, essays, lectures. 3. Securities—United
States—Addresses, essays, lectures. I. Amihud, Yakov, 1947–   . II. Ho, Thomas S.Y.
III. Schwartz, Robert A. (Robert Alan), 1937–
HG4910.M345   1985   332.64′ 273   83-48658
ISBN 0-669-07335-0 (alk. paper)

Published simultaneously in Canada
Printed in the United States of America on acid-free paper
International Standard Book Number: 0-669-07335-0
Library of Congress Catalog Card Number: 83–48658

Contents

Part II   Market and Regulatory Structure   117

Part III   Trading Systems and Automation   215

List of Figures and Tables

Figures

Tables

Foreword

The Securities Acts Amendments of 1975 broke the U.S. securities markets loose from structural moorings that had held for almost two centuries. A collection of autonomous markets was, by government fiat, to be transformed in some unspecified way into a national market system for which there was no design. The act laid out only a few guidelines for carrying out its mandate to foster competition in securities trading.

Many people in the securities industry thought they had been handed a recipe for chaos. In the years that followed, however, the individual markets—working together with their member firms and with the SEC—have evolved, and are still evolving, into a more competitive, stronger, and more innovative industry.

This book steps back to assess developments in this watershed period in securities-market history. Specifically, it focuses on the period from January 1977 to May 1984. This interval holds personal significance for me in that it spans all but a few months of my tenure as chairman of the board and chief executive officer (CEO) of the New York Stock Exchange (NYSE). In that position and as a public member of the Exchange's board of directors before then, I was an active participant in the flow of securities-industry events.

From the perspective of this front-line veteran, this compendium is a major contribution to the growing literature on securities-market structure. It not only recounts developments, but also places them in the broader framework of the theoretical and practical issues involved in market design and the regulatory structure. The book also provides some visions of how securities trading and the markets may be reshaped in the future by new electronic systems.

The success of this project is due to the astute selection of contributors—a mix of leading theoreticians and expert practitioners. Most of them I know personally; many of them I have worked with and hold in high esteem. All of them have well-regarded reputations.

Their contributions should be valuable both to students of the securities industry who want a theoretical backdrop to industry developments, and to the more general reader who wants to get a perspective on recent—and possible future—industry changes.

William Batten

Acknowledgments

This book and the conference that preceded it, have benefited substantially from the assistance of many people. In particular, we thank Arnold Sametz, Director of the Salomon Brothers Center, and Jeffrey Schaefer, Director of Research of the Securities Industry Association. We also thank Ligija Roze and Douglas Harvey of the Salomon Brothers Center, as well as Christine Schwartz; it would be difficult to envision the completion of this project without their extensive support. Lastly, we are indebted to John Teal, one of our doctoral students at the Graduate Business School, for his help in preparing the manuscript.

1
Overview of the Changing Securities Markets

Yakov Amihud
Thomas S.Y. Ho
Robert A. Schwartz

I n May 1984, a two-day conference on market making and the changing
structure of the securities industry was held at New York University's
Salomon Brothers Center for the Study of Financial Institutions. This
book is comprised of the papers presented at that conference. Its purpose
is to assess major developments in the structure of the U.S. security markets.
The key question is: Has the industry achieved the structure needed to meet
the technical, competitive, and regulatory challenges that lie ahead?

Once before, in January 1977, the Salomon Brothers Center sponsored a
conference that dealt with the evolving nature of the security markets.[1] Since
then, many changes have occurred. We have learned a great deal and made
sizable advances on several fronts. Now it is time to step back once again and
to assess the broader picture.

Intermarket Linkages and Intermarket Competition

In 1977 attention focused on the structure of the exchanges and on their
evolution into a national market system. Much importance was—and still
is—given to two issues: (1) integration of the various exchanges and the over-
the-counter (OTC) markets, and (2) promotion of competition in the industry.
By instituting appropriate intermarket linkages and by removing anticompetitive barriers, many felt the industry could improve its economic efficiency;
achieve greater fairness in competition between brokers, dealers, and market
centers; and realize a broader, more timely dissemination of information on
market conditions.

With regard to the first goal, two changes that occurred after 1977 have
done much to develop the intermarket linkages that were sought. The first
was the introduction in 1978 of the Consolidated Quotation System (CQS).

CQS now sends current trading price, quotation, and other market information to data vendors for display on various CRT systems throughout the country. The second was the introduction in 1978 of the Intermarket Trading System (ITS), which now electronically connects the trading floors of the two national and five regional exchanges. For some securities, ITS is also linked to the National Association of Securities Dealers (NASD) Computer Assisted Execution System (CAES). Without a doubt, the various market centers are now far more effectively joined together in an integrated network than they had been before.

Less apparent, however, have been changes on the second front: the promotion of competition between market centers. Of course, the ITS linkages themselves put the national and regional exchanges in direct competition for the order flow for cross-listed securities. With regard to competition, however, the Securities and Exchange Commission (SEC) and others had more in mind than this: They wished to remove the competitive restraint they saw in NYSE Rule 390 and AMEX Rule 5, rules that prohibit off-board trading on listed stocks by member firms. To this end, the SEC introduced Rule 19c.3, which, effective July 18, 1980, allows member firms to trade off-board all stocks listed after April 26, 1979. Further, to bolster competition between market makers within the exchange system, the NYSE has experimented with a system of competing specialists, and a few stocks have been cross-listed on the NYSE and the American Stock Exchange (AMEX). None of these experiments has met with success.

Immediately after Rule 19c.3 became effective, Merrill-Lynch, Bache, and a few other brokerage houses started making markets in what came to be known as 19c.3 stocks. For three years the SEC monitored the experiment, invited opinions about off-board trading, and considered various order exposure rules for the in-house markets. While the SEC pondered, by the summer of 1983 the brokerage firms had all ceased their 19c.3 operations.

Did the foray into in-house market making come to a halt because the operation is inherently unprofitable? Did the design of the experiment doom it to failure? Did the stock exchange specialists have more firepower, and so win the war? To an extent, the answer to each question is "yes." It may well be that the three yeses together caused Merrill, Bache, and the others to pull out. In any case, knowing why the experiment failed would tell us much about the nature of competition in the security markets. It is for this reason that a number of the chapters of this book discuss the 19c.3 experiment.

Competing specialists lasted for a while on the NYSE, and then that experiment also ended, as did the cross-listing of stocks between the AMEX and the NYSE. With regard to both in-house executions and on-board trading, the power of a single specialist to make the market for listed securities appears to be unbreakable. This impression is reinforced by the observation that, despite clear advances in the operating efficiency of ITS,[2] and a sharp increase in the volume of ITS transactions,[3] over 80 percent of the share volume and over 85 percent of the dollar volume of exchange trading still occurred on the floor of the NYSE.[4]

Apparently, for equity markets, what has been observed in the past continues to hold: Order flow attracts order flow.

System Development and New Product

In the past few years other issues have grown in importance relative to national market system matters, such as the development of intermarket linkages and intermarket competition. These include: (1) the major advances in the OTC markets; (2) the introduction and rapid expansion of trading in new financial instruments (in particular, options and futures contracts on market indexes); and (3) the continuing efforts to adapt computer technology to the needs of the trading floor.

Market Design

The introduction of the NASD's automated quotations system (commonly known as NASDAQ), has changed the fundamental structure of the OTC market. NASDAQ allows multiple market makers in diverse geographic locations to reveal their quotations to each other and to the public on a real-time basis. Such electronic interaction allows many dealers to compete for the order flow without an exchange floor.

Two technological developments with respect to NASDAQ affect market structure: the linkage of NASDAQ and the Intermarket Trading System (ITS), and the introduction of the Computer Assisted Execution System (CAES). Linking NASDAQ to ITS allows some of the OTC stocks to gain access to other market centers. Currently, there are over five hundred stocks whose quotations are readily available to any participant in ITS. CAES allows the NASDAQ market makers to execute their orders automatically. Although CAES is still in a developmental stage, it is expected to have increasing importance as an automatic order-routing, trade execution, and reporting system for NASDAQ National Market System (NMS) securities.[5]

The difference between the OTC market and the exchange-based market is not a simple distinction between a multiple dealer and a monopolistic dealer market. It also involves differences in the rules and principles of various self-regulatory agencies. For instance, OTC market makers can choose almost at will the stocks they wish to trade, which is not the case for a specialist on an exchange. Because of this, OTC market makers have greater flexibility in selecting the way they specialize in the market-making process. Some firms, for instance, have recently specialized in foreign issues; others have specialized in trading whenever there are trading halts on the exchanges.

There are other differences between the exchanges and the OTC markets. For one thing, OTC dealers are not constrained by the elaborate system of trading rules and market surveillance that regulates the specialists' operations. Further, market makers in the OTC are in direct contact with customers (or their agents), who originate orders by telephone. This access to the transacting public gives the dealers additional information on market conditions; such information in turn allows these market makers to provide greater liquidity to the public. Also, the OTC market makers deal in both primary and secondary issues. This dual role gives these dealers an additional incentive to make good secondary markets: the profits realized in the primary market when a favorable position with a corporation is maintained. Accordingly, the OTC dealers typically also maintain close relationships with corporate management. In contrast, specialists in the agency auction markets are not allowed to interface directly with the transacting public, and they generally maintain guarded relationships with the corporations whose stocks they handle in order to avoid any appearance of being able to profit from inside information.

On the other hand, the flow of public orders (most important, public limit orders) is a far more important source of liquidity in the agency auction markets than in the OTC markets. This is because public limit orders are exposed in the auction markets, and because of the auction market principle that, when public and floor traders' limit orders are tied at a price, the public transacts first. The consolidation of the public order flow also provides an informational advantage that the OTC markets do not enjoy. These are some of the features that further differentiate the exchanges and the OTC market.

The most sought-after quality in markets is liquidity. Liquidity encompasses many characteristics: low trading costs, the accuracy of price adjustments to new information, price continuity, continuity of trading, depth, and the ease and speed of execution. Although recent developments have greatly increased the liquidity of the securities markets, much is still desired. When all is said and done, we are still in search of a market design that will best serve the needs of customers—both the investors and the corporations whose securities are traded.

New Product

Another major development in the financial markets is the proliferation of new product. In just the last two years, the exchanges have introduced futures and options on stock indexes, interest-rate options, interest-rate futures, exchange-rate options, and commodity options. In the near future, we will no doubt see the introduction of more options and futures on various indexes. These new products have generated much interest on the part of the public, and their impact on the marketplace has been profound. The new-product market now represents a significant sector of the securities industry.

With this development, market professionals confront a new challenge. Market making in these new products differs in many ways from traditional market making. Because the new products are contingent claims on an underlying asset, their prices should follow some pricing relationship with the underlying asset prices. However, the contingent claims and the underlying assets are traded in different market centers, which function differently with respect to price formation.

In each market center, transaction prices reflect the contemporaneous supply and demand of the instruments that are traded in that locality. Yet transaction prices across the markets are not independently determined. This is because traders away from the market centers (for example, the so-called upstairs traders) integrate information from these markets and exploit arbitrage opportunities when underlying pricing relationships are violated. The ability of these traders to arbitrage effectively between markets depends on the quality of information they can obtain and on the efficiency with which their orders may be transmitted to the markets.

Whenever there are multiple related market centers, upstairs trading links the markets and thus is an integral part of the price formation process. Because linkages between the different market centers are especially crucial for the simultaneous trading of the contingent claims and the underlying assets, the introduction of new product has heightened the significance of upstairs trading. For market designers, it is important to understand the economic value of these linkages. The key questions are: In what sense might the linkages increase market efficiency? How do they affect price performance in each market? What is the role of market makers on exchanges with market linkages? In what ways do the upstairs traders compete with the floor traders, and with each other?

The Increasing Use of Computer Technology

Striking advances have been made in adapting computer technology to the trading floor and to the OTC markets. These advances have related primarily to information dissemination and display (for example, ITS and CQS for the exchanges, an improved NASDAQ system and CAES for the OTC markets) and to economizing on paperwork and processing costs associated with order handling and routing (for example, DOT, the NYSE's Designated Order Turnaround system; and OARS, the NYSE's Opening Automated Report Service).

Beyond the information and order handling/routing procedures, there have been relatively minor but continuing efforts to develop an electronic system that also gives trade execution. The Cincinnati Exchange is, of course, a computerized system, as is the Computer Assisted Trading System (CATS) first introduced on the Toronto Stock Exchange and later adapted for use by the Tokyo Stock Exchange. In addition, there is Intex, the electronic futures market that operates from a computer located in Bermuda, and Instinet, through which orders can be executed directly between parties.

Despite these developments and the inherent power of electronic technology, traders have remained wary of operating in a computerized system, especially with regard to equity orders in the major trading arenas. By and large, computerized trading has been successful only for markets comprising small orders and/or those that play off prices set in a primary market that is not computerized (for example, the Cincinnati Exchange, which operates within a context provided by the NYSE). The explanation may well be multifaceted: the aversion of market professionals to computerized trading (explained by the fact that the computer might take away some special advantage the professionals enjoy in our current system); the innate reluctance of the professionals to adapt to a radically different system; and, ultimately, the fact that, given the economic complexities of trading, we have not yet learned how best to structure a computerized system.

Challenges for the Future

The industry today faces three challenges. First, each trading arena will be challenged to keep its technology expanding faster than the demands made by an ever-increasing order flow. Second, and on the other hand, each trading arena will be challenged to preserve its order flow in the face of competition from other market centers. Finally, from a macro viewpoint, there is the challenge of regulating the industry so as to achieve a desirable competitive structure and to ensure the institution of appropriate technology. None of these challenges is new, but in certain ways each is keener now than it has been in the past.

Keeping Technology Ahead of the Order Flow

In 1977 the average daily trading volume on the NYSE was 20.9 million shares. In 1982 the average daily volume had increased to 65 million shares. August 18, 1982, was the first 100-million-share day in NYSE history. On the peak volume day in 1983, 129 million shares were traded; on August 3, 1984, over 236 million shares were traded. The very next trading day, volume was 203 million. The exchange is now thinking ahead to peak volume days of 300 million shares and more.

The sheer *size* of the order flow is one cause of concern; the *source* of the order flow may well be another. Again, the power and impact of institutional trading are emerging as important issues. Is there a move toward greater concentration in the brokerage industry? Toward greater market power on the part of the large traders? What demands will the unique needs of the large traders place on system design? Once again an old question is being raised by those who were never truly satisfied by the answers they received in the past: Is institutional trading a stabilizing or a destabilizing force in the market? On this point, perhaps only your market maker will ever know for sure.

Up to now the NYSE has handled the soaring order flow with facility. Meeting the first 100-million-plus day with a steady hand was a stunning accomplishment. The exchange succeeded because it saw the challenge coming, planned wisely to meet it, and had its systems (in large part DOT and OARS) in place when the volume peaked.

Will a super-DOT and a super-OARS be able to handle a daily volume of 300 to 400 million shares? What about the 500-million-share day that may be lying further down the road? Is there some outside limit to what a basically labor-intensive trading system can handle? Will we forever be able to push back the outer envelope of our current system? If not, what global change should be made, and how?

At this point, we will make only one observation. With more effectiveness than the regulators in Washington might ever have, and with a greater impact than might be expected from the forces of competition, it may well turn out to be the growth of the order flow that propels the security markets toward a new technology. To a modest extent, we have already seen this. CATS, the automated system currently in use on the Toronto and Tokyo exchanges, was instituted by both these exchanges for just one reason: They were running out of space on the trading floor.

Competition from Other Market Centers

Although the aggregate order flow might be increasing sharply, the order flow going to any individual market center might just as dramatically plummet. The reason is threefold. First, with the new electronic access systems, the various market centers have become close substitutes for one another for many investors. Second, when the public order flow starts to move from one center to another, the process might accelerate because order flow does attract order flow. Third, if one system proves superior to another, listings will be shifted appropriately.

Competition between the market centers is expected to evolve along three fronts:

1. There will be competition between the national exchanges and the regionals.
2. There will be competition between the exchanges as a group and the rapidly developing OTC markets.
3. At some point in the future, equity trading will doubtless become far more international than it is today. Then there will be clear competition between the domestic and foreign trading systems.

To a large extent, in the recent past competition between the various market centers has focused on the development of new product. This was clearly the case with the AMEX's expansion into option trading and the NYSE's expansion into the futures market. Introducing new product is only part of the story, however. The NYSE, AMEX, and NASD have also made notable progress in upgrading their systems. This is very important. Ultimately, the contest between the various market centers will be won not only with the packaging of new financial instruments; also crucial is the design of the systems that handle the market centers' main line of business—trading.

Intermarket competition for the order flow and for the listings is a tough challenge for the individual trading centers. It is, however, most desirable for the markets as a whole. What may be a painful challenge for each part of the industry is, for all together, a great opportunity. At present the industry truly appears to be moving ahead because of the challenge of intermarket competition. Seven years ago, it was not.

A Challenge for the Regulators

Traditionally, the SEC has been primarily involved with enforcement, rather than with regulating the structure of markets. Only after Congress passed the Securities Act Amendments of 1975 and thereby mandated the development of a national market system was the SEC forced to consider broader structural issues. Since then much of the SEC's involvement with structural design has centered on off-board trading and the possible imposition of an order disclosure rule. Allowing or not allowing off-board trading is, of course, a moot issue to the extent that brokerage firms choose not to make in-house markets. As we have noted, currently there are no in-house markets.

Having come full circle on the 390/19c.3 issue, however, in no way implies that the SEC's efforts with regard to design governance were a failure. For one thing, the threat of removing Rule 390 undoubtedly prodded the industry into action on a number of fronts. One could certainly argue that the deterioration of the NYSE's former clublike aura, and the development of the current intermarket linkages, were both substantially accelerated by the SEC's anti-390 stance.

In addition, although off-board trading never got off the ground, the results of the experiment could prove informative. We all realize better now just how complex the industry is. Now, understanding why the experiment failed should provide useful insight into the nature of competition in the industry.

Furthermore, it is unrealistic to expect that the SEC or any other group could simply step forth and begin regulating the industry with regard to structural design by blindly following an economics text that extols the glories of free competition. In fact, the SEC never did so (although it threatened to).

Despite impatience from some members of Congress, criticism from certain parts of academia, and various pointed comments from the press, the SEC took its time. Wisely, it waited, invited opinions, and moved with caution.

Nonetheless, major questions remain. Neither the SEC nor any other force in the industry should sit back in the belief that we now have a national market system, and hence no further problems. On the contrary, there remain major design issues—from order exposure rules to electronic trading, from competition with international markets to the introduction of new financial instruments. With respect to each of these issues, regulators will be challenged to specify appropriately the rules of the game. Competition in the free market might be relied on to bid away excess profits; but competition alone does not assure that an industry will ever achieve, or even evolve toward, the most efficient competitive structure. To achieve the best possible trading system for the financial markets, we need discretionary planning. To get such planning, we must look to the regulators.

The Academic Literature

Over the years, economists have studied many markets. We know of no markets that have received the breadth or depth of analysis that the securities markets have received. Current interest in these markets started in the 1960s with the first formal analyses of the dealership function. The literature has now expanded into an important subfield in financial economics. Increasingly, this subfield has come to be known as the *microstructure of securities markets*.

The academic attention given to the securities markets may be attributed to three factors. First, these markets are of tremendous importance to our economy: the efficiency of the secondary markets is vital to the health of the primary markets; a substantial amount of the nation's financial wealth is invested in the shares that are traded in the secondary markets; and the secondary markets are, both directly and indirectly, a major source of employment. Second, a voluminous amount of data is generated by the industry and is available in machine-readable form; this has facilitated much empirical research. Third, by its very nature, the industry is intriguing to economists. Undeniably, the challenges the industry faces provide irresistible grist for the economist's theoretical mill.

Two factors in particular are the source of the theoretical interest: (1) More visibly than in most other markets, price determination is concomitant with the trading process itself, and (2) market prices are continuously subject to change with the ever-shifting forces of demand and supply. Thus a primary function of the trading arena is to locate the clearing prices at which people trade. In fact, finding "the price" is every bit as important as handling the trades. Realization of this fact helps many pieces of the puzzle fall into place.

To date, much of the microstructure literature has focused on the role of dealers and specialists in price determination. Each of the three of us has contributed to the literature in this area. The dealer/specialist function is not the only issue, however (a fact to which recent history well attests). Fortunately, along with the continuing evolution of the marketplace, microstructure analysis itself has also developed over the past seven years. More emphasis is being given today to the role public investors play in the price determination process. Also emerging is an understanding of how, given individual demand/supply propensities, both the order flow and the market clearing price depend on the design of the trading system.

Extending the microstructure literature along these and other lines is important, and we hope the current trend continues. Perhaps the various chapters of this book will give some of us academicians a useful prod.

Overview of This Book

This book is divided into three parts. The first focuses on fundamental economic issues concerning market design and operations. The second deals with actual market systems and regulatory structure. The third considers recent developments in trading systems and automation.

Issues in Market Design

The first four chapters in this section deal with major issues concerning market design. The concluding chapter provides a comprehensive view of the quality of the markets and of the change that is currently being experienced.

Schreiber and Schwartz focus first on the fact that the complex function of a securities market is not so much handling the trades in itself, but, rather, discovering the prices at which the trades are made. They argue that, with respect to equity trading, improving the efficiency of price discovery is both a meaningful and an operationally viable goal. Schreiber and Schwartz also point out that, nevertheless, this goal has been neither clearly recognized nor widely used in the debates concerning market design and regulation. To illustrate the issues involved, they consider the relevance of efficient price discovery to two recent regulatory debates: off-board trading and shelf registration.

Chapter 3 by Ho and Macris deals with another primary issue concerning market structure: the number of market makers who would make the market in a stock if entry were not restricted by regulation. Ho and Macris show how trading volume and the cost structure of dealers combine to determine the number of market makers for a stock. They examine the interrelationship between the number of market makers and the liquidity of a market. They also highlight the implications of their analysis for the design of market rules and regulations, and for market structure.

One of the most important aspects of the financial markets is the operations of the market makers—the dealers and specialists. As noted, microstructure analysis has its origins in the dealer-specialist literature. Chapter 4 by Stoll next surveys various alternative roles of the market maker that have been presented in this literature. These include the market maker as auctioneer, price stabilizer, information processor, and supplier of immediacy. While presenting theoretical analysis and empirical evidence on these market-maker functions, Stoll also provides implications for the design of the securities markets.

Another fundamental consideration in market design is the consolidation of the order flow. This is the primary focus of chapter 5 by Cohen, Conroy, and Maier. As noted earlier, the consolidation question has been central to much of the regulatory debates; Cohen, Conroy, and Maier review the issues involved and examine the effect of market fragmentation on various measures of market quality. In concluding that a consolidated market structure is generally superior, they advance the policy implication that effective consolidation may be achieved in the presence of spatially fragmented markets, if a communications system and appropriate trading priority rules are established across the markets.

Stone, in chapter 6, introduces the views of an experienced professional in—and architect of—the industry. His chapter highlights several major recent developments—the proliferation of electronic equipment and trading systems, the enhanced competition from different market centers, and the increased importance of institutional trading. A key point advanced by Stone is that, by and large, these developments have substantially improved the quality of the markets.

Market and Regulatory Structure

In part II attention turns to more specific issues concerning the actual structure of the markets and of the regulatory system. Chapters 7–10 deal with market structure, chapters 11–14 with the regulatory structure.

In chapter 7, Phelan presents a comprehensive view of the accelerating pace of technological and economic change over the past decade in the securities industry and at the New York Stock Exchange. He highlights the intensification of competition among the financial service institutions (primarily banks and securities firms), the growth of the order flow and introduction of new products, the challenges presented by the OTC and international competition, and the development of a cooperative regulatory structure based on industry self-regulation and government oversight. Although he points to two events of 1975—the elimination of fixed commissions and the congressional mandate to create a national market system—as major catalysts for change, Phelan reminds us that the future will no doubt continue to bring new technological and competitive challenges that we cannot anticipate today.

In recent years the OTC markets have grown to an importance that, internationally, is third only to that of the NYSE and to the Tokyo Stock Exchange. Chapter 8 by Wall considers the features of OTC trading through NASDAQ that have accounted for this success. While highlighting the crucial role played by the competitive multiple market-maker system, Wall predicts that, with continuing improvements in NASDAQ and the growing institution of electronic trading, the OTC's position and share of the market will continue to grow forcefully.

The points of view of two major types of participants in the securities markets are presented in chapters 9 and 10: arbitrageurs, and the so-called upstairs traders. Hunter, in chapter 9, provides an in-depth look at arbitrage trading, which spurred by the development of the markets for contingent claims, has increased substantially in recent years, in terms of both sophistication and importance. Hunter shows how, in searching for arbitrage opportunities across markets and across assets, arbitrageurs mitigate the problems of market fragmentation and, in so doing, also make the markets more liquid.

Chapter 10 by Falk focuses primarily on the increasing importance of the trading desk in the block-trading operations of the major brokerage firms. This change is attributed by Falk to evolving economic conditions (lower trading costs and more volatile markets) and to various technological and regulatory changes that have reduced the impediments to trading. Falk's discussion, which reflects the expanding size and sophistication of the trading room, highlights the growing importance of effective market operations in generating noncommission income.

The four chapters that deal with the regulatory structure all touch on one issue: the multiplicity of the structure. In chapter 11 Bloch directly addresses this structural question as it pertains to the securities markets; to this end, he draws heavily on the historical experience gained with regard to banking, an industry that now overlaps with the securities industry in a number of important respects. In his analysis of the dynamic adaptations of multiple regulators, Bloch shows how the multiple regulatory structure can be beneficial to—and therefore be demanded by—the regulated firms. Essentially, he argues that this structure creates a market that enables firms to select the regulatory environment best suiting their own needs and goals.

Chapter 12 by Scarff presents a professional regulator's look at how two federal agencies, the Securities and Exchange Commission (SEC), and the Commodities Futures Trading Commission (CFTC) jointly determined their jurisdictional authorities over securities markets, commodity markets, and the newly developing derivative markets (futures and options). During the 1970s the accelerating product convergence created confusion over whether the SEC or the CFTC (or both) had—or should have—regulatory jurisdiction over the new products. Against this background, Scarff recounts how in late 1981 the agencies addressed this jurisdictional uncertainty and reached an unprecedented interagency accord, subsequently codified in amendments to both the securities and the commodities laws. He also points out how the notable success in removing jurisdictional uncertainty has itself served to highlight the lack of progress in addressing differences in the regulatory schemes governing the two industries.

Phillips amplifies on this discussion in chapter 13, while also noting a number of important ways in which securities trading differs from futures trading. In addition, she provides further elaboration of Bloch's and Scarff's chapters by applying Stigler's and Peltzman's analyses of an industry's demand for regulation.

Chapter 14 by White considers some of these same structural issues concerning regulation from the viewpoint of the economics of industrial organization. White highlights the need to analyze cases in which regulatory goals conflict, to assess the proposition that dual regulation is desirable, and to resolve the issue of market allocation between regulators.

Trading Systems and Automation

Our current trading systems are the product of many decades of evolution. In the past seven years the process of change has accelerated dramatically, with the changing economic and regulatory environment and with the introduction of electronic technology. The chapters in part III consider recent history and current systems design, with much emphasis on the use of automation in the trading systems.

In chapter 15 Amihud and Mendelson outline a proposition for a computerized trading system that will integrate and interface three subsystems: (1) an information system involving communication and data display; (2) an individual portfolio management system, which can be made automatically contingent on the information system; and (3) an order execution and exchange system. This last will include two alternative forms of exchange: a continuous open auction (dealer) market, and periodic clearings through a clearinghouse, which will take place a number of times a day, providing less costly trading. Amihud and Mendelson suggest that it be left for competition and market forces to determine the allocation of orders between these two trading mechanisms.

Chapter 16 by Whitcomb next presents a comprehensive international comparison of alternative stock exchange trading systems. Emphasis is given to features such as information dissemination and order handling procedures, stabilization procedures, and the use of electronic equipment. Although the largest exchanges internationally use a continuous trading system (as we do in the United States), many exchanges alternatively have a call market procedure where orders are batched for periodic execution at a single price; some exchanges use a blend of the two systems. In presenting the alternatives, Whitcomb reminds us that, although the U.S. markets are of high quality, viable alternatives do exist; we should not be myopic in our thinking. Furthermore, understanding the various systems used around the world will become more important as equity trading becomes more international.

Chapter 17 by Williams focuses more specifically on new developments in the U.S. securities markets as the industry evolves toward the national market system mandated by Congress in the 1975 Securities Acts Amendments. After reviewing the historical origins of the concept of a national market system, Williams summarizes the congressional goals that were set forth and describes the systems that have been instituted to satisfy them. He concludes by identifying likely future developments in systems design.

Chapters 18 and 19, by Davis and by Marshall and Carlson, consider more specifically various electronic trading systems that are currently in place. Davis discusses the Intermarket Trading System and the Cincinnati experiment (the computerized exchange that offers an electronic open-limit order book). The relative success of ITS, the difficulties faced by the Cincinnati Exchange, and the failure of both systems to attract substantial order flow from the major exchanges are analyzed in order to obtain guidance for the future.

Marshall and Carlson survey a wider array of electronic systems that have been instituted by the national and regional exchanges to service their own needs, as well as systems such as ITS that have been instituted to fulfill the demands of the regulators. These authors advance the thesis that a system will not be truly viable from an economic viewpoint unless it is developed in response to the market—in particular, to the users' needs.

Smidt then focuses in chapter 20 on the process of change itself. He points out that, rather than introducing competition so as to achieve a national market system, the national market system should itself be instituted as a means of appropriately strengthening the forces of competition. Stating the problem in this fashion leads Smidt to consider why the natural forces of competition may not themselves result in the institution of the most efficient trading systems. His answer highlights the problem of inertia (resistance of market professionals to technological change) and the difficulty of changing a complex technology all at once, rather than incrementally.

The concluding chapter in this book conveys the excitement of the brave new world toward which we are heading. As a seasoned professional, and as a pioneer in the adaptation of computer technology, Lupien directs our thoughts to two developments on the horizon. The first is the enormous potential for growth being opened up by the personal computer and systems that will give a broad spectrum of traders direct access to the market centers. The second, also being made feasible by today's computer technology, is the internationalization of the securities markets—a development that Lupien predicts will occur at a very rapid pace.

Notes

1. The papers presented at the 1977 conference are contained in *Impending Changes for Securities Markets: What Role for the Exchange?*, E. Bloch and R. Schwartz, eds., JAI Press, 1979.

2. The average turnaround time for placing an order in the ITS system and receiving a confirmation of trade was 37 seconds as of the end of 1982.

3. In 1982, ITS share volume increased by 52% while the consolidated tape volume rose by 40% (see the NYSE 1983 Fact Book).

4. See the NYSE 1983 Fact Book.

5. See the NASD 1982 Annual Report.

Part I
Issues in Market Design

2
Efficient Price Discovery in a Securities Market: The Objective of a Trading System

Paul S. Schreiber
Robert A. Schwartz

T he complexities of the securities markets do not pertain primarily to the process of physically matching buy and sell orders; rather, they are a manifestation of the difficulties involved in finding the prices at which trades should be made. This chapter focuses on price discovery as a primary function of a securities market. We suggest that, with regard to market design and regulation, increasing the efficiency of price discovery is an empirically measurable and operationally viable goal.

Here we give primary attention to the importance of efficient price discovery as a regulatory goal with respect to securities markets.[1] To this end, we briefly review the evolving focus of regulatory attention and, in light of the efficiency of price discovery, assess two recent regulatory issues: off-board trading and shelf registration.

The primary goals of regulation are as follows:

1. Assure a *fair and honest market*; that is, guard against manipulation of prices, trading volume, or information, and preclude abuses of position by professionals and insiders.
2. Increase *competitive efficiency* with regard to the provision and pricing of broker/dealer services; that is, keep bid-ask spreads, commissions, and other transaction costs at competitive levels.
3. Improve *market efficiency* with regard to the market's architecture as it affects the quality of prices established for shares that are traded.

The three regulatory objectives, though largely distinct from one another, are in many respects mutually consistent, and policy designed with regard to any one of them may be expected, to some extent, to affect the other two favorably. There are exceptions, however:

Greater competition between dealers and market centers, which will reduce commissions and tighten spreads, can fragment the order flow, which can result in trades occurring at prices that do not properly reflect overall supply-demand conditions.

Requiring that quotes be exposed on a consolidated system, which will facilitate price monitoring and tighten the inside spread, could put off-board market makers at a competitive disadvantage, which may result in bigger dealer spreads and an inflation of other transaction costs.

Prohibitions on trading based on inside information (which are intended to safeguard honesty and fairness) keep potential buyers and sellers out of the market, which delays the impact of new information on stock prices.

The imposition of trading halts, to stabilize the market and for reasons of fairness, also delays access to the market and thus, for some traders, represents a market inefficiency.

Given these and other trade-offs involved, and the fact that each regulatory objective is distinct, the overall impact of regulation will depend on which of the three goals is foremost in the minds of the regulators.[2] To date, the price-discovery objective has been the least considered of the three. In several respects this goal is the most difficult to attain, but it should not be overlooked. The first two objectives do not delineate adequately the attributes of the securities markets that make these markets unique, and they alone will give insufficient direction to the policymakers.

As the securities and commodity markets have increasingly overlapped, it is interesting to note that the importance of price discovery (and its derivative, price basing) has been a matter of direct regulatory review and consideration by the SEC's sister agency, the Commodity Futures Trading Commission (CFTC). Indeed, in determining whether or not to approve the trading of a new contract (or the establishment of a new market), one of the economic criteria the CFTC considers is the importance of that new contract (or market) to the quality of pricing in the cash market for the underlying commodity.[3] This interdependency of markets with regard to efficient pricing underscores the importance of efficient price discovery as a regulatory goal.[4]

This chapter is organized as follows. In the next section we discuss the price-discovery process. We first distinguish market clearing prices (which must be discovered in a market context) from intrinsic values (which are established outside the market in question). Next we assess the importance of the price-discovery process, and then consider the relationship between the efficiency of price discovery and the liquidity of a market. In the following section we review recent regulatory experience and examine in some detail two recent regulatory issues: off-board trading (NYSE Rule 390 versus SEC Rule 19c.3) and shelf registration (SEC Rule 415). A concluding section follows.

Trading and the Price-Discovery Process

Market Clearing Prices versus Intrinsic Values

Economists, lawyers, and others concerned with market systems generally believe that prices established on active markets properly reflect the balance of supply and demand. However, as a number of recent studies have indicated,[5] when trading costs (commissions, taxes, spreads, and the time and effort required to structure optimal trading strategies) impede the flow of orders to the market, and when instability of investor demand causes market clearing prices to be continuously subject to change, orders that are written depend on the prices at which investors expect to trade. As a result, transaction prices (which are based on the order flow), generally differ from equilibrium values that truly reflect the desire of all traders to hold shares of a stock. It is precisely for this reason that price discovery is an important function of a trading system.

Price discovery is requisite for a market, however, only if share prices are established within that market. When prices are established outside the market in which the shares are traded, the assets can be viewed as having an *intrinsic value*; then the market's role is solely to bring buyers and sellers together so that they may trade at prices that are reasonable in light of the intrinsic values. Such is the case with derivative pricing, as when one market (for example, the Cincinnati Exchange) operates within a context provided by another market (the NYSE). Similarly, if a set of assets can be objectively assessed as being in the same classification, then the price of each need not be independently discovered; such is the case for bonds that fall within the same risk/maturity class.

Do equity shares of IBM, General Motors, or other stock traded in the secondary markets, either on an exchange or OTC, have an intrinsic value? Security analysis, of course, is the process of determining what shares are worth in light of, for example, anticipated earnings, returns uncertainty, interest rate expectations, and the like. Clearly, good analysts do a good job of assessing a stock's value; in a good market, stocks trade at prices close to their underlying values. But are the underlying values intrinsic values? They are if, in assessing the information available to them, traders all derive the same expectations concerning the risk-return characteristics of various securities, and if, on the basis of their homogeneous expectations, they all group securities into equivalent risk-return classes. In this case the securities in each class would be perceived by the market as being perfect substitutes for each other. Hence market demand for each asset would be infinitely elastic at a price that could be discovered by objective analysis. Such a price could be considered an intrinsic value. The question then becomes: Do investors have homogeneous expectations, and do they therefore group securities in equivalent risk-return classes?

Much of the academic analysis in the investments literature has assumed that expectations are homogeneous.[6] This, however, has been largely for reasons of mathematical convenience; the assumption should not be blindly retained as a reasonable description of reality. Rather, even with a rich and widely available information set, stock advisory services rate various stocks differently,[7] and traders derive different expectations concerning a security's future price performance. Furthermore, evidence exists that some traders, on an ongoing basis, do outperform the market.[8] This would not be the case if expectations were homogeneous.

With heterogeneous expectations concerning a security's risk-return characteristics, to the extent that traders do not agree about how close any two stocks may be as substitutes for each other, and because traders in general have heterogeneous propensities to buy and to sell shares, market demand curves are downward sloping (that is, they are less than infinitely elastic).[9] When the demand curves to hold asset shares are downward sloping, prices on the secondary markets are set in the same way they are set for any other resource, good, or service: Be it diamonds, haircuts, or shares of ITT common, the market clearing price is the price that balances the aggregate of all buy/sell propensities. As a balancing mechanism, price reflects value on the margin. Because where the market is on the margin depends on the full array of buy/sell propensities, market clearing prices can be determined only within the market context. The fact that security analysts assess the value of a stock for their own portfolios does not imply that they undertake a treasure hunt to find some golden number which one might call an intrinsic value.[10] And, because stocks do not have intrinsic values, finding the market clearing price is a task which must be performed by the market's trading system. We have referred to this task as "the price discovery process." To the extent that this function is not performed perfectly, prices will deviate from their equilibrium values.

To illustrate the deviation of transaction prices from equilibrium values, let us consider the price history for a company called Liquidity Inc. (tape symbol, LIQ).[11] On the morning of March 28, 1984, we observed the following transactions for LIQ, along with the associated values of a market index:

Transaction price for LIQ:	45-1/4	45-1/4	45-1/2	46	45-1/2	45-3/8	45-5/8
Market index:	100	101	100	101	102	102	102.5
Time:	10:05	10:15	10:30	11:05	11:10	11:10	11:59

Five trading days later, on Sunday, April 1, LIQ closed at 47-1/4. At that time, the index was at 104.

We see that a price change for LIQ occurred on average every 17 minutes during the two-hour span on March 28. The average absolute price change was 27 cents, and the average price was 45-1/2. Interpreted as a rate of return, the average absolute return was 0.6 percent per 17 minutes. Ignoring compounding, 0.6 percent per 17 minutes is equivalent to 12.7 percent per six-hour trading day.

To put these seemingly innocuous brief-period price changes into perspective, consider an investor who, on buying a round lot of Liquidity Inc., expects to hold the shares for one year. By changing the timing of his order by as little as 17 minutes, the investor can on average alter the purchase price by 0.6 percent (plus or minus). If this same variability exists one year later, the investor's sell price would also be subject to a 0.6 percent variation over a 17 minute interval. This means that, when both buy and sell decisions are combined, if the investor were to buy this year at a relatively high price and to sell one year later at a relatively low price (within an equivalent two-hour interval), his return would be 1.2 percentage points less than the underlying price increase over the year. Alternatively, if he were to buy at a relatively low price this year and to sell at a relatively high price next year, the change in the timing of his order could add 1.2 percentage points to his realized return. Thus, if the investor expects the price of LIQ to grow by 12 percent over the year, a 17 minute change in the timing of his buy and sell orders would be likely to cause a 10 percent change (plus or minus) of the price appreciation expected over the entire one-year period.

What might account for brief-period price changes of this magnitude? It would appear implausible that either idiosyncratic liquidity changes, individual stock reassessments, or change in the publicly available information set could account for the succession of such large price changes.[12] Rather, these changes should also be attributed to the mechanics of the market: the bouncing of price between the bid and the ask quotations, the impact of new orders on a relatively sparse limit order book, and the dynamic process by which price finds a new equilibrium value after the advent of news.[13] In the short run, the last factor might be the most important of all; and, most important for the purpose of this analysis, it is a manifestation of the fact that price discovery is not an instantaneous process.

Importance of the Price-Discovery Process

If the buy/sell propensities of traders on a secondary market were sufficiently stable over time, the efficiency of the price-discovery process would not be a critical issue. As is true for any reasonably flexible and competitive market, prices would rise or fall with the pressures of unsatisfied demand or supply until any buy/sell imbalance was eliminated. Traders would then have an opportunity to observe market clearing prices and to adjust their orders appropriately to them.

The price-discovery function is key to the efficient operation of the securities markets precisely because—far more than is the case for most other markets—the demand to hold shares is continuously subject to rapid and unexpected shifts. Hence, if price discovery itself is not rapid, actual prices may never catch up to their underlying but unobserved values. In that case, trades will generally be made at inappropriate prices, and the transaction prices will generally signal false information to the investment community and to the firms whose shares are being traded.

Price discovery would, of course, be instantaneous if trading in the secondary markets were costless. The reason is that in the frictionless environment of no transaction costs, traders would continuously transmit updated buy/sell orders to the market, and the market would in turn instantaneously aggregate the order functions and execute trades at theoretically desirable, market clearing prices. With incomplete order transmission and rapidly changing prices, however, investors must decide the specific price, size, and timing of the orders they reveal to the market. For instance, if a buyer thinks he might get a lower price, he might submit a larger buy order; or, if some seller feels price is temporarily depressed, he might either delay transmitting his order or else submit a limit order rather than a market order; and so forth.

The strategic decisions of an investor depend on three things: (1) the investor's underlying demand to hold shares; (2) market design (how orders are handled and the rules by which they are translated into trades);[14] and (3) floor information (transaction prices, quotes, volume, and other indications of current market conditions). Because the trading strategies depend on trader expectations of what the transaction prices will be and on how orders are handled in the market, it follows that the order flow itself depends on the operations of the trading system. With the price, size, and timing of orders being dependent on the system, however, then so too must be the transaction prices that are given by the system.[15] Thus on the aggregate level, when incomplete orders are transmitted to the market, realized transaction prices will in general differ from their underlying equilibrium values; this difference also will depend on the design of the market and on the quality of floor information.

Ho, Schwartz, and Whitcomb (1985) have modeled short-run price determination in a way that comprehends the price-discovery process; their analysis suggests that theoretically desirable equilibrium prices will not be found after any single round of trading.[16] In support of this, observation of trading suggests that price discovery is a process that works over time. In addition, various features of market design can best be understood in relation to the price-discovery process: the special opening procedures of the exchanges, the role of dealers and specialists,[17] and the extensive information systems that provide rapid dissemination of floor information. Furthermore, the empirical evidence clearly indicates that, following the arrival of new information, prices for different stocks adjust nonsynchronously, and hence that at least some price adjustments must be noninstantaneous.[18] This is in fact suggested by the price history reported earlier for Liquidity Inc. That is, the price movements for LIQ and for the market index are quite disparate over the two-hour interval on the morning of March 28; however, the two adjustments appear related to each other over the five-day interval (by April 1, the market index had risen 4 points to 104, and LIQ was trading 2 points higher at 47-1/4).

We conclude that price discovery is a primary function of the major equity markets. This is true because shares traded in these markets do not have intrinsic or derivative values, because investor demand propensities are not stable over time, and because trading is not a frictionless process. Recognition of this has profound importance for the development of regulatory policy concerning the structure of a trading system.

The Efficiency of Price Discovery and the Liquidity of a Market

The liquidity of an asset market is typically defined as the ease with which shares of an asset can be traded in that market. There are two dimensions to the ease of trading: the cost in terms of time and money for buyers and sellers to find each other, and the reasonableness of the prices at which trades can be made. With regard to the U.S. securities markets (where best market quotes are continuously posted and widely announced), most trades can be made almost instantly at any time the market is open (if a buyer is willing to transact at the market ask, or if a seller is willing to transact at the market bid). Therefore, only the second dimension of liquidity is of concern.

However, this second dimension of liquidity is of paramount concern. Traders dislike and tend to avoid markets where, because of inefficiency in the price-discovery process and inadequate information systems, poor executions are prevalent. Experience suggests this. Before it was well structured on the Chicago Board of Options Exchange (CBOE), AMEX, and other exchanges, option trading was not popular. Similarly, trading on the OTC was at a far lower level before the advent of and then recent improvements in NASDAQ. In addition, the opinion has been expressed that the reason for the relatively sparse public participation in trading on the Paris Bourse is that the French system gives poor price information to nonprofessional traders; these traders therefore receive undesirable executions. Likewise, international trading is currently relatively limited; this may be in part because the more restricted dissemination of floor information outside of domestic markets puts foreign traders at a competitive disadvantage.

There are three ways in which the reasonableness of price is related to liquidity:

1. To any individual investor, a position in an asset may be considered illiquid if price volatility causes insufficient certainty concerning the convertibility of that asset into cash.

2. To an investor who holds a substantial portion of a stock's outstanding shares, the position may be viewed as illiquid if that position cannot be altered without adversely affecting the stock's share price.
3. From a macro viewpoint, a market may be considered illiquid if actual prices do not conform sufficiently well to the market clearing values that would prevail if the market were frictionless. The magnitude of the deviations of actual prices from frictionless market values depends on (a) the size of bid-ask spreads,[19] and (b) the location of the spread with regard to the frictionless market price.[20]

We refer to the third aspect of liquidity as *market liquidity*. Substantively, it is quite different from the first two. That is, whereas the price-volatility and market-power aspects focus on the magnitude of price changes, the third aspect of liquidity relates to the accuracy of price discovery. For this reason, the third aspect should be of particular concern to market regulators: Whereas price volatility and the market power of some traders are to a large extent exogenously determined, the conformity of prices to equilibrium values can be affected by market design (see Schreiber and Schwartz 1984).

The three aspects of liquidity are not unrelated to each other. As noted earlier, short-run price volatility results in part from transaction prices bouncing between the bid and ask quotations, and from the market searching for, but never quite catching up with, the desired equilibrium price.[21] Similarly, price changes brought about by the arrival of large orders may be attributable in part to temporary market thinness (which, like the bid-ask spread, is a manifestation of trading friction and imperfect price discovery).

In some respects, however, the different aspects of liquidity can lead to contradictory assessments. Assume new information causes equilibrium share prices to change. From the viewpoint of any individual investor, rapid adjustments of actual prices to new equilibrium values may cause his or her own investment to appear less liquid (with respect to aspect 1). From the macro viewpoint, however, the rapid adjustments of actual price would indicate *greater* market liquidity (re aspect 3). Further, as suggested in note 20, a trade-off might exist between the percentage magnitude of the bid-ask spread and the closeness with which the spread is positioned around the desired, frictionless market equilibrium price. Because the different aspects of liquidity can lead to contradictory assessments, special attention should be paid to the particular measure of liquidity that is used in an empirical study of a market.

The percentage magnitude of the bid-ask spread is one standard measure. Another measure of liquidity is the so-called *liquidity ratio*, the value of shares traded per a 1 percent change in a stock's price.[22] The larger the ratio, the more liquid the market, according to this measure. The reason is that the measure presumably shows how many shares a market can absorb per a 1 percent price change; a greater ability to absorb orders is associated with a more liquid market. As we have noted, however, if new information causes equilibrium prices to change, the transaction prices should change; in fact, the *fewer* the number of shares that trade before the new equilibrium price is reached, the *more* efficient is the market. Thus, with regard to information-ally motivated trading, the greater the market liquidity of a trading system, the smaller (not larger) will the ratio be.

The liquidity ratio is limited because it focuses on the instability of prices rather than on the relationship between actual prices and underlying equilibrium values. The bid-ask spread alone yields limited information because it reflects only part of the deviation of transaction prices from desired prices. Since equilibrium values are not directly observable, however, it might appear that market liquidity, as defined here, is not measurable. Fortunately, this is not necessarily the case. In brief, the closeness with which actual prices conform to unobservable equilibrium values can be inferred by assessing a stock's price movements in relation to change in the underlying economic factors that generate the price movements. These factors can be represented by change in a market index. More specifically, this empirical approach would be based on the following.

When data for monthly or longer intervals are used to measure price changes (returns), it has been widely observed that returns for individual securities are systematically related to change in the market index.[23] The stock return-market index relationships weaken, however, when shorter intervals are used for computing returns; and they deteriorate markedly when very short periods (for instance, daily intervals) are used. It has been shown that this deterioration is related to delays in the price-adjustment process.[24] These delays could not exist if stocks always traded at their equilibrium values. Therefore, by analyzing the deterioration of the accuracy with which the returns genera-tion relationships can be measured in very short period data, it is possible to obtain empirical evidence on the efficiency of a trading system. This evidence would give valuable guidance to the regulators of a system.

Recent Regulatory Experience

Historical Background

The federal regulation of securities commenced with the Securities Act of 1933 and the Securities Exchange Act of 1934.[25] This legislation was motivated primarily by the desire to prevent dishonesty and market manipulation.[26] As stated by Loss (1961), a leading commentator on the securities laws, "the prob-lems at which modern securities regulation is directed are as old as the cupidity of sellers and the gullibility of buyers." However, after fifty years of experience by the Securities and Exchange Commission in policing the markets, and given the computer technology that supports the current on-line surveillance and stock watch systems, protecting against manipulation and dishonesty is not the pressing policy issue it once was.[27]

Starting with the Institutional Investor Study (see U.S. Securities and Exchange Commission 1971), regulatory concern widened in the 1970s to include the competitive structure of the markets.[28] This change was motivated by a fact that had become patently obvious: The fees involved in handling large institutional orders had become exorbitant vis-à-vis the associated costs. Some institutions, of course, may have adapted to the rules and been able to fend for themselves; others, however, were not, and an important constituency—the shareholders of the registered investment companies—was viewed as being victimized. As a result, negotiated commissions were introduced and codified with the passage by Congress of the Securities Acts Amendments of 1975.

Along with recognizing fixed commissions as an unjustified competitive barrier, attention also focused on the quasi-monopoly position of various market makers, on restrictions on entry into certain market centers, and on the absence of spatial integration among various parts of the industry. In dealing with these issues, the goal emerged of establishing a national market system.[29] With this goal, the regulatory objective became one of improving the efficiency of order execution; of promoting competition between dealers and market centers; and of ensuring the wide dissemination of information on transaction prices, volume, and current bid/ask quotations.

The widening of regulatory attention beyond the issue of market manipulation was a manifestation of the maturing of our financial markets. Now, with the dismantling of competitive constraints and the electronic integration of various markets, the industry has truly started to come of age. As a consequence, further strengthening competition in the provision of dealer services is no longer the most crucial policy issue. Rather, we suggest that attention be turned to the third regulatory goal—improving the efficiency of the price discovery process by appropriate design of the trading system.

Recent regulatory experience has included two issues that are related to the efficiency of price discovery: off-board trading and shelf registration.[30] We next examine each of these briefly. Our primary purpose in so doing is not to derive firm conclusions with regard to the resolution of these issues; rather, we wish to call attention to the relevance of efficient price discovery as a regulatory goal.

Off-Board Trading

Traditionally, the U.S. exchanges have required that their members execute transactions in listed securities on an exchange. This has been accomplished through a variety of off-board trading restrictions (the best known being New York Stock Exchange Rule 390).[31] Clearly, such rules are by their nature anticompetitive in that nonmembers are restricted in their access to orders held by members, and members are restricted in seeking out markets provided by nonmembers.

The U.S. legal and economic system has, of course, always placed great store in the value of competition. Nonetheless, totally free competition is not always desirable, and rules and restrictions are typically imposed that have some anticompetitive effects. Traffic laws, for instance, restrict free competition (speed, positioning, access to certain roads by certain vehicles, and so on) in order to enhance the orderly flow of traffic, thereby enabling drivers to reach their destinations in a safer, more timely manner. With regard to the competitive structure of the securities markets, the focus of Congress and of the SEC was no doubt biased by the pricing excesses engendered by fixed commissions and by the industry's response to them.[32] Nevertheless, the legislative history of the Securities Acts Amendments did specify that the SEC must balance perceived anticompetitive effects "against the purposes of the Exchange Act." Thus it was not intended that competition "become paramount to the great purposes of the Exchange Act" but, rather, that it should be a factor in the balance.

We suggest that a principal underlying objective of the Exchange Act is also to assure that the securities markets optimally reflect the balance between supply and demand at any given time. In light of this, the most important test for off-board trading rules is an examination of whether they facilitate or impede the process of price discovery. Given the complexities involved, the SEC was wise to have moved as slowly as it has in eliminating off-board trading restrictions, and to have been cautious with regard to the potential for fragmentation. Nevertheless, the SEC's efforts could have been better guided if it had focused more clearly on the price-discovery issues that have been implicit in much of its considerations.

Too much time has now gone by, and too much has already been written on NYSE Rule 390, SEC Rule 19c.3, the 1975 amendments, and the pricing of dealer services, to warrant reviewing in detail the technical aspects of the arguments on either side.[33] Rather, our purpose here is to consider how issues concerning off-board trading relate to the efficiency of price discovery. The primary relationships are:

1. *Consolidation of the order flow*: The major fear that has been expressed about off-board trading is that, without forced consolidation, orders may not execute at the best prices (that is, there may be overreaching) and that orders may not be fully exposed to the market (that is, they may be internalized). Although these concerns might be alleviated by the development of a consolidated quotation system and by the institution of an appropriate order exposure rule, off-board trading by its very nature does imply market fragmentation. The costs and benefits that necessarily attend such fragmentation are intricate, and the trade-offs with regard to the quality of price

discovery are complex. We consider what is involved further in points 2–4 that follow.

2. *The consolidation of information*: For exchange-based trading, the consolidation of trades and of the order flow on the floor of an exchange, as viewed by a single specialist, facilitates the assessment of information concerning current quotations, order sizes, and the mood of traders. This in turn improves the specialist's ability to determine appropriate quotes. Because the specialist's quotes in turn provide important signals to public traders, better quotes generate an order flow that is in closer harmony with the price that best reflects the balance between demand and supply. Accordingly, the ability of the market maker to achieve a comprehensive assessment of market conditions is impaired by fragmentation, and the ability of the exchange-based system to achieve appropriate prices is hindered.

3. *The preservation of secondary trading priority rules*: Price is the universally accepted primary trading rule; orders that are consolidated within a trading system are also executed according to specified secondary trading priority rules when they are written at identical prices.[34] Fragmentation implicitly changes the secondary priority rules to, essentially, a rule of random selection. This change alters the manner in which orders are interfaced to give trades, and can also affect the order flow itself (see Bloch and Schwartz 1978; Cohen, Conroy, and Maier (chapter 5) and Cohen, Maier, Schwartz, and Whitcomb 1982). Although the effect of secondary priority rules on the order flow is only imperfectly understood, it is clear that these rules are important and that changing them does affect the prices that are discovered by the market. Surprisingly, however, these considerations have not received much attention in relation to the off-board trading issue.

4. *Intermarket competition*: As noted earlier, the primary impetus for allowing off-board trading has been the desire to reduce trading costs (spreads and commissions) by strengthening interdealer competition. There is another facet to competition, however—one that, in light of recent experience, may be recognized as the stronger of the two: competition between trading systems. Relaxing the constraints that help a market center capture order flow places that center in more direct competition vis-a-vis other trading systems. This gives other centers an incentive to upgrade their systems in an attempt to gain order flow, and puts pressure on the primary centers to upgrade in order to keep order flow. For instance, the development of PACE and SCOREX by the regional exchanges was met by the NYSE with the development of OARS, DOT, and super-DOT. The upgraded systems represent less expensive, faster procedures for physically handling the order flow; they also enable the various market centers to compete more effectively in terms of the quality of the prices they provide. In one respect, however, intermarket competition might adversely affect the quality of price discovery: Allowing off-board trading while exchange trading is closed following a major news announcement can force the

exchange to reopen markets too quickly so as not to lose an unacceptable amount of the order flow; as a consequence, investors may have insufficient time to digest news before trading is resumed.

Off-board trading has been the focus of the debates concerning fragmentation. In this context, *off-board* has meant the in-house execution of customer orders by member firms. The fragmentation issue, however, is potentially much broader. This is because the exchange-based system comprises two national and five regional exchanges (with many issues being cross-listed),[35] because large trades are typically negotiated "upstairs" before being brought to the trading floor, and because of the operation of third-market firms. To some extent the diverse markets are linked by information systems such as ITS, CQS, and the consolidated tape. These systems, however, do not consolidate all information (only last transaction prices and best market quotes), and do not permit the institution of presumably desirable secondary trading priority rules. To do this would require moving in a direction diametrically opposite to off-board trading, and returning to a proposal that was much discussed seven years ago in relation to a national market system: the consolidated limit order book (CLOB). Would a CLOB best serve the needs of the market with regard to efficient price discovery? There is still, unfortunately, much that we do not know about this issue.

Shelf Registration

A long-standing example of regulatory constraint has been the SEC's policy against shelf registration. The agency's position was that securities could be registered (a statutorily mandated prerequisite to public primary distributions) only if they were "presently intended to be offered." Underlying this policy was a belief that investors need to be furnished current information about the issuer and the securities to be offered, and that this may not happen when securities are sold off the shelf.

Registration, however, involves a massive concentrated effort by the issuer, underwriters, counsel, auditors, printers, and SEC staff themselves. This is true even for the most repetitive of public offerings involving major companies with widely traded stocks and debt securities. It often takes weeks, occasionally even months, to bring an offering to the market. Meanwhile, prices in the securities markets fluctuate, and no one knows what the payoff will be until the magic moment of clearance is reached. Not surprisingly in light of this, the issuing companies have pressed for a change in the regulatory constraint.

Both in response to the pressures brought by the issuing companies, and as part of its attempt to integrate the various disclosure systems under the federal securities laws, the SEC, on March 3, 1982, adopted a temporary "shelf registration" rule (Temporary Rule 415).[36] This allowed registered securities to be offered and sold on a delayed or continuous basis. The shelf registration was permitted for an insurer, its parent, or subsidiaries, for any security, in any amount that may be reasonably expected to be offered and sold within two years of the effective date of the registration statement.

After the adoption of Temporary Rule 415, the SEC sought and received numerous oral and written comments. Proponents of 415 emphasized the need of issuing corporations to raise capital on a timely basis and at reduced cost. Those who opposed the rule advanced two major counterarguments. First, they were concerned that, with the rule, the quality and timeliness of information disclosure to investors would be reduced. Second, they asserted that, with the rule, issuers would require underwriters to bid for an offering on such short notice that these firms would have insufficient time to form traditional underwriting syndicates. They felt this would give the large investment banking firms an unfair advantage over the smaller firms, and that this advantage would lead to a greater concentration of market power in the industry. Not surprisingly, the regional broker-dealer firms in particular were worried about this.

On November 17, 1983, the SEC approved Rule 415 by a vote of 4 to 1.[37] The major change in the final rule vis-à-vis the temporary rule is that the number of corporations eligible to use the procedure was significantly reduced.[38] It is, of course, too soon to tell whether or not the rule will improve the efficiency of the marketplace. In reviewing the debate, however, one can draw some inferences concerning the SEC's orientation to the various regulatory objectives.

The most striking observation is that, as was true with the off-board trading issue, the SEC continues to be far more concerned with the cost of trading than with the quality of the prices established for the trades that are made. In fact, the shelf-registration rule has implications for the price-discovery issue; but these appear to have received little attention in the debate.

We see what is involved as follows. Price uncertainty is undesirable for corporations, just as it is for traders. One value of the shelf-registration rule is that it enables corporations to reduce the cost of the price uncertainty involved in a new offering. In this sense, the rule effectively increases the liquidity of the markets for corporate issuers.

In addition, changing the procedure for selling new shares alters the relationship between the new-issues markets and the secondary trading markets. As a result, the aggregate order flow will be affected, as will be the prices of the shares that are traded. The implication of this is important. Allowing a corporation to work its offering will affect the prices that are discovered, those at which investors trade, and those that are used as pricing guides in related markets.

An issuing corporation essentially faces the same problem any trader confronts in the secondary markets: how to keep transaction costs low, and how to price, size, and time an order in light of current market conditions. As noted, the transaction costs involved in registering and selling a new issue are, indeed, far greater than the costs involved in bringing orders to the secondary market. It is not surprising that an attempt be made to reduce these costs.[39] However, the strategic decisions a corporation makes with regard to an offering are also far more complex than the trading decisions investors make when writing their orders for the secondary markets. For this reason, allowing greater flexibility in the timing of new issues may be just as important as reducing the costs of effecting the placement.

As was not the case with off-board trading, imposition of Rule 415 might be desirable with regard to both transaction efficiency and the efficiency of price discovery. However, Rule 415 could result in less information disclosure and in a greater concentration of market power in investment banking. Thus there are trade-offs involved. To assess these trade-offs properly, the impact on price discovery has to be considered.

Conclusion

Given the sophistication of our current trading systems, the complexity of the securities markets does not, for the most part, come from the process of physically interacting buy and sell orders. Rather, complexity with regard to trading is an expression of the difficulties involved in finding the prices at which trades should be made. If, however, trading were a costless process, transaction price uncertainty would not matter: Traders would simply submit continuously updated buy/sell orders to the market. If, on the other hand, transaction prices were not uncertain, transaction costs would have a straightforward impact on the order flow, and the objective of system design would be simply to reduce these costs as much as possible. Unfortunately, neither condition holds. That is why trading is a complex process, and systems design a crucial regulatory issue.

This chapter has considered the improvement of market efficiency as an objective of market regulation. To this end, it has focused on market liquidity (defined as the extent to which actual transaction prices conform to theoretically desirable equilibrium values) as an appropriate criterion for measuring efficiency. This definition, which focuses attention on the price discovery process, is attractive because it relates to a feature of securities-market performance that (1) is of concern to investors and to the firms whose shares are traded, (2) can be affected by appropriate structural design, and (3) can—we believe—be empirically measured and monitored by a regulatory organization (either the market centers themselves or a government agency).

The focus of regulatory attention has evolved since the inception of the Securities Acts of 1933 and 1934. This change can be explained by a developing understanding of competition in the securities industry, by the adoption of electronic technology starting in the 1970s, and by the attendant changing economic pressures—institutionalization of trading, for example, and the introduction of new products such as options and futures. With the expanding regulatory focus, more attention is currently being given to the importance of efficient price discovery—but not much more. Interestingly, the issue is recognized mainly in relation to the trading of futures contracts on commodities and certain market indexes, and by the regulatory agency that is exclusively concerned with futures trading, the Commodity Futures Trading Commission (CFTC).

Unfortunately, the greater generality of the efficiencies problem does not appear to have been recognized, and with regard to financial assets (e.g., the traditional equity shares), the role of markets and of market makers in the price-discovery process is, at best, only imperfectly understood. Indecision concerning regulatory policy could have been reduced appreciably if the objective of efficient price discovery had been more clearly recognized and used in the past; regulatory policy will be more effective in the future, if efficient price discovery is made a primary goal.

Notes

1. In a related paper (see Schreiber and Schwartz 1984), we also examine implications of the price-discovery process for various issues concerning systems design and empirical research in finance.

2. We use the word *regulators* broadly. The regulations we speak of include laws established by Congress.

3. See Commodity Exchange Act § 5a and appendix A to § 5.3 of the General Regulations under the Commodity Exchange Act. A recent *New York Times* article by Maidenberg (1984) highlights the influence futures prices have on the underlying cash markets: On March 16, 1984, a computer breakdown on the Chicago Mercantile Exchange directly affected both volume and prices in the securities markets for related instruments. As also reported by Maidenberg on March 29, the shortening of trading hours on the COMEX by a severe storm in New York City led one respected market professional to observe that, as a result of the abbreviated session, "the other bullion markets practically froze because they lost their key pricing guide." The same pricing function is performed by the interaction of market participants on the traditional trading floors, although the process has not been as clearly recognized with respect to these markets.

4. There are other examples of one market depending on another market for efficient price determination. Whenever an equity mutual fund issues or redeems its shares (as they do daily), public investors make or lose money on the basis of closing market prices, even though there may have been no disposition whatsoever of the securities by the fund. Similarly, prices established in secondary trading markets pro-

vide reference points for new issues of stock. In light of these interdependencies, the cost of market discontinuities or blockages caused by breakdowns in the trading system or by various regulatory requirements should be assessed not only with regard to execution costs, but also in terms of the quality of prices achieved in the related markets.

5. See, in particular, Goldman and Beja (1979); Hakansson, Beja, and Kale (1985); Cohen, Hawawini, Maier, Schwartz, and Whitcomb (1980); and Ho, Schwartz, and Whitcomb (1985).

6. For a discussion, see Elton and Gruber (1984).

7. For example, see the I/B/O/S/S Services, which are rankings of stocks by brokerage firms and financial institutions.

8. The evidence suggests that this is true, even aside from the possibility that some traders (for example, insiders) receive information before it is available on the market. See Givoly and Palmon (1983).

9. The academic literature on the microstructure of security markets has generally taken the demand curve to hold shares of an asset to be less than infinitely elastic. See, for example, Demsetz (1968); Garman (1976); Cohen, Maier, Schwartz, and Whitcomb (1978); Ho, Schwartz, and Whitcomb (1985).

10. In the microstructure literature as well, relatively little attention has been given to the fact that, with a downward-sloping demand curve, price discovery is an important function to be performed by a trading system. For an analysis of this process, see Ho, Schwartz, and Whitcomb (1985).

11. LIQ trades exclusively on the prestigious Canard Exchange, a totally unregulated, entirely electronic system based on OTC, pit-type double auction principles with a specialist (who moonlights as a French chef).

12. Bagehot (1971) was the first to distinguish between informational trading and liquidity trading. Cohen, Maier, Schwartz, and Whitcomb (1978) present a model of the price-adjustment process that builds on the informational change–liquidity change distinction. Their formulation differentiates between the idiosyncratic shifts of individual demand and aggregate-demand shifts. The idiosyncratic shifts are attributed to variation in individual liquidity and liquidity needs, and to individual reassessments of information; the aggregate shifts are due to generally known information change.

13. The mechanics of the market also include the interaction of new orders with orders in the crowd or on the limit order book, the rules of order execution, and special-handling procedures for block trades, the operations of market makers, and so forth.

14. The rules of order handling include: the specification of time, size, and other trading priority rules for orders placed at the same price; short selling and other restrictions; the types of orders that can be written (market, limit, stop-loss, and so on); and the ways in which orders might be worked (by a floor trader with discretionary power). The rules by which orders are translated into trades include: provisions for batching orders for simultaneous execution at periodic market calls; provisions for continuous trading; the affirmative obligation of designated market makers; and various price stabilization procedures (the imposition of trading stoppages, the time batching and spatial consolidation of orders, the intervention of dealers and specialists). See Whitcomb (chapter 16) for further discussion.

15. For further discussion of this issue, see Schreiber and Schwartz (1984).

16. Trading volume will also differ from its theoretically desirable equilibrium

value; and, immediately after any trading session, there will in general be a demand to recontract. It is therefore clear that immediately following any trading session, the realized distribution of shares across investors will not be Pareto optimal.

17. The market maker (dealer or specialist) has been recognized in the literature as having several functions. The market maker as a provider of immediacy was first modeled by Demsetz (1968). Subsequently, Hakansson, Beja, and Kale (1985) considered the market maker as a price adjuster (when, because of the discreteness of price, exact market clearing values are unobtainable). Barnea (1974) and Cohen, Maier, Schwartz, and Whitcomb (1977) analyzed the market maker as a price stabilizer. Following Ho, Schwartz, and Whitcomb (1985), we suggest the market maker can mitigate the divergent behavior of prices by stabilizing the market and improving the quality of signals that are transmitted to the investment community. See Cohen, Maier, Schwartz, and Whitcomb (1979) and Stoll (chapter 4) for further discussion. It may be noted that the futures markets, for structural and historical reasons, eschew specialists and depend on independent floor traders and the "crowd" to provide the needed liquidity. The notion of a specialist may be viewed as inconsistent with the mandates of the Commodity Exchange Act.

18. See Cohen, Hawawini, Maier, Schwartz, and Whitcomb (1983a,b) and Fung, Schwartz, and Whitcomb (1983).

19. Cohen, Maier, Schwartz, and Whitcomb (1981) have shown that the market spread for a stock (the inside quotas) will be nonzero only when trading is a nonfrictionless process. The bid-ask spread is the cost of a round trip when the stock is traded at market (bought at the ask quotation and then sold at the bid). Other transaction costs (such as commissions) might also be viewed as making a market illiquid; however, these costs are not uniquely related to the market for an individual stock, and they are not a direct manifestation of the trading characteristics of an individual stock.

20. It would not, of course, matter to a trader if his transaction price deviates from the frictionless market value because the bid-ask spread is large (though centered on the desired price) or because the location of the spread deviates substantially from the desired price (although the spread is tight). Analytically, however, it is useful to recognize that both reasons for a deviation exist and that, to some extent, they might exist as alternatives (that is, market makers may set spreads that are more appropriately placed in relation to the underlying equilibrium price if they are allowed, by regulation and by competition, to maintain wider spreads). For further discussion, see Ho and Macris (chapter 3).

21. See Goldman and Beja (1979) for a demonstration that deviations of actual prices from equilibrium values add to the volatility of transaction prices.

22. See, for example, Cooper, Groth, and Avera (1983). The NYSE and AMEX both assess specialist performance by analogous measures (for the NYSE, the magnitude of price changes per 1,000 shares traded).

23. It is, of course, from this relationship that market model betas, the well-known measures of systematic risk, are obtained.

24. See Cohen, Hawawini, Maier, Schwartz, and Whitcomb (1983a,b) and Fung, Schwartz, and Whitcomb (1983).

25. See Bloch (chapter 11) for a discussion of the evolving regulatory structure as it relates to both banking and the securities markets.

26. The Securities and Exchange Commission (SEC) administers several other statutes (such as the Investment Company Act of 1940) and has additional functions with regard to securities credit and certain bankruptcy situations, all of which can be ignored for present purposes. See Loss (1961, supplemented 1969). In a broader sense, it must be recognized that dishonesty is itself a gross and costly inefficiency.

27. A review of recent SEC enforcement actions supports this impression. The large preponderance of SEC cases relate, not to old-fashioned hard-core thievery and fraud, but rather to noncompliance with financial requirements such as net capital rules, to insider trading, and to various technical trading violations. Presumably, the SEC would prosecute more outright fraud if it existed; rather, for the time being at least, existing systems seem to have kept in check those gross abuses that the securities laws were intended to combat. Although it is of course possible for new avenues of dishonesty to be opened (primarily through computer fraud and manipulation if electronic trading is ever instituted on a wide scale), for now we can afford the luxury of keeping policy issues concerning manipulation on a back burner.

28. In response to this concern, Congress enacted the Securities Act Amendments of 1975, the most significant modification of the regulatory structure of the securities industry since the Security Exchange Act was adopted in 1934. The primary focus of these amendments was the removal of impediments to competition in the industry.

29. Among its other provisions, Section 11A of the Securities Exchange Act of 1934, which was added to by the Securities Act Amendments of 1975, directed the SEC to facilitate the establishment of a national market system (without, however, defining that concept).

30. Insider trading is a third issue that relates to the efficiency of price discovery, although it is beyond the scope of this chapter. Manne (1966) was one of the first to suggest that prohibitions on insider trading could lead to market inefficiency. See also Longstreth (1984).

31. See, generally, Parker (1980, vol. 13, no. 10, p. 919). Rule 390 was formerly known as Rule 394.

32. As noted earlier, concern about off-board trading restrictions arose in the context in the 1960s and early 1970s when fixed commissions resulted in execution costs for large transactions that were palpably and grossly out of line with the cost of effecting transactions. The exorbitant commissions in turn resulted in various mechanics for reducing transaction costs: third-market quotations, formation of captive brokers to recapture a portion of the excess, and various give-up arrangements.

33. See, for example, Parker (1980).

34. The NYSE, for instance, uses a complex combination of secondary priority rules that include time (first arrived, first executed) and size (larger orders are executed first). For further institutional description, see Whitcomb (chapter 16).

35. Off-board trading restrictions require member firms to execute orders on an exchange, but not on any specific exchange.

36. Securities Act Release No. 33-6383, "Adoption of Integrated Disclosure System." As stated by the SEC, the two principal objectives of its proposed integrated disclosure system and, as a part thereof, the promulgation of Temporary Rule 415 were: (1) a comprehensive evaluation of the disclosure policies and procedures under the Securities Act of 1933 and the Exchange Act of 1934 to identify the information

which is material to security holders and investors in both the distribution process and the trading markets, and (2) a determination of the circumstances under which information should be disseminated to security holders, investors and the marketplace. The stated goal of the SEC's integrated disclosure program has been to "revise or eliminate overlapping or unnecessary disclosure and dissemination requirements whenever possible, thereby reducing burdens on registrants while, at the same time, insuring that security holders, investors and the marketplace have been provided with meaningful, non-duplicative information upon which to base investment decisions." Ibid.

37. Securities Act Release No. 33–6499, Commissioner Barbara S. Thomas dissenting. The basis of Commissioner Thomas's dissent was her belief that the Rule should be limited to debt offerings exclusively. She stated that she was convinced that allowing shelf registration for equity offerings "jeopardizes the liquidity and stability of the primary and secondary securities markets."

38. Temporary Rule 415 was available to all SEC registered firms; however, Rule 415 is applicable only to (i) certain limited classes of securities that were traditionally allowed shelf registration prior to Rule 415 and (ii) securities to be offered on a continuous or delayed basis by a limited number of large, widely followed corporations. It does not apply to any other offerings. The SEC's stated reason for so limiting the application of Rule 415 is that concerns about disclosure and due diligence outweigh the benefits of Rule 415.

39. According to a memorandum prepared by the SEC's Office of the Chief Economist, "the issuing cost of equity securities sold under Rule 415 is about 29 percent less than that of comparable equity securities not sold under Rule 415." Cited in 15 *Sec. Reg. & L. Rep.* (BNA) p. 1955 (October 21, 1983).

References

Bagehot, W. 1971. The only game in town. *Financial Analysts Journal,* March–April.

Barnea, A. 1974. Performance evaluation of New York Stock Exchange specialists. *Journal of Financial and Quantitative Analysis,* September.

Bloch, E. 1985. Multiple regulation. Chapter 11.

Bloch, E., and Schwartz, R. 1978. The great debate over NYSE Rule 390. *Journal of Portfolio Management,* Fall.

Cohen, K.; Conroy, R.; and Maier, S. 1985. Order flow and the quality of the market. This volume.

Cohen, K.; Hawawini, G.; Maier, S.; Schwartz, R.; and Whitcomb, D. 1980. Implications of microstructure theory for empirical research on stock price behavior. *Journal of Finance,* May.

——— . 1983a. Estimating and adjusting for the interval-effect bias in beta. *Management Science,* January.

——— . 1983b. Friction in the trading process and the estimation of systematic risk. *Journal of Financial Economics.*

Cohen, K.; Maier, S.; Schwartz, R.; and Whitcomb, D. 1977. The impact of designated market makers on security prices: II. Policy proposals. *Journal of Banking and Finance,* December.

———— . 1978. The returns generation process, returns variance, and the effect of thinness in securities markets. *Journal of Finance,* March.

———— . 1979. Market makers and the market spread: A review of recent literature. *Journal of Financial and Quantitative Analysis,* November.

———— . 1981. Transaction costs, order placement strategy, and existence of the bid-ask spread. *Journal of Political Economy,* April.

———— . 1982. An analysis of the economic justification for consolidation in the secondary security market. *Journal of Banking and Finance.*

Cooper, K.; Groth, J.; and Avera, W. 1983. Liquidity exchange listing, and common stock performance. Unpublished Working Paper, Texas A & M University, August.

Demsetz, H. 1968. The cost of transacting. *Quarterly Journal of Economics,* February.

Elton, E., and Gruber, M. 1984. *Modern portfolio theory and investment analysis,* 2nd ed. New York: Wiley.

Fung, W.; Schwartz, R.; and Whitcomb, D. 1983. Adjusting the intervalling effect bias in beta: A test using Paris Bourse prices. Working Paper.

Garman, M. 1976. Market microstructure. *Journal of Financial Economics,* June.

Givoly, D., and Palmon, D. 1983. Insider trading and the exploitation of inside information: Some empirical evidence. Paper presented at the European Finance Association meetings, Fontainebleau, France, September.

Goldman, M., and Beja, A. 1979. Market prices vs. equilibrium prices: Returns variance, serial correlation, and the role of the specialists. *Journal of Finance,* June.

Hakansson, N.; Beja, A.; and Kale, J. 1985. On the feasibility of automated market making by a programmed specialist. *Journal of Finance,* March.

Ho, T., and Macris, R. 1985. Dealer market structure and performance. Chapter 3.

Ho, T.; Schwartz, R.; and Whitcomb, D. 1985. The trading decision and market clearing under transaction price uncertainty. *Journal of Finance,* March.

Longstreth, B. 1984. Halting insider trading. *The New York Times,* April 12.

Loss, L. 1961. *Securities regulation.* Boston: Little, Brown. (Supplemented 1969).

Maidenburg, H. 1984. Futures/options. *The New York Times,* March 19.

Manne, H. 1966. *Insider trading and the stock market.* New York: Free Press.

Parker, S. 1980. Off-board trading restrictions. *Review of Securities Regulation,* May.

Schreiber, P., and Schwartz, R. 1984. Efficient price discovery in a securities market: Implications for regulation, systems design, and the informational content of security prices. Working paper.

Stoll, H. 1985. Alternative views of market making. Chapter 4.

U.S. Securities and Exchange Commision (SEC). 1971. *Institutional investor study report,* Washington, D.C.: U.S. Government Printing Office.

Whitcomb, D. 1985. An international comparison of stock exchange trading. Chapter 16.

3
Dealer Market Structure and Performance

Thomas S.Y. Ho
Richard G. Macris

T rading rules in market making are designed to improve the performance of the market. That is, traders and/or the transacting public
benefit when market participants must abide by trading rules. Take
the exchange trading system, for example. Many rules are imposed on both
the market participants in this auction market: the consolidated limit order
book, the uptick-rule, and Rule 390, to name a few. Numerous debates and
discussions have been devoted to evaluating the impact of these individual
trading rules on market performance.[1] Yet few papers have analyzed the
market structure and performance of a dealer market, where there are
minimal trading rules.

Consider the National Association of Securities Dealers Automated
Quotation System (NASDAQ) of the over-the-counter (OTC) market. In this
trading system, each dealer may choose to trade in any NASDAQ stock, and
will encounter no constraints on the number of stocks in which he makes a
market. He chooses his own trading portfolio. For the market in each stock,
there is no limit to the number of market makers registered for the stock.
There is no barrier to dealers' entry or exit. (By contrast, in an exchange
market, each stock has a designated market maker, the specialist, whose
trading portfolio must be approved by the exchange.) In essence, the only
trading rule in the NASDAQ system is that the dealers must offer firm quotes
to the incoming orders. Market structure and performance are determined
through competition among the dealers to capture the order flow, not by
rules and regulations.

An important trading characteristic of a stock is the *float:* the number of
shares of the corporation not held by the management and, to an extent, by

The first version of this chapter was completed while Thomas Ho was visiting at the Owen
Graduate School of Management, Vanderbilt University. The research support there is gratefully
acknowledged.

The views and opinions expressed herein are those of the authors and do not necessarily represent the position of the First Boston Corporation.

institutions. One expects that the larger the float, the more often shares change ownership, resulting in greater transaction volume through the dealer market. The corporations, however, decide on the float for various managerial considerations; the market design has little impact on the float level. However, the converse is not true; the float significantly affects market structure and performance. When there is a demand to trade, there is a demand for dealers' services. The number of market makers averaging over time in a stock, given free entry and exit to the market, must depend crucially on the stock trading volume or the float.

The number of market makers in a stock is central to the dealer market structure. Market makers conceivably could differ significantly from each other in their capitalization and trading portfolio size and composition. Some might commit much capital to market making, trading a large number of stocks; others might only trade a few stocks with limited capital. Yet the capital committed to a particular stock and the trading strategy of a market maker must be more or less the same across the market makers. This is because there are few economies of scale to trading, and portfolio diversification is a secondary consideration. Therefore, each dealer must reach his optimal capitalization and pricing strategies for a specific stock. His optimal decisions depend more on the stock's trading characteristics than on the dealer firm's characteristics. For this reason, it is useful to view the dealers in each stock as being identical; hence the number of market makers for a stock becomes a meaningful measure of the market structure.

The extent to which a stock's trading volume induces dealers to register for the stock greatly affects the market performance. The trading volume determines the number of market makers, which in turn specifies the amount of capital committed to market making. The higher the trading volume, the larger the amount of capital committed to provide liquidity to the stock. Further, when there are more dealers competing for the order flow, each dealer's pricing strategy (bid and ask quotes) will be affected, which then affects the market bid-ask spread. In sum, the market bid-ask spread and market illiquidity as costs imposed on the transacting public are in large part endogenous to the market environment (for example, depending on the trading volume and the price risk of the stock). They are not set exogenously by trading rules of the market regime.

This chapter studies the nature of such endogenous market structure and performance. The purpose is twofold. First, it provides important insights into the organization of the NASDAQ system, and formulates a framework to analyze the stock market. Second, the chapter enables us to evaluate the impact of trading rules on market performance. Specifically, it shows that market performance can be measured both by the market bid-ask spread and by market liquidity (the capital committed to market making). The two attributes are not independent of each other, however, but interrelated. Therefore, a trading rule that seeks to narrow the spread may, as a result, reduce market liquidity; conversely, a rule that encourages more market makers to participate in the stock would lead to wider bid-ask spreads. From this analysis we draw some implications. We show that upstairs trading and block trading are integral parts of the market-making function. They arise from the inability of both the auction market and the dealer market to be sufficiently liquid and at the same time to set adequately tight market bid-ask spread for the transacting public. Also in this chapter, we discuss the differences between dealer markets and auction markets, describing their relative strengths and weaknesses.

The chapter is organized as follows. The next section describes the institutional framework used in later sections. The third section describes the salient features of the trading regime, so that our analysis can focus on the issues of the paper. The fourth and fifth sections contain the main theoretical results. To begin, we describe the optimal pricing strategies of a dealer under competition, and hence the structure of the bid-ask spread. Then we analyze the nature of market structure in equilibrium, and show how it is related to the competitive behavior of the dealers. Then, in the next section, we analyze the market bid-ask spread and the market liquidity of a stock, showing the interrelationship between the two market attributes. In the sixth section we report results of empirical studies of the NASDAQ market structure. There are four parts. First, we studied the distribution of portfolio size across market makers. Second, we examined the relationship between dealer firm size and trading portfolio composition. Third, we investigated the need for specialization in trading; finally, we considered the relationship between the number of market makers and transaction volume. In the seventh section we present the implications of the chapter. They provide an economic explanation of block trading and upstairs trading. This section also contains the conclusions. Here we compare and contrast the over-the-counter (OTC) trading system with the exchange system, and examine the impact of technological innovations on the future competition between the two trading systems.

Institutional Framework

This section presents the institutional background on which we base our analysis. We describe the existing NASDAQ system—specifically, the way the OTC market handles and executes an order. Also, we discuss the costs incurred by an OTC market maker. The cost structure of dealership forms the basis of our subsequent analysis.

NASDAQ System

The NASDAQ system is a communication system for the market makers in NASDAQ stocks, a subset of OTC stocks. The system, introduced in 1971, uses video display screens and a central computer file that allows dealers instant access to the quotes of other competing market makers, who subscribe to level III of NASDAQ. This service permits the dealer to enter bid and ask prices for any stock in which he makes a market. These quotes are available continuously for all market makers and for the transacting public. Hence the market makers compete directly for order flow. All quotes are firm for the normal unit of trading (usually 100 shares) at the prices quoted. When new quotations are entered into the system, they instantly replace the previous quotes.

Execution of NASDAQ orders is done via telephone since the system merely serves as an electronic bulletin board. Therefore, on the OTC market, there is at present no automated execution system. The NASDAQ level III system has allowed market makers from diverse geographical areas to compete effectively for incoming orders. Level II service allows the subscribers to view all the competing quotes in a particular security, but it does not allow the user to enter quotes. This service is used most frequently by firms that only deal in agency business (as brokers). The NASDAQ level I service allows the user to see the inside market in any security in the system. This service is the most common, and is the one most individual account executives use.

It is relatively simple for market makers to join the NASDAQ system. Perhaps the most stringent requirement is that they must maintain a minimum net capital of $100,000, or $2,500 for each security in which they make a market, whichever is less. Another requirement is that they must report daily and monthly trading volume. Trading volume is defined to be the larger of the dealer's purchases or sales. It follows that trading volume is more appropriately viewed as the flow of orders (somewhat overstated) passing through the market makers. The trading volume is not the aggregate of all the trades executed by the dealers. To register in a stock, the market maker needs only to notify NASD via a terminal one day ahead of time; therefore, the market maker can change his trading portfolio quite frequently.

Order-Handling Procedure

When a customer places a round lot market order to buy (sell), the order is sent to the OTC trading room of the stockbroker's firm. The OTC trader then seeks the lowest ask (highest bid) price among the competing market makers. Then he telephones the market maker who offers the best ask price to compete for the trade. This procedure closely resembles that for a listed stock. The only major difference is that on the OTC market, the trader seeks the best price on the NASDAQ system, whereas on the exchange, the market order would cross with the best quotes on the exchange floor.

However, a limit order on the OTC market is handled quite differently from one on the exchange. On the OTC market, there is no consolidated limit order book. Each trader handles the limit orders placed with him. Also, the trader is not obligated to reveal the limit order to the public. For example, even when the limit order buy price is higher than all the market makers' bids, the limit order may not be shown on the NASDAQ screen. The trader may execute the limit order only when the market ask quote is equal to or lower than the limit order price.

A customer's cost of transacting effectively may be separated into two parts. First, he must pay a commission to the stockbroker who transmits the customer's order to the trading room. Then he must also pay for the service of executing the order. For a market order, he pays for the bid-ask spread; for a limit order, he is charged on a commission basis.

The Cost Structure in NASDAQ Market Making

A variety of fixed and variable costs are incurred by market makers. We shall classify the costs as one of three types: variable costs, inventory costs, or fixed costs.

Variable costs are costs the market maker must bear for each trade. These include clearing and paperwork costs. The market maker has several options available for how this component is to be allocated. If the market maker clears his own trades, then clearing costs may be viewed as either fixed or variable costs. This is because the costs of an in-house clearing operation consist of salary expenses, which are usually independent of trading volume. When trading volume exceeds normal levels, however, the firm may seek additional clearing capacity, and thus increase costs.

The cost of carrying inventory is another significant variable. The ability of a market maker to carry large inventory positions is directly related to his capitalization. There are three components to inventory costs. First, while holding inventory (in a long or short position), there may be unanticipated changes in price level. Therefore, there is price risk imposed on the market makers.[2] Second, when the dealer must borrow (invest) at a rate higher (lower) than normal rate of interest, the dealer will pay for the financing costs. Third, the market maker, in offering firm quotes to the transacting public, is exposed to traders and investors who have special information about the price movement of the stock and thus can trade against the market maker.[3] For instance, some investors may be better informed because of exclusive access to more accurate and more thorough research on a particular issue. Possession of this research may allow certain investors to make a better informed trading decision. These investors will cause the uninformed market makers to incur additional costs.

Inventory costs are quite distinct from variable costs, though the inventory level will change after each transaction, and therefore the inventory cost relates to each transaction. The inventory cost is not fixed for each transaction, however. Instead it depends on the expected length of time the inventory will be held. The longer the market maker expects to hold the stock, the higher the inventory cost. Furthermore, the expected length of the holding period is dependent on the issue's trading volume. A thinly traded issue will not permit the market maker to turn over his inventory very often. Therefore, the dealer will not be inclined to assume the risk of holding a large position. In a thickly traded issue, the market maker bears less risk because the market has the significant order flow to allow for rapid inventory adjustments.

Another factor that would affect the expected inventory holding period for a market maker is competition. If there were many dealers making a market in a stock, it would be more difficult for any one of the dealers to adjust his inventory position. The more intense the competition, the higher the inventory cost imposed on each dealer. Therefore, inventory costs depend on the market environment, and vary across stocks.

A variety of fixed overhead costs are also associated with the costs of market making. These include such items as rent, salary, and equipment rentals. In recent years many firms have made a concerted effort to control and reduce these fixed costs in order to gain a competitive advantage. This trend has been noticeable among OTC firms that specialize in market making. Many of these firms moved from New York City to New Jersey initially to avoid a New York City security excise tax. After the tax was repealed, the vast majority of them stayed in New Jersey. These firms realized that because they did not engage in retail customer business, a New York City location was not of prime importance. The New Jersey location allowed them to make significant savings in rent. Other firms are reducing costs by developing in-house quotation and market information systems. It is felt that the initial cost of such an effort will be offset by the savings that result in reducing long-term equipment rentals.

Analytical Framework

The purpose of this chapter is to study the dealer markets in a competitive environment. To this end, we must make some simplifications to the institutional setup described in the previous section. These assumptions capture the essential features needed to describe the competitive environment in which the dealers operate, while at the same time suppressing minor institutional details. These assumptions are grouped into three categories: (1) dealership characterization, (2) specification of the order arrival process, and (3) cost structure of dealership and equilibrium conditions.

Dealership Characterization

For reasons given in the introductory section, we will focus our analysis on the market-making process of a particular stock. Unless otherwise stated, the term *dealer market* refers to the market of a particular stock, not to the OTC market as a whole. Also, we assume the market makers for a particular stock are identical. They commit the same amount of capital for the stock and share the same evaluation of the stock's share value and risk. There are *m* market makers. Each provides his ask price and bid price to the market for a round lot order of Q shares. Each dealer has a cash account and an inventory position such that when he buys at his bid price, he would pay from his cash account, and increase his inventory position. Conversely, when he sells at his ask price, he would lower his inventory position and put the proceed into his cash account. There is no short-selling constraint on the dealers, nor is there any limit to their borrowing capacity. It is costless for each dealer to submit his quotes to the market. The quotes are displayed continuously to all market participants, with the dealers monitoring their own quotes as well as those of their competitors.

Order Arrival

In this chapter we are not concerned with how a better market would attract more order flow but, rather, with how an exogenous demand to trade determines the market structure. For this reason we assume that all public orders are market orders seeking to buy or sell Q shares in each transaction, and that the arrival of orders is specified by two independent stochastic processes. The arrivals of orders depend only on the lowest asked price and the highest bid price displayed to the public. When the best ask price is higher than a price p^u, the public would not seek to buy. When the best bid price is below a price p^l, the public would not seek to sell. Otherwise, the orders would arrive on average at a rate of λ arrivals/unit time.

For the time being, we do not consider the impact of limit orders on the market. This issue will be examined later. We view limit orders as an alternative to market orders. Therefore, by examining where the dealer market fails to handle market orders, we can better understand the economic value of limit orders.

The Cost Structure of Dealership and the Equilibrium Conditions

As discussed in the previous section, there are three cost components to market making. We shall not repeat the details here except to state that each dealer bears fixed costs, denoted by C dollars/unit time; inventory costs, denoted by K dollars/share/unit time; and variable costs, denoted by c dollars/share. In this analysis, c is assumed to be negligible.

We assume that in this market, *m* is the equilibrium number of market makers. None of these dealers seeks to leave the market, and no other dealer seeks to register for the stock, although there is no regulatory barrier imposed on the dealers to entry into or exit from the market. In this situation, the revenue each dealer generates must just barely cover all the costs incurred to the dealer. We shall use this condition to determine the equilibrium solution.

The Market Structure

This section relates the equilibrium number of market makers in a stock to the cost structure of a dealership. To achieve this, we first describe the structure of a dealer's bid-ask spread. It shows how each cost component affects the bid and ask prices that the dealer quotes. Then we show the impact of competition on these quotes, and hence on the profitability of being a market maker. The market structure is then established.

The Spread Structure

Consider an individual market maker. He perceives that the underlying stock value is P dollars/share. To provide an ask price P^a is to make a commitment to sell at P^a when a public buy order arrives. P^a must be set higher than P so that $(P^a - P)$ would cover the inventory and variable costs. At no time would a trader submit a quote that would not cover these costs because otherwise a reduction in profit would result from the transaction. Meanwhile, a dealer's net revenue $(P^a - P)$, called the *surplus,* is generally positive. It is clear that the higher is P^a, the larger is the surplus to the dealer, suggesting that a dealer should set an ask quote significantly above P.

The foregoing argument, however, is conditional on a market order crossing the dealer's ask quote. As the dealer increases his ask quote, some investors may be deterred from submitting buy orders to the market. More important, his competitors who are willing to accept smaller surpluses will submit an ask price lower than his. Since market orders will only cross with the best dealer quote, his competitors have eliminated any possibility for him to transact with the next incoming order. These considerations prevent any dealer from setting an ask quote and similarly a bid quote significantly away from the underlying price P.

The foregoing discussion shows that a bid-ask spread structure may be decomposed into three parts: variable costs, inventory costs, and surplus. Figure 3–1 depicts the spread structure.[4] The variable costs portion is the same from one transaction to another. The inventory costs portion depends not only on stock trading volume and risk, but also on each market maker's inventory position. Therefore, the inventory cost portion would vary, not only across stocks, but also intertemporally for a particular stock. The surplus portion depends crucially on the prices of competing quotes. We shall discuss

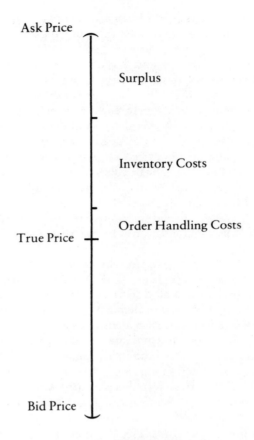

Figure 3–1. The Spread Structure

this surplus further in the following section. At this point we note only that an individual's bid-ask spread changes over time, varying with the inventory costs and the surplus portions.

Pricing Strategies under Competition
and the Market Structure

For simplicity, let us first consider the case of only two competing dealers. The insight gained in this analysis can be easily extended to any number of competing dealers. Suppose further, for the sake of argument, that they do not hold any inventory initially. At this time, each sets his quotes to maximize his expected surplus.

However, when dealer A finds his ask price higher than his competitor's (dealer B) ask price, he knows he will not capture the next incoming public sell order. For this reason, dealer A would lower his ask price to the extent that the quote is slightly below that of dealer B's. But dealer B, in response, will also lower his ask quote. As a result of this competition, dealers A and B both keep lowering their ask prices. As noted earlier, however, the surplus must always be positive; therefore, both dealers' quotes are lowered to the point where a transaction would yield either dealer a negligible surplus.

Analogously, the dealers compete on their buy side. In this case each dealer would raise his bid price to the level that a transaction with a public sell order would net him a negligible surplus. Therefore, under competition, in this case, no dealer can realize a significant surplus in either market buy or sell orders. More generally, when there are several market makers, we should find that, in many instances, competition eliminates the surplus to the dealers. The foregoing illustrates the one case when all market makers have no inventory.

There are other instances in which the marginal dealer (the dealer who offers the best quote) can realize a significant positive surplus. Consider the following case. Suppose all dealers except dealer A have accumulated large positive inventories. These dealers have less desire to buy for their inventory than does dealer A. As a result, dealer A's competitors will fail to raise their bid quotes high enough to eliminate dealer A's surplus. Meanwhile, dealer A will have no incentive to submit his highest (reservation) bid price to the market, but instead will submit the bid price that is slightly above the highest bid price of his competitors. In this scenario, when a public sell order arrives, he will cross with the order and will, by definition, realize a significantly positive surplus.

At equilibrium, the surpluses a dealer accumulates over a unit time on average must be approximately equal to the fixed costs per unit time that he bears. If the accumulated surplus exceeds his fixed costs, the market would induce more market makers to register for the stock. With more dealers entering the market, the excess surplus would be eliminated. Conversely, when the accumulated surpluses cannot cover the fixed costs, the market makers of the stock would not find it profitable to trade in the stock, and some of them would seek exit from the market. With fewer market makers in the stock, the remaining dealers may find it profitable to trade in the stock. This free entry to and exit from the dealer market is the mechanism by which to determine the equilibrium number of market makers in the stock. Denoting this equilibrium number by m and the transaction volume by V, we have shown that there is a functional form, F, such that

$$F(V, C, K, m) = 0 \qquad (3.1)$$

That is, the market structure m, the transaction volume V, and the cost structure (C, K) must all be interrelated. We shall study a model of the market structure in the following subsection.

The Market Structure

In a recent paper, Ho (1984) derived an explicit functional form of $F(.)$. Specifically, he showed that

$$V(\frac{\Delta L}{P}) = 2KQf(m) + m(2m + 1)C \qquad (3.2)$$

where

V is the dollar transaction volume traded through the dealer market (see the previous section).

$\Delta L = P^u - P^L$, the spread between the highest price and the lowest price that induce orders from the transacting public.

P is the underlying true price.

K is the inventory cost/share/unit time.

C is the fixed cost/unit time.

Q is the transaction size.

$f(.)$ is approximately a linear function; that is, $f(x) \cong - a + bx$ for some positive numbers a, b.

Equation 3.2 yields a number of interesting results. First, let us consider the effects on the dealer market of changes in the dealership cost structure. Suppose that, for technological reasons—automating order execution, for example— the fixed cost C is lowered. Then, holding V and K constant, equation 3.2 shows that m would increase $(\partial m / \partial C < 0)$. That is, the stock would induce more dealers to register for the stock. As a result, the market should perform better (to be discussed later), and that in turn should induce more order flow (V increases), leading to an even higher value of m. Reducing the fixed costs (through technological innovations) in the long run does not significantly benefit the market makers. It does lead to more agents becoming market makers, providing more liquidity to the market for the stock. In sum, at equilibrium, the transacting public benefits from technological innovations as market performance improves.

     Inventory costs can be analyzed analogously. Along with the changing technology in information systems, market makers are now bringing more current market information and research analysis to the trading room (see earlier in the chapter). This change reduces the risk of holding inventory and, hence, the inventory costs. As a result, according to equation 3.2, there should also be an increase in the number of market makers ($\partial m / \partial K < 0$). Once again, market performance improves and investors benefit.

Next we discuss the relationship between trading volume V and the number of market makers m, holding the cost structure constant. Alternatively, suppose that dealership cost structures are the same across all NASDAQ stocks (see the first section for the justification of this assumption), but that the trading volume differs among the stocks. Then equation 3.2 shows how m is related to different values of V, and figure 3–2 (curve A) depicts the values of m as a function of V. It shows that (1) m increases with V, and that (2) the function is concave, with the rate of increase negatively related to V.

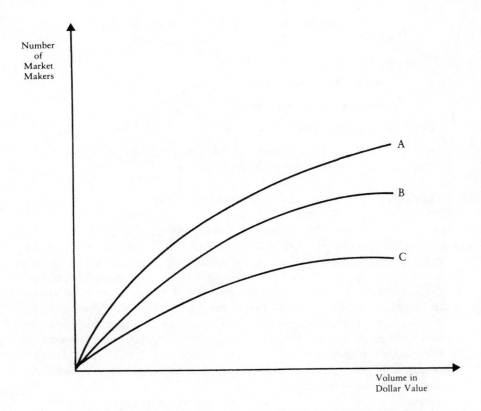

Figure 3–2. The Relationship between the Number of Market Makers and Transaction Volume

The first result can be explained simply: More trading volume should generate more revenues to the market makers, and therefore more dealers would become market makers for the stock. The second result needs more explanation. The result shows that an *n*-fold increase in trading volume would not induce an *n*-fold increase in the number of market makers in the stock. This is because the entry of an additional dealer to the market reduces the accumulated surplus/unit time to other dealers in two ways. First, additional participants will increase the competition, leading to a larger proportion of transactions that will yield negligible surpluses, and hence to a smaller proportion of profitable transactions for all the dealers collectively. Second, the newest dealer will also demand a share of the profits from the other dealers. The model shows that the combined effect will lead to a nonlinear relationship (a concave function).

The market structure depends crucially on the dealership cost structure. On the one hand, the extent of the nonlinearity depends on the fixed costs, with an increase in fixed costs leading to greater curvature, as depicted by figure 3–2 (curve *B*). That is, fixed costs affect the market structure more significantly for actively traded stocks than for less actively traded stocks. On the other hand, an increase in inventory costs does not significantly affect the curvature. Figure 3–2 (curve *C*) depicts the resulting market structure relationship with an increase in inventory costs.

In summary, this section shows how a market structure relationship is determined via competition among the dealers, and we describe the resulting equilibrium market structure as related to the trading volume and the cost structure of a dealership. It is interesting to note that whereas the fixed cost *C* is difficult to observe, the market structure relationship (equation 3.2) can be estimated. Therefore, the curvature of the estimated function can be used as an indirect measure of *C*.

Dealer Market Performance

In this section we consider only two attributes of market performance: the market bid-ask spread and market liquidity. For a public purchase, an investor must pay the ask price and, for a public sale, must sell at the bid price. The difference between the ask price and the bid price is the cost to the investor of a round-trip trade. It is therefore a desirable feature for a market to have a tight spread. Market liquidity measures the level of capital committed to market making. When there is a significant amount of capital attracted to stand ready to absorb any imbalances in buy and sell orders, the deviations of transaction prices from the true price would be reduced. In other words, when there is a block to sell in the market, and when the market is liquid, the sale would not significantly move the price. For this reason, it is also desirable for a market to be liquid. We have argued, however, that both the bid-ask spread and the market liquidity are endogenous to the market environment. Specifically, they are closely related to the transaction volume and the cost structure in market making. This section describes these relationships, and we show how the spread and the market liquidity are interrelated.

The Market Bid-Ask Spread

The market bid-ask spread is the difference between the lowest dealer ask price and the highest dealer bid price. As shown in the previous section, these prices are determined by direct competition among the dealers; therefore, the spread would change from one instant to another, depending on the inventory positions of the dealers. We shall discuss the behavior of the average market bid-ask spread.

To do so, we consider the impact of transaction volume on a representative dealer's bid-ask spread. Specifically, in the third section, we discussed the components of the market maker's bid-ask spread. Of these components, the inventory cost and the surplus depend on the trading volume of the stock. We shall discuss each of these costs separately. First, consider the inventory cost, which is directly proportional to the expected holding period. An increase in transaction volume, however, affects the expected holding period in two opposing ways. On the one hand, a higher level of trading volume induces more market makers to handle the stock. More intense competition will prolong the expected holding period of an inventory position. On the other hand, an increase in order flow will allow a market maker to turn over his inventory more often. Ho (1984) shows that, at equilibrium, the latter effect dominates the former, and that the expected holding period—hence the inventory cost—is negatively related to the magnitude of the order flow.

The impact on trading volume of the surplus is relatively straightforward. On average, surpluses for thickly traded stocks tend to be smaller because the dealer can recoup his fixed costs over many round-trip trades, whereas the market maker in a thinly traded issue must earn a substantial surplus on relatively few trades to cover his fixed cost. Therefore, average surpluses are higher for thin stocks than for thick stocks.

We have shown that a representative dealer's bid-ask spread is tighter for an actively traded stock than for a thinly traded stock. As a result, the market spread is negatively related to the transaction volume.

Market Liquidity

The previous section demonstrated that a market is more liquid (that is, more capital is committed to the market) when there are more orders passing through the dealer market. This section describes the relationship between transaction price movement and the market liquidity.

It is generally understood that the stock value changes because the market participants' evaluation of the stock value has changed. The stock price reflects the investors' expectation. On a transaction-by-transaction basis, however, stock price movements also depend on market liquidity. Consider figure 3–3. Figure 3–3a depicts the bid and ask quotes of dealers A and B, at time $t = 0$. Suppose they do not have any inventory, and hence are identical in all respects. It follows that their reservation prices are the same. Note that under competition, their reservation prices are their quotes (see the third section). We denote the asked price by P^a and the bid price by P^b. The midpoint between the asked price and the bid price is the perceived true price of the dealers.

At time $t = 1$, a market sell order arrives, and dealer B buys it, increasing B's inventory. After the purchase, dealer B lowers both his reservation prices, his reservation ask price becoming P and his reservation bid price becoming $P^{b'}$. In the previous section we argued that the dealers in this case would not quote the reservation prices. Indeed, we have shown that dealer A's bid price is slightly higher than $P^{b'}$ and dealer B's ask price is slightly less than $P^{b'}$. Notice that the market cannot observe price P or P^b. The market bid is $P^{b'}$, and the market ask is P^a. The mean of the bid ask is no longer P but a lower price, although the perceived true price has not changed at this time.

At time $t = 2$ another market sell order arrives. Figure 3–3c depicts the resulting quotes of the dealers. Dealer A would make the purchase, and his reservation price would also be lowered. Now, both dealer A and B have the same inventory level, and their reservation prices are the same. Under competition, they would submit quotes equaling their reservation prices. Now, the mean of the bid-ask quotes is $P' = (P + P^{b'})/2$, even lower than that depicted in figure 3–3b. Figure 3–3 shows how two consecutive market sell

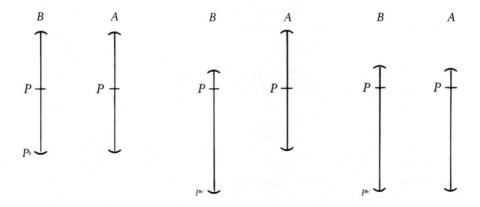

Figure 3–3. Market Liquidity

orders result in the lowering of market quotes. This argument can be extended to any number of dealers. Indeed, if there are m dealers, it would require m consecutive sell orders to add positive inventory to m dealers, and the mean of the market quotes to move from P to P'. It is in this sense that for large m, the transaction price is less likely to be moved by imbalances between buy orders and sell orders.

The Bid-Ask Spread and Market Liquidity

Although both the bid-ask spread and market liquidity are important attributes of market performance, they are not independent of each other. The bid-ask spread represents the portion of the value of the transaction that pays for dealer services. Meanwhile, the revenue to the dealer market determines the number of dealers, and hence market liquidity. Therefore, as long as there is free entry into and exit from the dealer market, and as long as there are no subsidies to dealers for their market-making activities, we must have a direct relationship between the spread and the number of market makers.

Ho (1984) shows that the relationship is given by the following equation:

$$(\tfrac{1}{2})Vs = QK\psi(m) + Cm \tag{3.3}$$

where

s is the percentage spread = [(ask price-bid price)/(average price)].
V is the dollar value of the transaction volume, flowing through the dealer market/unit time.
K is the inventory cost/share/unit time.
Q is the transaction size.
m is the number of market makers.
C is the fixed cost/unit time.
ψ is some increasing function of m.

Equation 3.3 says that the revenues to all the dealers (left-hand side) must equal the costs to all the dealers of staying in the market (right-hand side). Notice that the proportion of the flow of transaction value that goes to the dealer is $(\tfrac{1}{2}s)$, not s. This is because s is only the quoted spread, as distinct from the realized spread $(\tfrac{1}{2}s)$ (see Stoll 1984b for a more detailed discussion on this point). The first term on the right-hand side represents the inventory costs, and it increases with m. The reason for this is given in the section entitled Market Liquidity, and that is, when there are more dealers, the market is better suited to absorb imbalances of buy and sell orders. Consequently, in such a market, all of the dealers would together pay higher inventory costs for being able to carry more inventory.

Consider equation 3.3. Suppose we keep the transaction volume constant, and increase the percentage spread s. As a result, the number of market makers would be affected. Specifically, differentiating equation 3.3 with respect to m, we get

$$\tfrac{1}{2} V \frac{\partial s}{\partial m} = QK \frac{\partial \psi}{\partial m} + C \qquad (3.4)$$

But

$$\frac{\partial \psi}{\partial m} > 0$$

as noted earlier, and therefore

$$\frac{\partial s}{\partial m} > 0 \qquad (3.5)$$

Equation 3.5 shows that the spread is positively related to market liquidity when transaction volume is kept constant. That is, if there is some trading rule that requires a tight spread, the revenues to the dealers will decrease, and some of the dealers will leave the market, leading to a less liquid market—that is, a decrease in (s) resulting in a decrease in (m). This analysis clearly shows a trade-off between the spread and market liquidity in the design of trading rules. Unless dealers are subsidized, a market cannot achieve any specified degree of liquidity and market spread.

Empirical Investigations

Before we proceed to discuss the implications of the analysis of the paper, we present some empirical investigations of the NASDAQ market. The purpose of this section is to provide some empirical evidence of our theory and some empirical description of the NASDAQ market.

We obtained the list of stocks in the trading portfolio of each market maker in the OTC NASDAQ system as of December 14, 1983. There are 442 market makers altogether. The data allowed us to analyze the characteristics of the trading portfolios and the determinants of the equilibrium number of market makers in each stock.

The Distribution of the Trading Portfolio Sizes

The sample consists of the complete list of market makers and their trading portfolios. In this section, unless otherwise stated, the trading portfolios considered consist of both NASDAQ stocks and Consolidated Quotes System (CQS) stocks.

First, we studied the distribution of the market makers in terms of their trading portfolio sizes, measured by the number of stocks they traded. The distribution is depicted in figure 3–4. It shows that most market makers trade fewer than ten stocks, and few market makers hold large trading portfolios. Indeed, the distribution is monotonically decreasing with portfolio size.

Although the average portfolio size across these market makers is 79.2 stocks, there is no evidence of any optimal portfolio size that the market maker would seek to maintain. There is no region of portfolio sizes where the distribution tends to cluster.

It is also interesting to observe the large variance in portfolio size. Whereas there are over fifty market makers trading only 1 stock, there are five market makers with portfolio sizes of over 1,000 stocks, and one of over 2,000 stocks. The significant number of market makers with few stocks in their trading portfolios (over half the market makers have fewer than 30 stocks) suggests there is little economy of scale in trading. Meanwhile, the fact that there are market makers with extremely large trading portfolios shows that the NASDAQ system also attracts large firms as market makers.

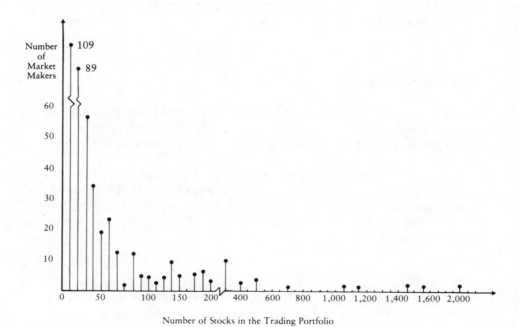

Figure 3–4. The Distribution of Trading Portfolio Sizes

Wire Houses, Trading Houses, and Specialization in Trading

Generally speaking, there are two types of market makers in the NASDAQ system: wire houses and trading houses. In the traditional sense, a wire house is a brokerage firm with a large retail branch system. For the purposes of this chapter, institutional firms with large customer bases will also be included in the wire house category. As market makers in NASDAQ securities, wire houses have direct access to the OTC market. They can therefore effectively facilitate the execution of both market and limit orders originating from their customers. Market makers in wire houses engage in dealer activities primarily for the purpose of earning commissions from customer order flow (see the description of commission income earlier in this chapter).

One may hypothesize that in a wire house the market maker's objective may be to facilitate in-house trades. The main portion of profits arises not from trading as described in this paper but from commission earned on each customer trades.

A trading house specializes in providing liquidity to the market. Their profits derive primarily from competition for order flow and other aspects of the market making function. In most cases, there is a negligible order flow generated from in-house brokerage activity, and hence a low level of agency commission revenues. The distinction between these two types of market making suggests that there may be some relationship between the firm's size and the type of stocks that the firm trades.

Specifically, since wire houses tend to be larger firms with significant customer order flow, they are more likely to hold thick stocks and have larger portfolio sizes. In contrast, trading houses may deal in thinner issues and have a smaller trading portfolio. This hypothesis was then investigated.

We formed pairs of observations (X, Y) as follows. Consider each trading portfolio in the sample. For the ith trading portfolio in the sample, let X_i be the portfolio size, the number of stocks in the portfolio. Let Y_{ij} be the number of shares outstanding for the jth stock, $1 \leq j \leq X_i$. Y_{ij} is used as a proxy for the liquidity of the stock. Then we formed the pairs (X_i, Y_{ij}) for all i and j; that is, the observations of all the trading portfolios are merged together. The correlation between X and Y is investigated.

The empirical tests show that there is no correlation between portfolio size (the firm size) and the shares outstanding (stock liquidity). Scatter plots of X and Y confirm the empirical estimations. Correlations of X and Y for different sample groups (large/small firms, thick/thin stocks) are also studied. They show that there is no tendency for large firms to trade thick or thin stocks, nor for small firms to specialize in either thin or thick stocks.

While there is no evidence that large firms tend to trade thick or thin issues, there is strong empirical evidence that firms do specialize in trading foreign or ADR stocks.[5] An ADR (American Depository Receipt) is a receipt that evidences shares of a foreign corporation. Transactions take place in the ADR instead of the actual shares, which is usually held by a trustee. Transaction prices for ADRs are dollar-denominated. The ADR is usually issued by a foreign branch of a U.S. bank. While most large firms with over 500 stocks in their trading portfolios deal with some foreign or ADR stocks, most market makers do not participate in them. However, there are firms that clearly specialize in these stocks. For example, one firm trades 291 stocks of which 97 are foreign or ADR issues. And one small firm trades 20 stocks, of which 17 are foreign/ADR.

One possible explanation for this apparent specialization is that these firms have built up personal relationships with certain overseas securities firms which make markets in the underlying securities. This would permit the U.S.-based firm to engage actively in arbitrage between the ADR and the actual foreign security. The evidence suggests that ADRs and foreign stocks are not homogeneous as trading instruments, thereby requiring a certain degree of specialization.

Equilibrium Number of Market Makers in a Stock

Now we investigate the determinants of the number of market makers in NASDAQ stocks. From the data described in the last section, we determined the number of dealers in each of the OTC stocks with NASDAQ symbols starting with the letter A. Included in our sample were foreign stocks, ADR stocks, warrants, and firms in bankruptcy. There were 126 observations in our sample. It is interesting to note that large numbers of stocks attract few market makers. Indeed, fewer than 15 percent of the stocks have over ten market makers. On average there are approximately seven market makers per stock, and the distribution is quite symmetric around the mean.

For each of 126 stocks, we determined the cumulative volume (in shares) of transactions (v) from July through September 1983 (three-month period). The data were obtained from the Standard and Poors OTC stock report. We then determined the value on December 16 of each stock P. The transaction volume is defined to be Pv.

The transaction volume for a stock varies significantly over time. Therefore, there is much noise in the volume observations. Part of the noise can be suppressed by grouping all the stocks with the same number of market makers, and calculating their average transaction volume per week. The relationship between the average transaction volume and the number of dealers was then plotted. The results are presented in figure 3–5. They provide strong support for the hypothesis of the analytical results.[6]

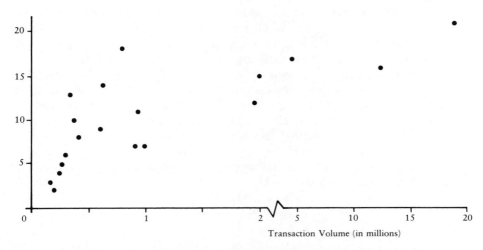

Figure 3–5. The Relationship between the Number of Market Makers and Transaction Volume

Specifically, the scattered plots show that thick stocks attract more market makers. Stocks with a transaction volume of over $2 million each week will attract over fourteen market makers. On the other hand, stocks that have less than $0.2 million of transaction volume per week attract fewer than three market makers. The nonlinearity of the graph is substantial. Whereas stocks with a weekly transaction volume of $2 million attract about fourteen market makers, stock with tenfold transaction volume ($20 million/ week) attract only four additional market makers. Apple Computer was the most active stock in our sample. Its trading volume, in our sample period, averaged $75 million/week. Yet it has only twenty-four market makers. This evidence is consistent with our hypothesis that fixed costs are significant in the cost structure of market making.

By way of comparison, casual empirical analysis shows that the trading volume of a majority of the NYSE stocks is in the order of $20 million/week. Figure 3–5 suggests that these stocks would attract over ten market makers in the stock if they were traded on NASDAQ. Also noteworthy is that for the most active stocks on the NYSE, for example IBM and GM, trading volume is around $500 million/week, about ten times greater than one of the most active stocks on NASDAQ.

Implications and Conclusions

This paper has studied the structure and performance of dealer markets as endogenous to the order flow intensity and the cost structure in market making.

Specifically, we show that the market bid-ask spread and market liquidity depend crucially on the trading characteristics of the stock. Actively traded stocks have tighter bid-ask spreads, and they are more liquid than less actively traded stocks. Also, riskier stocks attract fewer dealers to make a market and they have wider spreads than less risky stocks. Trading rules often result in a trade-off between a tighter market spread and a more liquid market.[7] From this analysis, we argue that a dealer market cannot achieve any degree of liquidity while at the same time maintaining a sufficiently narrow market spread, since both attributes are endogenous to the trading environment. This analysis suggests that the way to improve market performance is to reduce the costs incurred in market making. Also, it shows that the trading rules meant to regulate the market spread or the number of market makers in a stock may not be always beneficial.

Upstairs Trading

Upstairs trading here refers to investors or market professionals buying and selling shares on a frequent basis. They do not in general supply quotes to the market as dealers do. Instead, they often send market orders to the market makers. These upstairs traders' specialized skill is the timing of order executions. Our analysis shows how market timing may be profitable. Earlier we showed that the capital committed to make a dealer market in a stock is limited. In the event that there is a sequence of buy or sell orders generated by liquidity investors, the market quotes would be affected; they may be above or below the underlying true price. Upstairs traders are best able to recognize these price movements during a trading day. They seek to buy when there is downward pressure on the price by sell orders originated by uninformed traders; similarly, they seek to sell when buy orders from uninformed traders push the market quotes upwards. This model of a dealer market recognizes that the market makers alone cannot provide an efficient market. The reason is that the dealers' capital is limited at any instant in time, and therefore the dealers cannot exploit all profitable opportunities. Thus when investors seek to trade, it may not be desirable for them to send their orders to the market without monitoring the price movements; but they should execute the orders in a timely fashion. Such profit opportunities induce upstairs trading.

Block Trading

Our analysis also provides some insights into "block trading."[8] For the sake of argument, we dichotomize the clients for dealer services into two types: retail traders and institutional traders. Retail traders send small orders to the market, whereas institutional traders transact in large blocks. These two groups have different concerns with respect to the market. Retail traders' orders can often transact at the market quotes, so the cost imposed on them (by the market) is primarily the bid-ask spread. By contrast, institutional traders' orders are often block transactions. They demand that a market possess a significant amount of capital to provide the opposite side of the trade. They seek liquidity and timeliness in completing a transaction. We have argued, however, that any market has to make a trade-off between the market spread and the market liquidity; as a result, the market fails to satisfy the two groups of traders. For this reason, block trading has evolved to deal with the demands of institutional traders. The creation of two markets has essentially allowed the retail traders and the institutional traders to self-select, resulting in a more cost-efficient trading system.

Dealer Markets and Auction Markets: A Comparison

In a dealer market, for a sufficiently thick issue, the order flow will induce many dealers to participate in the market. The competitive forces of the market will ensure that the market spread is tight. Further, the diversity of opinions among the various market makers will ensure market liquidity.

Meanwhile, competitive forces alone cannot provide an adequate market for thin issues. First, these issues attract few market makers; as a consequence, relatively less capital is committed to trading. The market is therefore less liquid. Second, the dealers must demand a significant surplus in each trade to cover fixed costs, which will result in a relatively wide bid-ask spread. Third, when there are few market makers, the structure of the NASDAQ system may allow these market makers to act noncompetitively. When they do not act competitively, other dealers would be induced to register for the stock. In the final analysis, each dealer is still indifferent between making a market in a thinly traded stock or in another thickly traded stock. The end result may be that the spread of these thin stocks is greater. Finally, in the NASDAQ system, there is not at present a consolidated limit order book. As a consequence, an investor cannot effectively reveal his quote to the public.

Now consider the auction market (for example NYSE, AMEX, and the regional stock exchanges). The specialist system is well equipped to trade thin issues. There is a consolidated limit order book and rules requiring that public orders be exposed to the market place. Also, there are many types of orders available to the investors, and that should encourage transactions from a broad spectrum of customers. The exchanges have also introduced a variety of different technological improvements that greatly speed the handling and executing of small orders. These systems (such as DOT) have permitted wire houses to operate with far fewer floor brokers and other associated personnel than would be required if these systems were not in place.

Finally, the exchange floor provides a way to monitor the business conduct of the specialist. The specialist, for the privilege of having exclusive access to the limit order book, is under an affirmative obligation to maintain a fair and orderly market, and is also prohibited from making destabilizing transactions for his own account. The exchange monitors all transactions that take place on the floor for violations and trading irregularities, and floor officials observe trading and mediate disputes during the trading day.

After comparing the NASDAQ system to the exchange system, it would seem that the exchanges should lower their listing requirements so that many of the stocks that do not attract enough market makers in the multiple dealer market (thin issues) can be traded on an exchange system.[9] At present, listing requirements for the NYSE tend to favor thick issues. For a company to be listed, it must meet some stringent criteria.

Why, then, are most thick issues traded on the NYSE? The answer is complex. First, historically there is prestige associated with being listed on the NYSE (recently, however, some firms with actively traded issues choose to stay in the OTC market). Second, an NYSE rule makes it very difficult for a firm, once listed on the exchange, to be voluntarily delisted (see Wall 1984). A final reason concerns technological innovations. In principle, allowing dealers to trade in diverse geographical locations represents a viable alternative to the auction market. In practice, the trading system is technologically complicated. The NASDAQ system, though proved to be a successful system, remains an electronic bulletin board. Although more efficient electronic trading systems are being developed for dealer markets, these systems remain in the future.

Our final discussion deals with the trading of new instruments. The recent plethora of proposed new products and trading vehicles has been received with some skepticism by many members of the securities industry. There is, however, significant economic value to be gained by trading some of these products. Instruments such as futures on the wheat, cotton, or auto output indexes, or on the housing start index, to name a few, should be important to particular segments of the economy; many of these narrowly based products would permit commercial users to transfer risk to the capital markets. Unfortunately, market designers face the significant problem of attracting adequate public order flow to these new products. The problem arises because many of these instruments are complex and unfamiliar to the transacting public. We argue that these innovative new instruments would be best suited to trade under a specialist system.

In the past, many futures and other instruments have failed or become very inactive soon after their introduction. Most of these instruments were traded under an open outcry or dealer market. Since many trading vehicles require an extended period of time to allow for the education of the public and commercial users, the exchange system is in a position to nurture a new product until sufficient external order flow develops. Recently, the Philadelphia Stock Exchange proposed the trading of futures under a specialist system. This recent development is consistent with our hypothesis. In sum, the exchange should maximize the utility of the specialist system, and become a major factor in new-product developmnt and implementation.

Notes

1. The study of market making and trading systems has generated much interest in academic literature. See, for example, Cohen et al. (1979), Demsetz (1968), Garman (1976), and Stoll (1984).

2. The cost of inventory risk has been considered in Amihud and Mendelson (1980); Ho and Stoll (1983); O'Hara and Oldfield (1982); and Stoll (1978, 1984).

3. Inventory costs as a result of asymmetric information has been considered in Copeland and Galai (1983) and Glosten and Milgrom (1982).

4. The spread structure is first discussed in Stoll (1985). Chapter 4.

5. The primary difference between foreign stocks and ADRs concerns the transfer of shares. Since ADRs are held by U.S. banks, the transfer of shares is quite simple. For foreign stocks, the certificates are held by a bank in the country in which the company is based. For example, a Japanese company will have its shares held by a Japanese bank. Another difference concerns the computation of round lots. For most U.S. stocks, a round lot consists of 100 shares. The round lot amount for ADRs is also 100 shares. For foreign stocks a round lot may consist of an amount other than 100 shares.

6. There are other empirical studies of the relationship between transaction volume and the number of market makers, but they do not focus on any particular theoretical model (Stoll 1978b).

7. This trade-off between the spread and the liquidity should be an important consideration for empirical studies on market bid-ask spreads (Benston and Hagerman 1974; Newton and Quandt 1979; and Stoll 1984).

8. Many institutional block trades (orders greater than 10,000 shares) are handled by a brokerage firm's block trading department, rather than by the market makers alone. The following scenario outlines a general framework for the handling of block orders. In general, an institution will relay an order through the institutional salesman who covers the account for the brokerage firm. The salesman will then give the order to his block execution department. Sales traders will then contact other institutions and attempt to find buyers for the block (or sellers, if the order was a buy). If enough interest can be found to take the other side of the order, the block will be crossed. In the event that the sales traders cannot solicit enough interest, the balance of the order will be turned over to the market maker. The market maker will then determine whether to position the block or whether to execute the uncrossable portion of the order flow through other competing market makers.

9. For a company to be listed on the NYSE, it must meet some of the following criteria. First, the company must have demonstrated earning power of at least $2.5 million annually before taxes for the most recent year, and $2 million for each of the two preceding years. The company must also have net tangible assets of at least $16 million in market value of publicly held common stock, 1 million publicly held common shares and at least 2,000 holders of 100 shares or more.

References

Amihud, Yakov, and Mendelson, Haim. 1980. Dealership market: Market making with inventory. *Journal of Financial Economics 8* (March):31–53.

Benston, George, and Hagerman, Robert. 1974. Determinants of bid-asked spreads in over-the-counter market. *Journal of Financial Economics.*

Branch, B., and Freed, W. 1977. Bid-asked spreads on the AMEX and the big board. *Journal of Finance* (March):159–163.

Cohen, Kalman; Maier, Steve; Schwartz, Robert; and Whitcomb, David. 1979. Market makers and the market spread: A review of recent literature. *Journal of Financial and Quantitative Analysis* (November):813–835.

Copeland, Thomas, and Galai, Dan. 1983. Information effects on the bid-asked spread. *Journal of Finance* (December).

Demsetz, Harold. 1968. The cost of transacting. *Quarterly Journal of Economics 1* (February).

Garman, Mark. 1976. Market microstructure. *Journal of Financial Economics* (June).

Glosten, Lawrence R., and Milgrom, Paul R. 1982. Bid, ask and transaction prices in a specialist market with heterogeneously informed traders. Working Paper, October.

Ho, Thomas. 1984. Dealer market structure: A dynamic competitive equilibrium model. Working Paper, New York University.

Ho, Thomas, and Stoll, Hans. 1983. The dynamics of dealer markets under competition. *Journal of Finance 3* (September).

Newton, William, and Quandt, Richard. 1979. An empirical study of spreads. Research Memorandum No. 30, Financial Research Center, Princeton University, January.

O'Hara, Maureen, and Oldfield, George. 1982. The microeconomics of market making. Working Paper, Cornell University, October.

Schleef, H.J., and Mildenstein, E. 1983. A dynamic model of the security dealer's bid and ask prices. *Journal of Finance* (March).

Stoll, Hans. 1978a. The pricing of security dealer services: An empirical study of NASDAQ stocks. *Journal of Finance 33* (4).

——— . 1978b. The supply of dealer services in securities markets. *Journal of Finance* (September).

——— . 1984. The New York Stock Exchange specialist system. Working Paper No. 83-129, Owen Graduate School of Management, Vanderbilt University, February.

——— . 1985. Alternative views of market making. Chapter 4.

Tinic, Seha, and West, Richard. 1972. Competition and the pricing of dealer services in the over-the-counter market. *Journal of Financial and Quantitative Analysis 7* (June).

Wall, John. 1984. The competitive environment of the securities markets. In Amihud, Ho, and Schwartz, eds., *Market Making and the Changing Structure of the Securities Industry.*

4
Alternative Views of Market Making

Hans R. Stoll

This chapter analyzes alternative views of market making and reviews academic research on this subject, most of it produced in the last ten years. In this period, technological, economic, and regulatory forces have brought about significant changes in the structure of securities markets. Academic research has improved our understanding of the operation of market makers and of the short-term behavior of securities prices—behavior determined in part by market makers.

The paper begins with a discussion of the trading environment and the criteria for judging market-making performance. Several alternative views of market making are then considered: the market maker as auctioneer, as price stabilizer, as information processor, and as supplier of immediacy. As auctioneer, the market maker is an agent who organizes and runs a call auction market according to rules that influence the efficiency of the outcome. As price stabilizer, the market maker trades for his own account as principal to eliminate market price deviations that he feels are unjustified. As information processor, the market maker processes market information inherent in the order flow that gives a signal concerning the changes in the underlying price. He is the fulcrum through which new information is reflected in the market price. As supplier of immediacy, the market maker is a service organization that supplies liquidity to investors at a cost reflected in the market maker's bid-ask spread.

Although these views differ, they are not mutually exclusive and are, indeed, frequently complementary. The chapter also contains a section on empirical tests of the bid-ask spread and a section on the market for market makers that discusses the industrial organization of market-making services, and a concluding section.

The Trading Environment and Criteria of Market-Maker Performance

The fundamental price of a security is determined by the public's willingness to hold the existing supply of that security. Trading arises whenever any investor is unwilling to hold his initial portfolio at the initial price, either because the investor has information that leads him to believe the fundamental price of the security has changed or because he desires liquidity to meet consumption or savings objectives or otherwise wishes to rebalance his portfolio. Although the motives for trading by information traders and liquidity traders are different, both types of traders interact in the trading process to arrive at a new market equilibrium price at which all trading and nontrading investors are willing to hold the outstanding shares of the security in question. If the new price makes someone unhappy, trading will continue.

Assume that the price at the beginning of a trading period is P_0, and assume that this price is correct and represents the consensus of opinions at which all investors are willing to hold the existing shares of the security. Assume further, for the purposes of this illustration, that the fundamental price at the end of the trading interval, at which the public would continue to hold the shares of the security, remains at P_0. In other words, assume that investors trade for a variety of reasons, but in the end would agree on a fundamental value that is the same as the value at the beginning.

In a perfectly efficient market the transaction price, P_T, at the end of the trading interval would be P_0. In actual markets, however, the demand to buy shares at P_0 may not equal the supply of shares at P_0 during a particular trading interval. As a result, a discrepancy between P_T and P_0 that would not exist in a frictionless market might exist in actual markets. For example, in figure 4–1, $P_T > P_0$ because there is an excess of buyers over sellers at P_0. The structure of real-world markets, real-world communication costs, order-processing costs, and the like can cause deviations of P_T and P_0.

The market maker is at the hub of the overall market mechanism. He processes orders, establishes transaction prices, and—in some but not all regimes—bears risk. The processing of orders is affected by the level of trading volume and the degree of volatility in the rate of order arrivals and the size of orders. The establishment of transaction prices is related to investor beliefs about the fundamental true price, the level of uncertainty about future changes in the true price and the degree to which investors disagree about the true price. The price and the degree of price uncertainty are also affected by the characteristics of the market structure and the role of the market maker.

The performance of a market-making system is judged by its pricing and transaction efficiency. Most fundamentally, a desirable market-making system is one that minimizes the difference between P_T and P_0—in other words, one that reveals the true price, P_0. If this is so, investors who observe this price will not wish to trade again. In practice, it is difficult to evaluate market makers' systems directly according to this criterion, since P_0 is not observable.

The second criterion, transaction efficiency, means that the market-making system provides its services at minimum cost. One reason for the discrep-

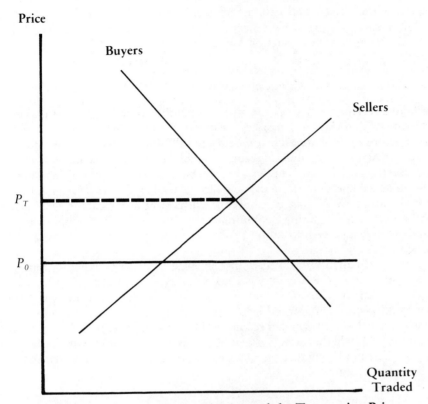

Figure 4–1. The Fundamental Price and the Transaction Price

ancy between P_0 and P_T is the cost of the market-making system itself. If these costs are as low as possible, then one argues that the market-making system facilitates transactions efficiently.

The Market Maker as Auctioneer

A call auction market is a periodic market in which orders to buy and sell are batched over time and traded at a price, P_T, that is equal to, or better than, the order price specified by each trader. The market maker as auctioneer is the coordinator of this process. Under certain arrangements, he may participate actively. Unlike the case in dealer markets, however, there is no bid or ask price in a call auction market.

Thin secondary securities markets are often organized as call auction markets. For example, until 1870 the New York Stock Exchange was a call auction market. Even today the opening on the NYSE is handled as a call auction market. Major foreign markets—the Paris Bourse and the Tel Aviv Stock Exchange—are call auction markets.

The Market Maker as Walrasian Auctioneer

Until quite recently, economic analysis ignored the process of market making and assumed that transaction prices are determined so that $P_T = P_0$. Justification of this result is achieved by reference to a *Walrasian market* in which the Walrasian auctioneer knows *all* traders' demands and supplies for *each* asset, conditional on *each* possible price of each asset. Furthermore, the auctioneer is disinterested and does not participate in the trading process. Given all this information, the Walrasian auctioneer can determine a transaction price such that $P_T = P_0$. Although this view of market making is a useful simplification in understanding certain economic problems, it is not an accurate view of real markets.

Real-world auction markets do not provide the voluminous set of information that allows the fictitious Walrasian auctioneer to determine the true market clearing price in one sitting. Actual auction markets may diverge from the ideal, depending in part on the particular rules under which they operate. These rules include (1) whether recontracting is possible before a final price is announced, (2) whether orders are publicly disclosed before the final price is announced, and (3) whether the auctioneer can solicit orders or enter orders for his own account.

The Market Maker as Order Clerk

The simplest, and most extreme, real-world call auction market is one in which orders arrive anonymously and are batched without public disclosure, in which recontracting is not permitted, and in which the auctioneer acts as a clerk who accumulates orders and announces the market clearing price without either soliciting additional orders or entering orders for his own account. In other words, this market is like a black box that accumulates orders and calculates a price at which the flow of buy orders is offset by the flow of sell orders. In an insightful paper, Ho, Schwartz, and Whitcomb (1985) analyze this market in detail.

Although a call auction market is supposed to take place at intervals such that sufficient volume is generated to cause the trade price P_T, to represent closely the true price P_0, there is no guarantee in fact that $P_T = P_0$ for any particular auction. Indeed, Ho, Schwartz, and Whitcomb show that a black-box auction generates order placement strategies that may induce increased instability of P_T relative to P_0.

There is a further complication when the underlying true price is changing and investors have different information. In a rational-expectations equilibrium (see, for example, Grossman 1981), the market price aggregates all available information. When investors observe the result of an auction, they received new information which may cause them to trade again. Thus a single black-box auction does not generally reach a satisfactory market clearing price. This will also be true of a Walrasian auction, where the auctioneer uses all prior information but fails to use the information implicit in the price that he calculates.

Several mechanisms exist for resolving the difficulties posed by a one-shot black-box call auction market. First, one can permit recontracting after the posting of a trial clearing price. Although this is an acceptable solution in a world of costless trading, in actual markets such recontracting would be costly and time-consuming. Recontracting does not occur in any formal way in actual call auction markets—although additional orders can usually be solicited by the auctioneer if he observes that the market clearing price is likely to be incorrect.

A second modification of the black-box auction would be to provide for the public disclosure of orders as they are submitted to the auctioneer. This procedure would allow all market participants to calculate the likely clearing price, P_T, and to submit additional orders or modifications of existing orders. In practice, no auction markets have this feature. Part of the difficulty in implementing this solution is that all traders would want to see all other traders' orders before placing their own. This would lead to postponement of orders until the last minute. Alternatively, if multiple orders were permitted in a single auction, investors might want to modify their orders continuously as other orders were observed. This would be costly in the same way that frequent recontracting is costly.

The Market Maker as Active Auctioneer

A third modification of the black-box auction would be to allow certain traders, such as the auctioneer, to observe the order flow and to take positions for their own accounts to lessen any discrepancy between P_T and P_0. Real-world markets seem to utilize this solution. On the Tel Aviv Stock Exchange, banks accumulate the order flow and are in a position to observe order imbalances that might lead to an unjustified clearing price. Then, using the information they have gleaned from the observed order flow, they are able to trade for their own accounts. In U.S. exchange markets, the specialist behaves in this manner at the opening and after trading halts, when orders are batched in the manner of a call auction market. The specialist also has the advantage at all times of being able to observe the orders on his book of limit orders—information that is not available to other traders.

This procedure of allowing the auctioneer to make up some portion of the imbalance that he observes after all other investors have finalized their orders gives the auctioneer a tremendous economic advantage over other traders. Having observed all orders, he has more information than any other trader in the market about the discrepancy between P_T and P_0, and he can offer to make up that part of the excess demand or supply that maximizes his profits. In other words, he is a monopolist with respect to the excess demand existing just before the auction price is announced. Gould and Verrecchia (1982) examine a rational-expectations equilibrium price under a regime that gives the auctioneer this power.

It should be noted that there is a significant difference between meeting an imbalance after the fact and establishing a price before the fact at which any imbalance will be met. In the second case the participating auctioneer faces much greater risks since he has not been able to observe the information implicit in the order flow itself.

Call Auction Versus Continuous Markets

Call auction markets have several drawbacks. First, they impose on investors the cost of waiting to trade since the trading takes place at periodic intervals. Second, there is uncertainty about the price at which the investor will trade. As Ho, Schwartz, and Whitcomb (1985) have shown, this uncertainty can cause investors to place orders that are too large and that are away from the price at which they expect the market to clear. This order placement strategy can in turn bring about unnecessary additional price uncertainty. Third, because of the periodic nature of call auctions, new information is conveyed to the public with delay. Between auctions, and before the new information is revealed in the price, investors may take inappropriate actions, including the placement of orders that are inappropriate.

A benefit of a periodic call auction market is that it economizes on supervision costs in comparison with a market that is open continuously. Therefore, in a thin market, a call auction procedure may be the most effective mechanism for handling the order flow. A second benefit of a call auction market may be that it is an effective mechanism for dealing with asymmetric information, a problem discussed in greater detail below. The problem arises from the fact that information traders gain only at the expense of traders without information—liquidity traders. A market cannot be successful if liquidity traders do not receive reasonable protection against information traders. A call auction market, by imposing delay, may be a mechanism that forces information traders to reveal, through their order placements, the existence of information. Indeed, in continuous markets such as the NYSE, periods of apparent informational asymmetry, manifested by an imbalance in orders, cause a trading halt and put into process a call auction procedure.

Successful real-world securities markets tend to be (most of the time) continuous markets, not call auction markets, perhaps because of the significance of the drawbacks of call auction markets as compared with their benefits. Beja and Hakansson (1977, 1979) have discussed the costs and benefits of continuous call markets as well as other aspects of market structure. Modifications to make call auction markets continuous have generally taken one of two forms. One approach is a continuous market without a designated market maker. In such a market, individual investors may continuously place limit orders to buy or to sell, thereby providing liquidity and preventing the price from deviating from its true value. This type of market may be called a continuous double auction market—*double auction market* because auctions occur both on the buying side and on the selling side; *continuous* because investors can place limit orders at any time and may execute against any existing limit orders observed in the marketplace. Cohen, Maier, Schwartz, and Whitcomb (1981) analyze this type of market. Some recent experimental literature indicates that these double auction markets work quite well (see, e.g., Forsythe, Palfrey, and Plott 1982; Plott and Sunder 1982; and Friedman 1984). Making trading continuous solves the problems of call auction markets. First, the cost of waiting is eliminated. Second, each trader knows the market price at each instant of time and can trade his preferred quantity at that price. The possibility of increased price volatility as a result of order placement strategies, noted by Ho, Schwartz, and Whitcomb (1984), is thus eliminated. Third, the information implicit in price changes is continuously revealed to the market. In effect, a continuous market allows for continuous recontracting that is not possible in a call auction market. All investors are able to perceive the evolution of market prices as orders are received, something that is not possible when orders are batched over time.

There is no intention in this survey to examine in detail the operation or the costs and benefits of continuous double auction markets without designated market makers. Suffice it to say that the final result is quite similar to that of a continuous market *with* designated market makers. This is because limit orders placed by knowledgeable investors in the market without market makers will provide the same function as the bid and ask prices provided by market makers (see Ho and Stoll 1983).

A second modification that will be pursued in greater detail in this survey is the introduction of a market maker who trades for his own account on a continuous basis to eliminate discrepancies between P_T and P_0. The role of market makers in the transition from call auction markets to continuous markets is discussed by Garbade and Silber (1979).

In the next three sections we turn to three alternative views of the market maker acting as principal: as stabilizer, as information processor, and as supplier of immediacy.

The Market Maker as Price Stabilizer

Recognition that the public-order flow may result in a price that deviates from its fundamental value generates economic incentives for professional traders to benefit from this price deviation. On futures markets, scalpers trade against the public-order flow. In the securities markets, dealers, such as the New York Stock Exchange specialist, trade against the public-order flow and are viewed as price stabilizers (or criticized as price destabilizers). The emphasis of analyses of the market maker from this perspective is not on the bid-ask spread of the market maker but, rather, on the effect the market maker has in keeping transaction prices from deviating from their true values. Although market makers as stabilizers can play important roles in meeting imbalances in certain call auction markets, they are essential factors in the operation of continuous markets. Several approaches have been taken to the market maker as price stabilizer.

The Market Maker as Mechanical Stabilizer

Because trading is in lumpy quantities and at prices that change discretely, transactions differing slightly in quantity or price may not be executed. For example, a seller of 300 shares at $20 per share cannot trade with a buyer of 200 shares at $20 per share, since quantities are different. The objective of the market maker as mechanical stabilizer is to facilitate these kinds of transactions and to eliminate temporary discontinuities in demand; that is, the market maker performs the function of demand smoothing (Beja and Hakansson 1979). This perspective sometimes leads to recommendations that the function of the market maker be automated or otherwise given to an employee of the exchange. Such a recommendation, however, fails to recognize that price fluctuations are due to more fundamental reasons than the mechanics of the trading process and can result in significant risks that a computer or an employee of the exchange has no interest in minimizing. Some of the arguments for and against automating the specialist are presented in Black (1971).

The Market Maker as Passive Stabilizer

The most common view is that of market maker as a passive stabilizer who buys when prices are depressed below their true value and sells when prices are pushed above their true value. The market maker is passive in that he does not anticipate price movements. Instead, the market maker reacts to the order flow, buying when there is an excess supply and selling when there is an excess demand. When the fundamental price (P_0 in figure 4–1) does not change, passive stabilization is a profitable strategy.

The New York Stock Exchange's tests of the specialist's performance in maintaining a "fair and orderly market" are tests of stabilizing behavior in this sense. The NYSE finds that the specialist buys on down ticks and sells on up ticks in over 90 percent of all transactions (NYSE 1980). The SEC's *Institutional Investor Study* (U.S. SEC 1971, vol. 4) also found that the specialist bought on price declines and sold on price increases. A similar pattern is observed by Stoll (1976) for competing NASDAQ dealers. Barnea (1974) argues that a stabilizing specialist will reduce the short-term variance of a stock relative to the long-term variance of the stock as compared with a non-stabilizing specialist. Schwartz and Whitcomb (1976) note that Barnea's measure of stabilization depends on the degree of serial correlation in a stock's return, which may be affected by other forces as well as by the specialist.

It is important to distinguish between an ex post stabilizer and an ex ante stabilizer. As noted earlier, an auctioneer acting as an ex post stabilizer in a call auction market, after seeing all other orders, has a substantial advantage and stands to earn a monopoly rent. An ex ante stabilizer is one who sets a price before seeing the order flow and agrees to buy or sell at that price (or at two prices—the bid and ask). In this second case of ex ante stabilization, the market maker can go bankrupt in trying to absorb the random order flow as Garman (1976) has shown. In the real world, the market maker protects himself against this possibility by limiting the size of his transaction at his quote and adjusting his quote over time to avoid excessive accumulation or decumulation of inventory. In other words, although the dealer is passive and responds to the order flow, he learns from the order flow and adjusts his prices accordingly. The possibility of earning a monopoly profit still exists if competing market makers are not present; but there is greater uncertainty for a market maker willing to set ex ante prices, even for limited quantities, than for a market maker who sets prices after observing the order flow.

Cohen, Maier, Schwartz, and Whitcomb (1977) argue that the activity of stabilization has external benefits that cannot be captured by the market maker doing the stabilizing. As a result, they argue there should be a single stabilizer in each stock who is rewarded over and above his profits from stabilizing for performing the social service of stabilization. This position is consistent with the NYSE view that the specialist has an affirmative obligation to maintain a fair and orderly market and should be subject to special standards, in return for which he receives special benefits such as a privileged position on the floor and knowledge of the book of limit orders.

The opposing view is that the specialist, like any other dealer, is a profit-maximizing entity that provides stabilization as a by-product. The fact that

90 percent of specialist transactions are stabilizing may simply reflect the fact that buying on price declines and selling on price increases is generally profitable. Stoll (1976) finds that the stabilizing behavior of unregulated NASDAQ market makers is the same as that of regulated exchange specialists, and concludes that market makers behave roughly the same way with respect to their stabilization whether they are regulated or not.

Goldman and Beja (1979) model transaction prices as a noisy adjustment process relative to a stochastic and unobserved true price. The role of the specialist is viewed as one of speeding the adjustment process and/or reducing the noise in the system. However, they propose no direct theoretical link between the stabilizing activities of the specialist and the observed transaction prices.

The Market Maker as Active Stabilizer

The market maker is sometimes viewed as an active stabilizer who foresees market trends and moves prices in the correct direction. He does not respond to the inflow of orders. Instead, he initiates transactions in order to move the price in a particular direction.

Whether a dealer is an active stabilizer, a passive stabilizer, or both can be inferred on the basis of the following regression framework (Stoll 1976):

$$\Delta Q_t = a_0 + a_1 r_t + a_2 r_{t+1} + a_3 \Delta Q_{t-1}$$

where

ΔQ_t = inventory change during day t.

r_t = percentage price change during day t.

Passive stabilization implies $a_1 < 0$—that is, inventory changes opposite to the price change during the day. Active stabilization implies $a_2 > 0$—inventory changes in the same direction as the next day's price change. Stoll found $a_1 < 0$ but $a_2 < 0$. This result implies that inventory changes of dealers respond to the same day's price change in a passive manner and do not anticipate the following day's price change. Indeed, because dealers tend to buy on days prior to a price decline and sell on days prior to a price increase, they make losses with respect to the next day's price change. The coefficient, a_3, is negative, which means there is a tendency for inventory to return to a normal level.

The Market Maker as Destabilizer

A frequently stated popular view of the market maker, particularly of the NYSE specialist, is that he has the power to destabilize or manipulate prices. A well-known statement of this view is Richard Ney's book *The Wall Street*

Jungle (1970). Congressional critics and the SEC have, on the basis of this view, called for increased regulation of the specialist (see, e.g., U.S. SEC 1963 chap. 5).

Economists generally argue, however, that absent fraud, deceit, or other nefarious practices, market makers have an incentive to be stabilizing, not destabilizing, because stabilizing is profitable. As long as investors have alternatives to trading with a particular market maker—such as a competing market maker or the placement of a limit order—and as long as there are a large number of investors willing to trade, the powers of a market maker to take advantage of any individual investor or to drive prices away from their equilibrium is limited. Regulatory policy, as reflected in the Securities Acts Amendments of 1975, appears to have moved in the direction of allowing competition rather than regulation to protect investors.

The Market Maker as Information Processor

Underlying the view of the market maker as price stabilizer is a view of his information set. A passive stabilizer believes the true price is unchanged. An active stabilizer has information that leads him to believe a price change is warranted. Thus the actions of the market maker are conditioned by the information he possesses, and certain academic researchers have focused more directly on the information processes underlying market makers' actions.

Two kinds of information may be distinguished: company information and market information. Company information is fundamental information about a security, such as earnings forecasts, new contracts, or new management. Although market makers have a good understanding of the fundamentals of the security they trade, there is general agreement that market makers do not spend time in security analysis and therefore do not process company information directly. Instead, other investors enter orders to trade based on company information. These are the information traders in the sense of Bagehot (1971). The market maker, then, is an information processor only in the sense that he infers information from observed transactions.

Market information is information about the prices and quantities of past, current, and pending transactions in the immediate market and related markets. Being at the hub of the market, the market maker is in a position to collect and properly interpret market information. Market information includes knowledge of pending block transactions or other large orders in the process of being traded, knowledge of price quotes by other dealers in the same security or in closely related securities, and knowledge of limit orders. Conroy and Winkler (1981) emphasize the benefits to the specialist of the exclusive knowledge of the book of limit orders. This exclusive knowledge increases the profitability of being a specialist and allows the specialist to narrow the bid-ask quote.

Following Bagehot (1971), Copeland and Galai (1983), and Glosten and Milgrom (1982) examine how the market maker establishes rational bid and ask prices in light of the fact that some investors may have superior information. The basic principle is that the bid price and the ask price are set to reflect all the available information, including the information conveyed in the next transaction. Thus the bid price is a rational price conditional on a sale to the dealer, and the ask price is a rational price conditional on the purchase from the dealer. Since a sale to the dealer has some probability of being placed by an information trader who has adverse information rather than by a liquidity trader who has no information, it carries with it information of an increased probability of a stock price decline. Conversely, a purchase from the dealer carries with it information of an increased probability of a stock price increase. This implies that the ask price must exceed the bid price as Copeland/Galai and Glosten/Milgrom show.

As in other markets with asymmetric information, it is evident here that the dealer faces an adverse selection problem. The market maker establishes a bid and ask price based on the average information contained in a sale to him or a purchase from him. Those investors with superior information (information traders) can trade at the dealer's price and make a profit, whereas those without any information (liquidity traders) incur a loss by trading at the dealer's quotes. If liquidity traders could find other mechanisms for trading that bypass the market maker, the market maker would be left to trade only with information traders. This would require the market maker to widen his spread; however, only those information traders who would be able to make a profit at the quoted spreads would trade. As a result, an equilibrium spread could never be reached because the market maker would not make a profit at any spread, and the market would collapse. In real-world markets this collapse has not occurred, and it is an interesting research question to explain why.

Several explanations are possible. First, it may be difficult for liquidity traders to distinguish themselves in a believable manner. See Black (1971), however, for a suggested method. Second, certain institutional arrangements, such as trading halts, may limit the effect of informational trading. Third, the importance of informational trading may be exaggerated in the sense that only a small fraction of traders have truly useful information, although many traders trade in the belief they have useful information.

The Market Maker as Supplier of Immediacy

The market maker is said to supply immediacy when he specifies, at all times, a bid price at which traders may sell to him and an ask price at which traders may buy from him. The willingness to quote prices before seeing public orders brings about continuity of markets because traders can trade at any time with the market maker. This is quite different from certain call auction markets in which the market maker as auctioneer observes an order imbalance and responds to it after the fact. The theory of the market maker as supplier of immediacy emphasizes the determinants of the bid-ask spread—the price of immediacy—rather than the determination of the price of the security. In the process of supplying immediacy, market makers also stabilize and process information; but these activities are now more properly related to the model of the dealer organization itself.

The extensive literature on market makers as suppliers of immediacy is reviewed in detail in Cohen, Maier, Schwartz, and Whitcomb (1979). Demsetz (1968) coined the term "supplier of immediacy" and proposed that this is a costly activity related to certain characteristics of the stock and market structure that he identified and examined empirically. Additional theoretical contributions in the spirit of Demsetz were made by Tinic (1972), who also carried out certain empirical tests. Stoll (1978a) developed an explicit theoretical model of the dealer in a single period framework. Ho and Stoll (1981) placed the dealer in a continuous time framework with return uncertainty and transactions uncertainty.

A number of theoretical papers adopt an approach to modeling the spread that is not so directly in the spirit of Demsetz in the sense that they are less concerned with the factors that determine a dealer's cost. Instead, they model the behavior of the dealer over time in a world with stochastic transactions and prices and certain assumptions about the objectives of the dealer. Garman (1976) is concerned with the bankruptcy of the dealer who maintains ex ante quotes. Amihud and Mendelson (1980) and Mildenstein and Schleef (1983) show that the dealer will adjust prices on the basis of his inventory. O'Hara and Oldfield (1982) model the determination of bid and ask prices in a multiperiod framework in which the dealer maximizes utility of his expected profits and a terminal value of inventory.

The factors that affect the price a dealer charges for providing the service of immediacy are now considered.

The Market Maker as Order Processor

Important costs in market making include the clerical costs of processing orders. These costs can be placed into three categories:

1. Costs fixed over a particular planning horizon such as a month or year: These include the cost of space, the cost of communications equipment and most labor costs, and the cost of the dealer's time.
2. Costs that are fixed with respect to a particular transaction but may vary with the number of transactions: These costs might include a fixed mini-

mum communication cost for a transaction, such as a minimum computer terminal charge per transaction and a fixed minimum clearing charge per transaction.

3. Costs that vary with the size of the transactions: Larger transactions have larger clearing charges and may require more attention from the dealer.

The price charged on a particular transaction by the dealer must cover those costs incurred in carrying out the transaction. Stoll (1978) models order costs on the basis of a fixed and variable component associated with a particular transaction. The price of a particular transaction need not include costs that are incurred regardless of the transaction, but over time the competitive environment of the dealer must permit him to charge a price sufficient to cover these fixed costs. Otherwise, the dealer could not stay in business. Ho (1984) determines the equilibrium number of competing dealers by the condition that each dealer have sufficient opportunity to earn a surplus over the variable costs associated with any particular transaction to allow the fixed costs associated with entering the business of being a dealer to be covered over the long term.

The Market Maker as Risk Bearer

Stoll (1978a) and Ho and Stoll (1981) model the dealer as a risk bearer, who, by taking on unwanted inventory, assumes a portfolio he would rather not have and additional risk he would rather avoid. The cost of holding an unwanted inventory position is reflected in a bid price below the dealer's estimate of the true price and an ask price above the dealer's estimate of the true price. This bid-ask spread is larger the larger the return variance of the stock, the larger the transaction size, the more risk-averse the dealer, and the lower the capitalization of the dealer.

Ho and Stoll (1981) and Stoll (1978a) show that the dealer's spread is largely independent of his inventory position. This is because the dealer lowers both the bid price and the ask price when he acquires inventory and raises both the bid price and the ask price when he reduces his inventory or takes on a short position. Shifting the spread relative to the true underlying price creates incentives for traders to place orders that will tend to move the dealer back to his desired inventory position. Amihud and Mendelson (1980) and O'Hara and Oldfield (1982) develop models in which the spread itself, not just its position relative to the true price, is a function of inventory.

The Market Maker as Victim of Information Traders

Because the dealer quotes prices at which he will trade a stated amount, he can be victimized by traders who possess superior information. Thus a trader with information justifying a price below the dealer's bid price will sell to the dealer at the bid price, and the dealer will lose to this information trader. As noted earlier, the dealer must widen his spread so that losses to information traders are offset by gains from those traders without information.

Jaffee and Winkler (1976) show that the dealer must lose to information traders. As already indicated, the papers of Copeland and Galai (1983) and Glosten and Milgrom (1982) establish a spread based on the need to offset the adverse effects of information trading. In these models the spread exists whether or not a dealer is risk-averse because the bid and ask prices are based on the expected value of information contained in a sale to the dealer or a purchase from the dealer. This contrasts with the view of market maker as risk bearer, in which risk aversion is necessary.

The Market Maker as Monopolist

A single market maker in a stock has some degree of monopoly power with respect to incoming market orders. The extent of this power depends on the elasticity of demand for immediacy—that is, the urgency with which traders wish to trade and the range of other alternatives available to them (such as placing limit orders or going to other markets). In general, one expects a dealer with monopoly power to place his bid price below his reservation buying price and to place his ask price above his reservation ask price, where the reservation price is the price that just covers the dealer's costs and is expected to leave him no worse off after a trade than he was before.

Theoretical papers by Ho and Stoll (1981), Amihud and Mendelson (1980), O'Hara and Oldfield (1982), and others examining the behavior of a single dealer all include a monopoly surplus in the spread equation they derive. Even when there is some competition among dealers, a surplus will arise periodically when the dealer is temporarily in a favorable position relative to competing dealers. For example, a particular dealer may have a short inventory position while other dealers all have long inventory positions. This enables the dealer to outbid other dealers while still earning a surplus over and above his reservation bid price (see Ho and Stoll 1983).

The Market Maker as Financial Intermediary

A financial intermediary borrows at one rate and lends at a higher rate, which compensates the intermediary for its costs of doing business. These costs include the cost of processing loans and sources of funds, costs of bearing the risk of unmatched maturities, and costs of dealing with asymmetries of information between the borrower and lender. In addition, a financial intermediary, like a dealer, may have some monopoly power. A bank can thus be viewed as a more complicated dealer; or, conversely, a dealer can be viewed as a simple form of bank. Like a bank, a dealer frequently borrows short and lends long. He borrows short term to finance stock purchases, a long-term investment. Unlike a bank, but more like an insurance company, a dealer can also borrow long (by selling stock short) and lend short. Aside from the similarity in the risks assumed, the other costs of the dealer are similar in kind to those of a bank, albeit different in magnitude, since the extent of asset transformation and repackaging is much greater for a bank than for a dealer. Although a beginning has been made in applying the theory of dealers to banks (Ho and Saunders 1981), this appears to be an area for further research.

Empirical Evidence on the Bid-Ask Spread

Factors Affecting the Quoted Spread

In addition to the theoretical works cited earlier, a large body of literature is concerned primarily with empirical analyses of the bid-ask spread. In addition to the paper of Demsetz (1968) and Tinic (1972), papers by Benston and Hagerman (1974); Branch and Freed (1977); Ho and Macris (1984); Stoll (1978b); and Tinic and West (1972, 1974) fall in this category.

These studies have examined the relationship of the quoted bid-ask spread to a variety of variables that tend to measure the factors discussed earlier—processing costs, risk, adverse information, monopoly power. The bid-ask spread is usually measured as a proportion of the stock price, and the key variables explaining variations in the proportional spread across stocks include:

1. An activity variable such as volume of trading, shares outstanding, or number of shareholders. Justification for this variable is that the greater the activity, the shorter the dealer's holding period and, therefore, the lower his risk. The variable may also be related to economies of scale in order processing.
2. A risk variable such as variance of return of the stock or the components of the variance—systematic risk and unsystematic risk. For a given holding period, the greater the variance, the greater the risk to the dealer and, therefore, the greater the spread. It has also been argued that the level of unsystematic risk may be related to the level of informational trading in a stock.
3. A measure of competition such as the number of competing markets (in the case of the New York Exchange specialist) or the number of competing dealers in NASDAQ.

These three variables tend to be significant in explaining the spread. The activity variable has a negative sign, the risk variable a positive sign, and the competition variable a negative sign (greater competition implying lower spread). Several other variables, such as the price per share or the level of institutional trading, are sometimes included in these regressions. Most studies have a policy emphasis and are therefore concerned with the third variable listed earlier—the effect of competition. In general, the studies conclude that competition reduces the spread, although direct comparisons of different markets are difficult.

The empirical studies, though explaining a substantial fraction in the cross-sectional variability of the spread (Stoll 1978b explains 82 percent of the variation), are less successful in testing the validity of alternative theories of market making. They do not thus far permit us to distinguish, for example, whether the view of market maker as risk bearer or as victim of information traders is correct. This is because the variables used in the empirical tests proxy for more than one theoretical concept and because the theories of market making are complementary.

Realized versus Quoted Spread

Whether the dealer earns the spread he quotes depends on how his bid and ask prices change after a transaction. If bid and ask prices do not change systematically according to whether a transaction is a dealer purchase or a dealer sale, the spread realized by a dealer—the realized spread—will equal the quoted spread of the dealer. In this case, a dealer who buys at P_t^b, the bid price at time t, can expect on average to sell at P_t^a, the ask price at time t. On the other hand, if bid and ask prices have a tendency to fall after a dealer purchase and a tendency to rise after a dealer sale, the realized spread will fall short of the quoted spread. In other words, the dealer who buys at P_t^b cannot expect to sell at P_t^a. Instead, he sells on average at an ask price at time $t + 1$, P_{t+1}^a that is less than P_t^a.

Both the views of the market maker as risk bearer and as victim of information traders suggest that bid and ask prices change in a systematic way to reduce the dealer's realized spread below his quoted spread. In other words, assuming the dealer can reverse a position in one period, these views suggest that

$$P_{t+1}^a - P_t^b < P_t^a - P_t^b$$

and

$$P_t^a - P_{t+1}^b < P_t^a - P_t^b$$

where

$$P_t^a - P_{t+1}^b = \text{quoted spread at time } t.$$

$P_{t+1}^a - P_t^b =$ realized spread, dealer purchase followed by dealer sale.

$P_t^a - P_{t+1}^b =$ realized spread, dealer sale followed by dealer purchase.

The explanation for these inequalities is as follows. As risk bearer, the market maker lowers both P^a and P^b after a dealer purchase because he is less anxious to buy additional shares, which would increase his inventory position; and he is more anxious to sell those shares he has just acquired. Similarly, he raises P^a and P^b after a dealer sale because he is less eager to increase his short position and more eager to buy so as to cover the existing short position he has just taken. As victim of information traders, the market maker lowers his bid and ask prices after a dealer purchase because such a purchase conveys information that the true price of the stock has fallen. Similarly, he raises his bid and ask prices after a dealer sale, which conveys information that the true price has risen. Note that both the bid and ask price change in the same direction, with the result that the spread may remain unchanged over time even though the bid and ask prices are changing continuously.

Empirical evidence supports the view that the realized spread falls short of the quoted spread. Stoll (1976) shows that there is a systematic tendency for prices to fall after a dealer purchase and to rise after a dealer sale. Stoll (1984) calculates a weighted-average realized percentage spread for all NYSE specialists, based on SEC data for the period 1975–1980. He finds that the realized spread in this period is about 0.33 percent, which is approximately one-half the average quoted spread of 0.65 percent during this period. Roll (1984) proposes a method of inferring the realized spread from the covariance of returns of successive transactions. Using daily returns (not transaction returns), he calculates a realized spread of 0.32 percent for New York Stock Exchange stocks in the period 1963–1981, which is also significantly less than the quoted spread in this time period.

The realized spread measures what the market maker earns. The difference between the quoted and realized spread measures what he loses to informed traders and what price concession he makes to induce the public to take unwanted inventory off his hands. Those traders who possess superior information can, in effect, cut the quoted spread by realizing trading gains from their knowledge. Those traders that do not possess superior information pay the full quoted spread. On average, the dealer's losses to information traders are offset by the fact that he earns the full quoted spread from liquidity traders who do not possess superior information. This point was first made by Bagehot (1971).

The Market for Market Makers

Models of market makers usually consider the case in which there is only one market maker in a security, as in the case of the NYSE specialist. In many markets, however, there are multiple dealers in a given security. This is true of the NASDAQ system, the government securities markets, the foreign-exchange market, and other markets. In such markets there is a market for market makers in the sense that firms must choose whether or not to enter the business of market making in a particular security. An important regulatory issue is whether the market for market makers should be regulated in some way or whether it should be allowed to operate freely. For example, is it desirable to limit the number of dealers in a security, as is done in the case of the New York Stock Exchange? Should market makers be constrained in their ability to leave markets? Should a minimum number of market makers be established?

To analyze policy questions of this type, one must understand how markets with competing market makers operate. Second, the factors that determine the number of market makers in free markets must be understood. These issues are considered in turn.

Behavior of Competing Market Makers

Based on their model of the individual dealer as supplier of immediacy, Ho and Stoll (1983) model the behavior of competing dealers. They show that dealers will trade with each other if inventories diverge too greatly, but they also show that the inflow of orders from the public will be distributed among dealers in such a way that interdealer trading is unlikely. They determine the market spread, the highest bid of any dealer, and the lowest ask of any dealer as these relate to the reservation spread of any dealer. The reservation spread is the minimum spread such that trading at either the bid or the ask does not change the dealer's expected utility of wealth. If dealers have the same utility function, the market spread is shown to be the reservation spread of any dealer, even though different dealers will have different bid prices and different ask prices because of different inventory positions. Since a monopolistic dealer will always charge more than his reservation spread, the market spread under competition is expected to be less than the spread of a single dealer who provides the same degree of liquidity (depth of market) as the competing dealers.

Empirical work by Newton and Quandt (1979) suggests, however, that spreads are larger on NASDAQ, a market with competing dealers, than on the NYSE, when similar stocks are compared. Explanations for this difference are offered by Ho and Stoll (1983) and by Stoll (1984). One explanation is that the specialist quote is frequently on behalf of his book of limit orders, not for his own account. These limit orders act as competing dealers. In addition, to the extent that limit orders close to the market are slow to be changed as market conditions change, limit orders periodically may result in much narrower spreads than the specialist would offer for his own account. On NASDAQ, limit orders are not exposed to the market in the same way, in part because there is no consolidated limit order book; and they do not have the same effect of narrowing the bid-ask spread. Second, the specialist has greater control over the total order flow; this may explain the lower spread. The specialist quote is good for a limited number of shares. If additional shares are traded, his quote can be changed. For example, if his quote is good for 300 shares, the first 300 shares will be purchased by the specialist at his quoted bid price. The second 300 shares, however, would be purchased only at a lower bid price. In NASDAQ, however, if each dealer is good for 300 shares and there are ten dealers, 3,000 shares may be sold before any dealer can adjust his quote. The NASDAQ market would thus provide greater liquidity (depth of market) at its quote than the specialist would at his quote. Each NASDAQ dealer has less control and knowledge of the market, and each protects himself by quoting a larger spread than he would if he were a single dealer, as is the specialist. This line of reasoning implies that a NASDAQ dealer could provide a better price than the quoted price if he were assured that no other shares were about to hit the market.

The evidence in Benston and Hagerman (1974), Demsetz (1968), Stoll (1978b), Tinic (1972), and Tinic and West (1972) shows empirically that competition tends to reduce spreads. The Newton and Quandt (1979) results may be reconciled with these findings by controlling for the impact of limit orders and for the differences in the depth of market provided by the quotes in NASDAQ as compared with the specialists' quotes.

Optimal Number of Market Makers

In a free market the maximum number of dealers in a security is the number that demand (volume of trading) can support if each dealer is operating at minimum average cost. Using this criterion, and assuming certain economies of scale that arise from the existence of fixed order costs, Stoll (1978a) derives an equation for the optimal number of dealers in a stock. An interesting implication of the model is that, the riskier the stock, the greater the number of market makers. Empirical work (Stoll 1978b) supports this implication: The number of dealers in NASDAQ is positively related to the variance of return of a stock. As expected, the number of dealers is also positively related to the volume of trading and negatively related to turnover, which is viewed as a proxy for informational trading. These results imply the existence of an optimal number of market makers, which is related to characteristics of the stock. Hamilton (1976, 1978) analyzes similar issues. He concludes that although economies of scale exist for market makers, they are not so great as to preclude the existence of competing market makers.

In a recent paper, Ho (1984) builds an elegant model predicting that the number of dealers in a stock increases at a decreasing rate with the volume of trading in the stock. A dealer enters a market if he can cover his fixed costs of doing business. Given volume, the greater the number of dealers, the less the frequency with which a dealer has the opportunity to trade at an advantageous price. Ho's model balances the number of dealers and the volume of trading such that each dealer can expect just to earn sufficient profits to cover his costs of entering the market.

Conclusions

In this chapter the market maker has been viewed in a number of ways. He has been portrayed as the organizer of a call auction market in which the efficiency of price determination depends on the rules of the auction market and the nature of participation by the market maker. Call auction markets and continuous markets have also been contrasted. Although continuous markets can exist without the presence of a market maker if individual investors continuously update limit orders, the role of the market maker in maintaining a continuous market is emphasized. In a continuous market, the market maker is frequently viewed as a stabilizer (or destabilizer). This approach to market makers deals with important policy issues related to the pricing efficiency of markets; however, it provides little understanding of the fundamental economic forces that determine the behavior of an individual market maker.

Only when the market maker is portrayed (1) as information processor or (2) as provider of immediacy is an explicit theory of the market maker developed that is grounded in maximizing behavior by the market maker. Only under these two approaches is an explicit model of the bid-ask spread of an individual market maker derived. Models of optimizing behavior by the market maker suggest that the following variables influence the market maker's welfare and therefore the spread he charges for his services: (1) processing costs, (2) cost of risk associated with holding an inventory, (3) the cost of dealing with informed traders, and (4) the monopoly surplus. The empirical work shows that quoted spreads are related to variables that proxy for these four factors. Although the analysis of quoted spreads seldom distinguishes the relative importance of the four factors, the fact that realized spreads are less than quoted spreads suggests that dealers lose to informed traders, which implies that the cost of dealing with informed traders is important. The fact that the realized spread is not zero suggests the dealer also bears inventory costs and processing costs. The influence of monopoly surplus is reflected in the fact that quoted spreads decline with increases in competition among market makers.

The last section of this chapter examines briefly some topics bearing on the broader issue of market structure—the behavior of competing market makers and the optimal number of market makers. The emphasis of this chapter, however, has been on the individual market maker and factors explaining his behavior. In that sense, this chapter treats only one part of the broader issue of the evolving structure of the securities industry to which this book is devoted.

References

Amihud, Y., and Mendelson, H. 1980. Dealership market: Market making with inventory. *Journal of Financial Economics 8* (March):31–53.

Bagehot, Walter (pseud.) 1971. The only game in town. *Financial Analysts Journal 27* (March–April).

Barnea, Amir. 1974. Performance evaluation of New York Stock Exchange specialists. *Journal of Financial and Quantitative Analysis 9* (September).

———. 1976. Reply: Specialists' performance and serial dependence of stock price changes. *Journal of Financial and Quantitative Analysis* (December):909–911.

Barnea, A., and Logue, D.E. 1975. The effect of risk on the market maker's spread. *Financial Analysts Journal 31* (November–December):45–49.

Beja, Avraham, and Goldman, M. Barry. 1980. On the dynamic behavior of prices in disequilibrium. *Journal of Finance 35* (May):235–248.

Beja, Avraham, and Hakansson, N.H. 1977. Dynamic market processes and the rewards to up-to-date information. *Journal of Finance 32* (May):291–304.

———. 1979. From orders to trades: Some alternative market mechanisms. In E. Bloch and R.A. Schwartz, eds., *Impending changes for securities markets: What role for the exchange?* Greenwich, Conn.: JAF Press, pp. 144–161.

Benston, G., and Hagerman, R. 1974. Determinants of bid-asked spreads in the over-the-counter market. *Journal of Financial Economics 1* (March).

———. 1978. Risk, volume and spread. *Financial Analysts Journal* (January–February):46–49.

Black, F. 1971. Toward a fully automated exchange I, II. *Financial Analysts Journal* (July–August, November–December).

Bradfield, James. 1979. A formal dynamic model of market making. *Journal of Financial and Quantitative Analysis* (June):275–291.

Bradfield, James, and Zabel, E. 1979. Price adjustment in a competitive market and the securities exchange specialist. In J. Green and J. Scheinkman, eds., *General equilibrium, growth and trade.* New York: Academic Press, pp. 51–77.

Branch, Ben, and Freed, W. 1977. Bid-asked spreads on the AMEX and the Big Board. *Journal of Finance 32.*

Cohen, K.; Hawawini, G.; Maier, S.; Schwartz, R.; and Whitcomb, D. 1980. Implications of microstructure theory for empirical research on stock price behavior. *Journal of Finance 35* (May).

Cohen, K.; Maier, S.; Ness, W., Jr.; Okuda, H.; Schwartz, R.; and Whitcomb, D. 1977. The impact of designated market makers on security prices. *Journal of Banking and Finance* (December):219–235.

Cohen, K.; Maier, S.; Schwartz, R.; and Whitcomb, D. 1977. Impact of designated market makers on security prices: II. Policy Implications. *Journal of Banking and Finance 1* (December):236–247.

———. 1979. Market makers and the market spread: A review of recent literature. *Journal of Financial and Quantitative Analysis 14* (November).

———. 1981. Transaction costs, order placement strategy, and the existence of the bid-ask spread. *Journal of Political Economy 89* (April).

Conroy, R.M., and Winkler, R.L. 1981. Informational differences between limit and market orders for a market maker. *Journal of Financial and Quantitative Analysis 16* (December):703–724.

Copeland, T.C., and Galai, D. 1983. Information effects on the bid-ask spread. *Journal of Finance 38* (December):1457–1469.

Demsetz, H. 1968. The cost of transacting. *Quarterly Journal of Economics 82* (February).

Forsythe, R.; Palfrey, T.; and Plott, C. 1982. Asset valuation in an experimental market. *Econometrica* (May):537–567.

Friedman, Daniel. 1984. On the efficiency of experimental double auction markets. *American Economic Review 74* (March):60–72.

Garbade, K. 1978. Effect of interdealer brokerage on transactional characteristics of dealer markets. *Journal of Business of the University of Chicago 51* (3):477–498.

Garbade, K., and Silber, W. 1976. Price dispersion in the government securities market. *Journal of Political Economy 84* (4):721–740.

———. 1976. Technology, communication, and performance of financial markets 1840–1975. *Journal of Finance 33*, 3 (June):819–832.

———. 1979. Structural organization of secondary markets: Clearing frequency, dealer activity and liquidity risk. *Journal of Finance 34* (June).

Garbade, K.; Pomrenze, J.; and Silber, W. 1979. On the information content of prices. *American Economic Review 69* (1):50–59.

Garman, Mark. 1976. Market microstructure. *Journal of Financial Economics 3* (June).

Glosten, Lawrence R., and Milgrom, Paul R. 1982. Bid, ask and transaction prices in a specialist market with heterogeneously informed traders. Working Paper, October.

Goldman, M.B., and Beja, A. 1979. Market prices vs. equilibrium prices: Return variance, serial correlation and the role of the specialist. *Journal of Finance 34* (June).

Gould, John P., and Verrecchia, Robert E. 1982. The specialist as economic agent. Working Paper, Center for Research in Security Prices, Graduate School of Business, University of Chicago.

Grossman, S. 1981. An introduction to the theory of rational expectations under asymmetric information. *Review of Economic Studies 48:*541–559.

Hamilton, J. 1976. Competition, scale economics and transaction cost in the stock market. *Journal of Financial and Quantitative Analysis 11* (December):779–802.

———. 1978. Marketplace organization and marketability: NASDAQ, the stock exchange, and the national market system. *Journal of Finance 33* (May):487–503.

Ho, Thomas. 1984. Dealer market structure: A dynamic competitive equilibrium model. Working Paper, March.

Ho, Thomas, and Macris, Richard G. 1984. Dealer bid-ask quotes and transaction prices: An empirical study of some AMEX options. *Journal of Finance 39* (March):23–45.

Ho, Thomas, and Saunders, A. 1981. Determinants of bank interest margins: Theory and empirical evidence. *Journal of Financial and Quantitative Analysis* (November).

Ho, Thomas; Schwartz, R.A.; and Whitcomb, D.K. 1985. The trading decision and market clearing under transaction price uncertainty. *Journal of Finance* (March).

Ho, Thomas, and Stoll, Hans R. 1980. On dealer markets under competition. *Journal of Finance 35* (May).

———. 1981. Optimal dealer pricing under transactions and return uncertainty. *Journal of Financial Economics 9* (March).

———. 1983. The dynamics of dealer markets under competition. *Journal of Finance 38* (September):1053–1074.

Jaffee, Jeff, and Winkler, Robert. 1976. Optimal speculation against an efficient market. *Journal of Finance 31* (March):49–61.

Logue, D. 1975. Market making and the assessment of market efficiency. *Journal of Finance 30* (March).

Mildenstein, E., and Schleef, H. 1983. The optimal pricing policy of a monopolistic marketmaker in the equity market. *Journal of Finance 38* (March):218–231.

Newton, William, and Quandt, Richard. 1979. An empirical study of spreads. Research Memorandum No. 30, Financial Research Center, Princeton University.

New York Stock Exchange (NYSE). 1980. The quality of the New York Stock Exchange marketplace in 1979. Report of the Quality of Markets Committee of the Board of Directors of the New York Stock Exchange, March 6.

Ney, Richard. 1970. *The Wall Street Jungle.* New York: Grove Press.

O'Hara, Maureen, and Oldfield, George. 1982. The microeconomics of market-making. Working Paper, Cornell University.

Plott, C.R., and Sunder, S. 1982. Efficiency of experimental security markets with inside information: An application of rational expectation models. *Journal of Political Economy 90* (August):663–698.

Roll, Richard. 1984. A simple implicit measure of the effective bid-ask spread in an efficient market. *Journal of Finance 39* (March):1127–1139.

Santomero, A. 1974. The economic effects of NASDAQ: Some preliminary results. *Journal of Financial and Quantitative Analysis* (January):13–24.

Schwartz, R.A., and Whitcomb, D.K. 1976. Comment: Assessing the impact of stock exchange specialists on stock volatility. *Journal of Financial and Quantitative Analysis 11* (December):901–908.

Silber, W.L. 1975. Thinness in capital markets: The case of the Tel Aviv Stock Exchange. *Journal of Financial and Quantitative Analysis 10* (March):129–142.

Smidt, S. 1971. Which road to an efficient stock market? Implications of the SEC institutional investor study. *Financial Analysts Journal 27* (September–October).

———. 1979. Continuous versus intermittent trading on auction markets. *Journal of Financial and Quantitative Analysis 14* (November):837–866.

Smith, V. 1974. Effect of market organization on competitive equilibrium. *Quarterly Journal of Economics 78* (May):181–201.

Stigler, G.J. 1964. Public regulation of the securities markets. *Journal of Business 37* (April):117–134.

Stoll, Hans R. 1976. Dealer inventory behavior: An empirical investigation of NASDAQ stocks. *Journal of Financial and Quantitative Analysis* (September):359–380.

Stoll, Hans R. 1978a. The supply of dealer services in securities markets. *Journal of Finance* (September).

———. 1978b. The pricing of security dealer services: An empirical study of NASDAQ stocks. *Journal of Finance* (September).

———. 1984. The New York Stock Exchange specialist system. Working Paper No. 83-129, Owen Graduate School of Management, Vanderbilt University.

Tinic, S. 1972. The economics of liquidity services. *Quarterly Journal of Economics* 86 (February):79–93.

Tinic, Seha, and West, R. 1972. Competition and the pricing of dealer services in the over-the-counter market. *Journal of Financial and Quantitative Analysis* 7 (June):1707–1728.

———. 1974. Marketability of stock in Canada + USA: Agent vs. dealer markets. *Journal of Finance* 29 (3):729–746.

U.S. Securities and Exchange Commission (SEC). 1963. *Report of the special study of securities markets*. 88th Congress, 1st Session. Washington, D.C.: U.S. Government Printing Office, chap. 5.

———. 1971. Institutional investor study report. 92d Congress, 1st Session. Washington, D.C.: U.S. Government Prnting Office.

5

Order Flow and the Quality of the Market

Kalman J. Cohen
Robert M. Conroy
Steven F. Maier

Market making plays an important role in the efficient functioning of markets in which assets are traded. The key factor affecting the market maker is the structure of security markets, which, like everything else, has been affected by the revolution in the processing and communication of information. Understanding the potential impact of changes in market structure, such as the question of consolidation versus fragmentation, can help us deal more effectively with a changing environment. The impact of change on security markets is also the underlying theme of this book. The interaction between market structure and the quality of the price discovery process is discussed in Schreiber and Schwartz (chapter 2). The different roles of market makers are considered in Stoll (chapter 4). Ho and Macris (chapter 3) explicitly examines the relationship between market structure and the role of the market maker. In this chapter the issues underlying the consolidation/fragmentation debate are considered.

Competition has long been viewed as a positive force for the quality and evolution of security markets. In fact, the Securities and Exchange Commission (SEC) has mandated many forms of competition and has sought to remove anticompetitive barriers where they exist. Moreover, whereas there are some things that can be done to promote competition in a market composed of only one trading arena with many traders, some people contend that the most effective form of competition occurs when there are multiple trading arenas.

The U.S. securities markets are dominated by a single trading arena, the New York Stock Exchange (NYSE). Much of the effort to promote competition over the past ten years has been directed at loosening the grip of the NYSE on security trading. Its famous Rule 390, limiting the trading of NYSE member firms on listed securities, has been a focal point of the SEC's anticompetitive concern. In passing its own Rule 19c-3, the SEC attempted to break down the barrier to the creation of other marketplaces for security trading.[1] Though unsuccessful, this experiment by the SEC clearly placed the principal regulatory body for the securities industry in a position of actively promoting multiple trading arenas for the same security.[2]

Other efforts to promote competition between markets have been the institution of the Consolidated Quotation System (CQS) and the Intermarket Trading System (ITS). These linkages provide communication between different marketplaces, but they have not diminished the importance of the NYSE as the dominant trading arena. An experiment in a totally computerized trading system has been developed as the National Securities Trading System (NSTS) on the Cincinnati Stock Exchange. A discussion of the implications of the ITS and the NSTS for fragmentation is found in Davis (chapter 18). All these efforts have had as their primary objective the increase of competition among marketplaces.

The academic literature has long favored and promoted the existence of competitive marketplaces. Some of the arguments in favor of competitive marketplaces are:

1. By having multiple market makers who compete with each other, the overall market for the security would be of better quality as measured by such statistics as the size of the bid-ask spread.
2. By introducing securities to regional exchanges and/or in-house brokerage markets, the attractiveness to the sales forces of the broker-dealer firms that are not NYSE members would increase, thereby inducing more customers to trade the securities and increasing the overall order flow.
3. The existence of competitive markets would accelerate the process of innovation and thereby provide greater variety in the types of securities traded and the mechanisms for trading.

Earlier researchers disagree concerning whether market fragmentation is, on balance, desirable or undesirable. For example, Hamilton (1979) concludes that the beneficial competitive effects of fragmentation outweigh the harmful effects. Cohen, Maier, Schwartz, and Whitcomb (1982) (hereinafter cited as CMSW) conclude that fragmentation has a detrimental effect on market quality. Mendelson (1984) concludes that, in general, market fragmentation is undesirable since it results in the expected quantity traded being lower, the price variance faced by any individual trader being higher, and the expected overall gains from trade being lower.

The focus of this chapter is a discussion of consolidated versus fragmented markets. We concentrate on the potential for loss in the quality of markets when the order flow is fragmented among several trading arenas.

We believe the net effect of the creation of multiple markets is negative, especially when there is no realized increase in the order flow and the creation of multiple trading arenas simply splits an existing order flow. Our more fundamental objective, however, is to promote a more balanced view on the value to the public of multiple trading arenas.

Measures of Market Quality

We begin by specifying the parameters by which one may measure the quality of a security market. The concept itself would appear simple, in that what we seek are measures of speedy execution at the best possible price. Unfortunately, the literature on the microstructure of security markets has taught us that this criterion generally is not directly measurable. Instead, we must use surrogates from which to deduce the quality of the marketplace. The following are reasonable surrogates for market quality:

1. *Size of the bid-ask spread:* The general argument is that the smaller the difference between the lowest ask price and the highest bid price, the better the marketplace. Many, in fact, regard the bid-ask spread as a principal cost of trading via market orders in security markets, since an investor will usually both buy and then sell a security over some period of time, and therefore incur as a cost the bid-ask spread.

2. *Length of time until a limit order executes:* An investor who seeks to trade by a limit order instead of a market order is engaging in a trade-off between getting a better price and waiting longer for execution. To the extent that this waiting time is reduced, all other things being equal, the market is better for the investor.

3. *Probability that a limit order will execute:* When an investor places a limit order in the market, he often sets a time and date at which he will withdraw the order. Typically, withdrawal occurs at the end of a trading day if the order has not executed. The greater the probability that a limit order will execute before it is withdrawn, the better the quality of the market from the standpoint of the investor, since a withdrawn limit order represents an unfulfilled demand to trade the security.

4. *Preservation of price priority:* Investors generally seek to execute their trades at the best possible price, taking into account all transaction costs. In the presence of multiple trading arenas, investors will seek to have their trades executed in the arena offering the best price.

5. *Preservation of secondary priority:* Many trading arenas seek to maintain time priority (first come, first served) among orders that wish to execute at the same price. From an investor standpoint, this secondary trading priority rule is valuable since it reduces the variability of the time an order

must wait to execute. For a discussion of other possible secondary priority rules, see CMSW (1982).

6. *No autocorrelation patterns:* In viewing the prices at which successive trades occur, most investors would prefer to see an absence of short-term price trends or reversals, which we refer to as an *autocorrelation pattern*. If such patterns exist, the investor might reasonably conclude that insiders or others with significant security holdings were distorting the process of price formation and/or using inside information. Ideally, there should be a large number of investors, none of whom has significant market power, and each of whom forms his own assessment of the worth of the security based on a common body of information.

The rest of this chapter will return to these measures of market quality, except for the last, to examine the trade-off between single and multiple trading arenas. Since the chapter uses theoretical models that assume atomistic competition among traders, the phenomenon of autocorrelation, which in part is traceable to market power, cannot be addressed.

Theoretical Foundation

Multiple trading arenas may cover a broad spectrum depending on the information exchanged between the various marketplaces. At one extreme, the marketplaces could exhibit little or no common information and order sharing. In such an instance one would depend on arbitrageurs to maintain market quality. These traders would observe price differences in the markets and simultaneously buy and sell to eliminate price differentials. The quality of such markets would then depend on the ability of the arbitrageurs to obtain accurate information on a timely basis and the transactions costs they incur.[3] Such activities are always imperfect, since transactions costs exist and arbitrageurs extract an economic profit for their activity.[4]

The other end of the spectrum of multiple marketplaces would be a structure in which both price priority and secondary priority rules are preserved by technologically linking multiple trading arenas. In such an ideal system a number of things would have to occur:

1. Limit orders would have to be exposed on all markets simultaneously.
2. Market orders would always have to be directed to the arena that offered the best price.
3. Where a price tie occurs, the earliest arriving limit order would have to be executed first, regardless of which arena it was in.

In this latter system there would be little need for arbitrageurs. In fact, the marketplace would always appear to the investor as being a single consolidated arena, even though the trading activity might be taking place in several geographically diverse locations. Thus any reduction in the size of the bid-ask spread or increase in order flow from a larger sales force would be clearly beneficial. Unfortunately, no current system for linking markets provides for this level of interaction.

The lack of maintaining *both* price priority and secondary priority rules across markets may result in a deterioration in market quality, and this may not be offset fully by the improvements in the bid-ask spread and order flow. Of particular concern to us is that all proposed schemes for linking markets completely ignore the desirability of preserving secondary priority rules. That is, despite attempts to link markets so as to maintain price priority, no one is concerned with the secondary priority rules that determine one's position in the limit order queue relative to other orders that have come in at the same price. We believe it is important to examine, in terms of the market quality measures discussed earlier, the potential effect of violating a secondary priority rule, specifically time priority. To this end we appeal to the mathematics of queueing theory to structure a model that will permit us to examine the issues of fragmentation and consolidation, in particular the violation of secondary priority rules.

A Queueing Theory Model

The key elements of a public trading arena are orders and the existence of market makers—for example, specialists on the NYSE. In the remainder of this section we will use the terms *market maker* and *specialist* interchangeably. Note, however, that exchange procedures on the NYSE and AMEX usually limit each security to one specialist.

Essentially, the public can submit two forms of orders through a security broker. The first is a *limit order,* which specifies a minimum sales price or a maximum purchase price. If these orders cannot be immediately executed at these prices or better, they are left with the specialist in charge of the security to be executed if and when the stock price reaches the specified level. There are a number of variations on the form of a limit order, but the foregoing serves as a general definition. The other form of an order is a *market order,* which authorizes the sale or purchase immediately at the best prevailing price. The majority of transactions in which the specialist is not acting as a dealer involve the matching of a market order and a limit order.

All limit orders that have been left with the specialist are recorded in the specialist's book. These limit books form queues at different prices and are matched with market orders, first on the basis of price and then by time of arrival, the earliest arriving order executing first. For simplicity, we assume that time priority is the secondary priority rule; this is literally true of the AMEX, but only partially true of the NYSE.[5]

The specialist has the option of buying or selling at a better price for his own account, but not at the current market quote price. In other words, at any given price, public limit orders have priority over the specialist. In fact, the continuity requirements of the organized exchanges cause the specialist to enter quotes to buy or sell for his own account when the closest public limit orders are priced too far from the last transaction price. The percentage of time the specialist must or can participate as a dealer is clearly related to the order flow of public limit orders.

In our simple queueing model of trading activity, we assume limit orders arrive randomly to the floor of the exchange. Formally, we assume that they follow a Poisson process with parameter λ, which specifies the average arrival rate per unit of time. Once an order arrives at the market, it enters the limit order queue until it is crossed with a counterpart market order. We assume market orders also arrive at the market randomly and follow a Poisson process with parameter μ. This model formulation views the limit orders as being in a queue while they are waiting for service, and this service comes when market orders arrive and execute against the limit orders.

The assumptions of Poisson arrival processes for both limit orders and market orders means that the associated queueing system can be modeled as an M/M/1 system. The attributes of this well-known model are fully described in any standard queueing-theory text (see, e.g., Gross and Harris 1974, pp. 38–89). Key attributes of this system are as follows:

1. The intensity is $\rho = \lambda/\mu$.
2. The probability that the specialist and not a limit order currently sets the markets quotes is $P_0 = 1 - \rho$.
3. The expected number of limit orders in the system is $L_s = \rho/(1 - \rho)$.
4. The expected time a limit order must wait until it is executed against an incoming market order is $W_s = 1/(\mu - \lambda)$.

It should be noted that the existence of a specialist in the marketplace does not affect the use of the queueing model. Instead of concentrating on the entire limit order flow, however, we count only those limit orders where prices are placed inside the specialist's quotes. The other limit orders are disregarded, since any market orders arriving with no limit orders inside the specialist's spread are executed against his bid or ask quotes. We are abstracting from the dynamics of changes in the specialist's spread and concentrating on the interaction within the specialist's spread as if his quotes were fixed over time. In this situation we expect that the total market order flow would exceed the limit orders set within the specialist's spread; in other words, the intensity parameter ρ just described would be less than one.

The simplest possible model of market fragmentation is to assume that the total order flow currently going to one trading arena is on average split equally between two arenas. We further assume that each investor who places a limit order directs that order randomly to one of the two equal markets. Moreover, market orders are directed randomly between the two markets for execution. Such a situation would violate both price priority and time priority between markets. Arbitrageurs would tend to maintain prices for both markets at the same level as long as it is profitable for them to do so (but transaction costs might cause some inequality in prices between the two markets; see note 4).

From the standpoint of our model, each trading arena could be separately modeled by reducing the average arrival rates for limit orders and market orders to $\lambda/2$ and $\mu/2$, respectively, where λ and μ are the relevant order flow parameters in a consolidated market. The measures of effectiveness for each of the new (fragmented) markets is shown below. (Primes indicate values for the two market setting.)

1. The intensity is $\rho' = \lambda/\mu$ and is unchanged.
2. The probability that the specialist sets the market quotes is $P_0' = 1 - \rho'$ and is also unchanged.
3. The expected number of limit orders in the system is $L_s' = \rho'/(1 - \rho')$ and is also unchanged.
4. The expected time a limit order must wait in the queue before it executes is $W_s' = 2/(\mu - \lambda)$ and is *twice* the waiting time for a single consolidated market.

In other words, in this simple model the one visible effect of fragmentation is to cause the average waiting time for limit orders to increase by a factor of two. Moreover, if the markets are further fragmented, the average waiting time for a limit order would increase proportionally. For instance, if there were n markets, the average waiting time would be n times that of a single market. The increase in order flow required to offset this increase in waiting time would in turn have to be n times that of the original consolidated market. The intuition underlying this result can be seen by considering the simplest case. An individual order that arrives when no other orders are present must wait twice as long when the arrival rate of market orders is halved. If this is the case with the first arrival, it is also true for all other arrivals. Thus if we look at the expected waiting time, it will on average be twice as great when we halve the service rate.

In addition, consider the situation where the order flow split between two separate markets was not 50/50 but rather 85 percent of the order flow randomly going to one market,[6] and the remaining 15 percent going to the other market. As before, the probability that the specialist sets the market quotes remains unchanged, as does the expected number of limit orders in the system. There is, however, a significant effect on expected limit order waiting time. The market with the larger order flow has an expected waiting time $W'_s = 1.18/(\mu - \lambda)$, or 1.18 times that of the consolidated market. The smaller market has an expected waiting time $W'_s = 6.67/(\mu - \lambda)$, or an expected waiting time that is 6.67 times that of the consolidated market and 5.65 times that of the market segment with the larger order flow. This is a significant difference in the quality of the two markets, and it is clear that most orders would get better execution in the market with the larger order flow. To the extent that orders are not randomly assigned but have some choice, we would expect that most (if not all) orders would go to the larger market. This supports the common belief that "order flow attracts order flow."

The analysis to this point has implicitly assumed that once a limit order arrives in the trading arena, it remains there until it executes. In reality, limit orders have expiration times and will leave the queue because of either a completed execution or an expiration. This leaving before service completion is known in queueing theory as *reneging*. In order to incorporate this behavior into the analysis, we will assume that limit orders expire on a random basis. In the context of our previously defined model, we assume the time to expiration is exponentially distributed, and we define a new parameter α so that $1/\alpha$ is the average time a limit order is valid. We should note that as the parameter α is permitted to go to zero, reneging disappears and the market is the same as we had previously analyzed. The measures of market quality with reneging may be derived by consulting the literature of queueing theory (see Ancker and Gafarian 1962). We show the derivation of the key parameter, P''_0, in appendix 5A. The major results are:

1. The intensity is $\rho'' = \lambda/\mu$ and is unaffected.
2. The probability that the specialist sets the market quotes is:

$$P''_0 = 1/(1 + \left[\sum_{n=1}^{\infty} (p'')^n / \prod_{i=1}^{n} (1 + (\alpha/\mu)i) \right]$$

where we note that $P''_0 > P_0$, which means the specialist is more active in a system in which reneging occurs, all other things equal.

3. The expected number of limit orders in the system is:

$$L''_s = (1/\alpha)\left[\lambda - \mu(1 - P''_0) \right].$$

4. The expected time a limit order must wait in the queue before it executes or reneges is:

$$W''_s = L''_s/\lambda$$

where both L_s'' and W_s'' are lower than L_s and W_s, meaning that with reneging the limit order book has been reduced in size and becomes less important to the trading process, other things being equal.

5. The inclusion of reneging introduces a new consideration, the probability of executing before reneging, which is:

$$P_s'' = (\mu/\lambda)(1 - P_0'')$$

Although comparing a market with reneging to one without reneging would reveal differences in market quality, such a comparison is not meaningful in a practical sense (since there are no markets where limit orders cannot be canceled), and hence we do not make it. An important issue, however, is the impact of market fragmentation when limit orders have expiration times. To examine this question, we again assume we have two markets, each with equal expected order flow, and without either price or time priority being maintained between markets. This again may be modeled by halving the parameters λ and μ. The reneging factor α is, however, not affected since it seems reasonable to assume traders would not be willing to wait any additional time in the presence of multiple markets.

Because of our assumption of Poisson arrival processes for both limit and market orders and the assumption of exponential reneging, queueing theory tells us that dividing the marketplace in half is mathematically equivalent to doubling the size of the reneging factor. In other words, each market will behave exactly as if it were a single market but with limit orders willing to wait only on average one-half the time for execution that they would have waited in the consolidated market.

Since a greater number of limit orders would now renege, the major conclusion is that in a fragmented market the specialist would set the market quotes a higher proportion of the time. Notice that without reneging our result was that $P_0' = P_0$, which implies that there was no change in the percentage of time the specialist sets the market quotes. Thus the existence of reneging would appear to cause a further deterioration in the quality of the market when the order flow is split between multiple market arenas. Another result is that the size of the limit order books will decrease, thus reducing price stability for the underlying security.

The analysis obtained from this simple queueing model of security trading is applicable only in a fragmented market setting which fails to maintain both price and time priorities across market segments. Obviously, the degree to which price and time priorities across market segments can be maintained (by suitable communication linkages) will mitigate the deterioration in market quality.

Queueing Model Simulation

The simple analytical queueing model described in the last section does not give us sufficient insight into what happens to the quality of markets if we are able to maintain price priority, but time priority is not maintained across market segments. Since most communication systems linking fragmented markets (for example, ITS and NASDAQ) maintain some form of price priority, a key issue in the fragmentation of markets is the loss of time priority. Because of the assumptions of Poisson limit and market order arrival and our exponential assumption on reneging, the issue of time priority is almost irrelevant in our basic queueing model.

In particular, the probability of a market order being served by the specialist, the expected waiting time for a limit order to execute, the expected number of limit orders in the limit order book, and the probability of a limit order executing are unaffected by the existence or nonexistence of a secondary priority rule if markets are fragmented, but price priority is maintained. This is because the basic assumptions of our queueing model provide for what is known as the *memoryless property* of the exponential distribution; that is, once a limit order arrives on the limit order book, its expected time to reneging is still the same regardless of whether the order has waited on the book for five minutes, five days, or whatever.

Given this unrealistic characteristic of the simple Poisson and exponential assumptions we have used up to this point, the reader may ask why we chose them in the first place. The answer is that these assumptions (which are reasonable for the arrival processes of market and limit orders but are somewhat questionable for reneging times) are the only ones that are tractable for a closed-form analytical model. To continue our investigation of what occurs when secondary priority rules are violated, we now turn to a computer simulation model that incorporates a more realistic assumption of reneging times.

The simulation model we constructed parallels closely the analytical framework presented in the last section. Again we have a Poisson arrival process assumed for limit orders that are placed inside the specialist's quotes. Again we assume that market orders are governed by a Poisson arrival process and that the number of market orders exceeds the number of limit orders placed inside the market maker's quotes. However, we now assume that reneging occurs after a constant and fixed amount of time instead of being governed by an exponential distribution. We feel this latter assumption is more realistic; the limit orders we are modeling are therefore similar in concept to, but generally of shorter duration than, so-called day orders, which are automatically withdrawn at the end of the trading day.[7]

Our simulation test compares two markets. Both are assumed to observe price priority, and prices are discrete in both markets.[8] In one market we assume time priority is strictly observed, and in the other market we assume a market order is matched randomly with any of the existing limit orders which are tied at the best price (if there is only one best-price limit order, then of course it is the one that executes against the market order). In table 5–1 we present results for one of our typical simulation runs. The market modeled in this simulation has limit orders arriving on average every five minutes and market orders arriving on average every four minutes. If a limit order does not execute after seventeen minutes, it is automatically withdrawn from the limit order book (it reneges). The four key market-quality parameters are shown in table 5–1.

Notice that the violation of time priority causes: (1) an increase in the bid-ask spread (since the specialist sets the market quotes more frequently and there are fewer public limit orders within the specialist's quotes), (2) a reduction in the expected waiting time in the queue for limit orders, and (3) a reduction in the probability that a limit order will eventually cross with a market order. Of particular interest is the significant drop in the probability that the limit order will execute: from over 88 percent of the time to 83 percent of the time. It is also important to note that the waiting time to execution or reneging does decrease, as does the actual waiting time for those orders that do execute. Although this is an improvement for those orders that execute, this is offset by the reduction in the probability of actually getting execution

Table 5–1
A Comparison of Market Trading Parameters as Observed with Both Time Priority and Random Limit Order Selection

	Time Priority Maintained (standard error)	Random Limit Order Selection (standard error)	t-Test of Difference in Means
Average time the specialist sets the market quotes	31.09% (.49%)	33.43% (.52%)	− 3.29
Average number of limit orders within the specialist's quotes	1.69 (.018)	1.50 (.017)	7.37
Average time a limit order waits before execution or reneging	8.34 min (.058)	7.51 min (.065)	9.55
Average percentage of limit orders that execute	88.43% (.34%)	83.03% (.41%)	10.13

Note: λ = 12 orders per hour, μ = 15 orders per hour, and $1/\alpha$ = 17 minutes. The difference in means of all four statistics are significant at the 99 percent confidence level.

before reneging. In other words, orders that execute have a lower waiting time, but fewer orders execute. These overall changes in market-quality parameters clearly demonstrate the deterioration that occurs in a fragmented market when time priority is violated across market segments, even when price priority is maintained.

A limited amount of sensitivity analysis was performed by varying the values of λ, μ, and α. In general, the results for each combination of parameter values parallel those presented in table 5–1. In all cases the average time a limit order waits before execution or reneging and the average percentage of limit orders that execute had t-values that were significant at the 99 percent confidence level; in one case out of six, however, the t-values for the average time the specialist sets the market quotes and the average number of limit orders within the specialist's quotes were not significant. These results imply that the effects of violating time priority might vary with parameters, but are nonetheless significant.

Conclusion

The queueing theory and simulation models show that fragmented markets, when compared to consolidated markets with the same expected total order flow, have:

1. A smaller probability of there being any limit orders within the market maker's quotes, and therefore a greater probability that the market maker will set the market quotes.
2. A smaller average number of limit orders within the market maker's quotes.
3. A lower probability that a limit order placed within the market maker's quotes will execute.
4. A greater average length of time to execute for any limit order placed within the market maker's quotes, assuming it executes rather than expires.
5. Larger bid-ask spreads in fragmented markets (because of items 1 and 2).

It should be noted that these conclusions can apply *even when price priority is fully maintained between markets*. Where price priority is not maintained across market segments, we analyze the situation with a simple queueing model and showed that the conclusions listed here would hold. If price priority is maintained but time priority is violated across market segments, the deterioration in market quality that then occurs is related to the presence of reneging (that is, to limit orders being withdrawn before they execute). If the expiration (withdrawal) of limit orders were a purely random process with the time to expiration following an exponential distribution, we would see no systematic effect due to market fragmentation. If limit orders have a fixed time to expiration, however, then the effect of violating time priority is very similar to that of violating price priority in that all the conclusions listed (except for item 4) would still hold. Moreover, as illustrated in table 5–1, these effects can be significant in size.

An important part of our demonstration is the distribution of expiration (or reneging) times of limit orders. The deterioration in market quality from violation of time priority under market fragmentation occurs when expiration times are constant, but not when expiration times are exponentially distributed. We have chosen these distributions as polar extremes. The actual distribution of limit order expiration times can be approximated by a mixture of these two distributions. But as long as there is a significant positive correlation between the probability that a limit order will soon expire and the length of time it has already been on the book (a correlation that empirically we would expect to exist), then violation of time priority can cause a deterioration of market quality.

Our simulation model analysis is the first demonstration we know of that violation of time priority can lead to a deterioration of market quality. In particular, we have shown that when time priority is used as the secondary (tie-breaking) rule, then the violation of this rule that could occur from market fragmentation can be harmful to market quality even though price priority is strictly maintained over the fragmented submarkets.[9] Thus even if ITS were to operate perfectly with respect to maintaining price priority, since it does not also maintain time priority, the resulting (partially consolidated) market would be less desirable than a market linking separate trading arenas by means of a consolidated limit order book (CLOB), which maintains both price and time priority.

Obviously this chapter has not answered the key question concerning whether consolidated or fragmented markets are better on an overall basis. What we have addressed, however, is that fostering competition through the fragmenting of markets can lead to some deterioration in market quality. In our worst case, if both price and time priority were violated across submarkets, then the order flow would have to increase by n-fold if the market were fragmented into n submarkets in order to restore market quality; such an increase in order flow seems highly improbable. Furthermore, to the extent that this deterioration in market quality interferes with the price discovery process (as suggested by Schreiber and Schwartz in chapter 2), there could be an overall decrease in the order flow, which would further reduce market quality. Of course, if (as was pointed out originally) fragmentation were instead to lead to an overall increase in the order flow (or to a decrease in the market maker's posted spread), then the effects documented here would be mitigated.

Our analysis has various implications for the design of a securities-market trading system in the context of the issue of consolidation versus fragmentation. A key element of the discussion has been the issue of what a fragmented market is. As discussed earlier, a market with multiple trading arenas is not fragmented if there is full communication between the trading centers. Full communication in this framework means maintaining price priority and any secondary priority rules across the multiple trading centers. In this case, the market dynamics are identical to those of a single trading center with a consolidated order flow. This analysis should serve to focus discussion of the issue of consolidation versus fragmentation. Any proposed design of a security-market trading system with multiple trading arenas must incorporate full communication as an integral element in order to avoid the detrimental effects of fragmentation. Such communication is an important part of a number of proposals (see, for example, Amihud and Mendelson, chapter 15). In the absence of full communication, some discussion of the loss in market quality resulting from fragmentation is necessary.

In the section of the chapter dealing with queueing-model simulation, we considered the situation of a market in which price priority, but not time priority, is maintained across trading centers. The resulting loss in market quality is a direct result of the lack of full communication. One obvious way to avoid this is to maintain time priority. Another, less costly way may be to allow trading at more refined price units such as cents rather than eighths (of a dollar), as suggested in CMSW (1982). By allowing more refined pricing, ignoring time priority would have less of an impact on market quality. In fact, if trading could take place at continuous prices, time priority would have almost no impact, because orders would rarely be tied in price. By understanding how communication affects market quality, we can, as evidenced earlier, go a long way toward resolving the debate concerning consolidation versus fragmentation.

In conclusion, we would argue that in the real-world marketplace—where price priority across markets is only partially maintained and time priority is not maintained at all—it would take significant additional order flow and competitive pressure on market makers in order for those markets to have the same degree of market quality as if the order flow were consolidated in a single trading arena. Perhaps this explains why the old axiom that order flow attracts order flow still holds, and why the NYSE still dominates trading activity.

Notes

1. For further background, see Cohen, Maier, Schwartz, and Whitcomb (CMSW) (1982) and Schreiber and Schwartz (chapter 2).

2. A more recent phase of the Rule 19c-3 controversy involves a proposed (but never implemented) order-exposure rule requiring that (some or all) orders be exposed on all competing markets before a broker-dealer could trade against them (see SEC 1982). This is an attempt to limit to some extent the fragmentation resulting from Rule 19c-3.

3. Garbade and Silber (1978) examine empirically the impact of improvements in communications technology on the integration of decentralized markets. There is evidence that the faster information and order flows brought about by the introductions of the domestic telegraph and the trans-Atlantic cable in the nineteenth century increased arbirtrage activity, resulting in rapid and significant narrowing of price differentials between markets.

4. Suppose the same security is simultaneously traded at $50 per share in one market and $52 per share in a second market. In the absence of transaction costs, we would expect arbitrageurs to buy in the lower-priced market and to sell in the higher-priced market, thus driving the prices to equality in both markets. Positive transaction costs will limit the extent to which such arbitrage is profitable; and the larger the transactions costs, the bigger the price discrepancy across markets that might remain. Moreover, it should be noted that the arbitrageurs' profits arise at the expense of ordinary traders. For example, suppose an arbitrageur buys from an ordinary seller at $50 per share in one market and then sells to an ordinary buyer in the other market at $52 per share; if the two markets were consolidated, the ordinary buyer and the ordinary seller might have transacted together at $51 per share. Thus the arbitrageur's gross (before transactions costs) profit of $2 per share comes partly at the expense of the ordinary seller (who sells at $1 per share less than he otherwise could have) and partly at the expense of the ordinary buyer (who buys at $1 per share more than he otherwise could have).

5. The secondary priority rule on the NYSE involves a combination of what is officially called "priority, parity, and precedence," reflecting both time and size priorities. When two or more NYSE limit orders are tied at the same price and could cross an incoming order: (a) *priority* is applied first (but for only one order), meaning that the earliest of the tied limit orders executes; (b) if there still are unfilled shares of the incoming order, then *parity* is applied, meaning that from the subset of tied limit orders that are large enough to satisfy the remaining portion of the incoming order, the earliest of that subset executes; (c) if the parity rule is inapplicable because none of the tied limit orders are large enough to satisfy the remaining portion of the incoming order, then *precedence* is applied, meaning the largest of the tied limit orders executes (and if there is more than one such largest order, the earliest of these executes); (d) after precedence, as described in (c), is applied one or more times, as soon as there is at least one tied limit order large enough to satisfy the remaining portion of the incoming order, then parity, as described in (b), is applied. The application of parity and precedence on the NYSE reduces the number of transactions necessary to satisfy an incoming order, while still allowing time priority to play some role.

6. The NYSE in 1981 had approximately 81 percent of the volume and 85 percent of the dollar value of shares traded on registered stock exchanges in the United States; see NYSE (1982).

7. Note that the thinness of the limit order book in our simulation might not vary in exactly the same way as it does when day orders predominate. All day orders are withdrawn at the end of the trading day, regardless of when they are placed. In our

simulation, each order is withdrawn after some specified number of minutes (for example, 17 minutes in the run whose results are reported in table 5–1), regardless of when the end of the trading day occurs.

8. Actual security markets have discrete prices. For example, on the NYSE, the minimum price change for most stocks is one-eighth (of a dollar). Clearly the coarser the minimum price change unit, the more likely there are to be orders that are tied in price, and hence the more important time priority is likely to be. This is consistent with extensive simulation runs that we have made but do not report in detail here; the impact of violating time priority decreases as the size of the minimum price change unit decreases. Note that in the queueing theory models discussed earlier in this chapter, it does not matter whether prices are discrete or continuous.

9. This result would generalize to any other secondary priority rule for which violating the tie-breaking criterion used by that rule increases the probability of a limit order reneging.

References

Amihud, Yakov, and Mendelson, Haim. 1985. An integrated computerized trading system. Paper presented at the Conference on Market Making and the Changing Structure of the Securities Industry. (Chapter 15.)

Ancker, C.J., Jr., and Gafarian, A.V. 1962. Queueing with impatient customers who leave at random. *Journal of Industrial Engineering* 13:84–90.

Cohen, Kalman, J.; Maier, Steven F.; Schwartz, Robert A.; and Whitcomb, David K. 1982. An analysis of the economic justification for consolidation in a secondary security market. *Journal of Banking and Finance* 6:117–136.

Davis, Jeffry L. 1984. The intermarket trading system and the Cincinnati experiment. Paper presented at the Conference on Market Making and the Changing Structure of the Securities Industry, Salomon Brothers Center for the Study of Financial Institutions, New York University, May 17–18. (Chapter 18.)

Garbade, Kenneth D., and Silber, William L. 1978. Technology, communication and the performance of financial markets: 1840–1975. *Journal of Finance* 33:819–832.

Gross, Donald, and Harris, Carl M. 1974. *Fundamentals of queueing theory.* New York: Wiley.

Hamilton, James L. 1979. Marketplace fragmentation, competition, and the efficiency of the stock exchange. *Journal of Finance* 34:171–187.

Ho, Thomas S.Y., and Macris, Richard G. 1985. Market structure and performance. Paper presented at the Conference on Market Making and the Changing Structure of the Securities Industry. (Chapter 3.)

Mendelson, Haim. 1984. Consolidation, fragmentation and market liquidity. Paper presented at the Conference on Trading Mechanisms in Securities Exchanges: Towards the Era of Sophisticated Automation, Tel Aviv, January 30–31.

New York Stock Exchange (NYSE). 1982. *1982 fact book.* New York: NYSE.

Schreiber, Paul S., and Schwartz, Robert A. 1985. Regulation and marekt efficiency. (Chapter 2.)

Securities and Exchange Commission (SEC). 1982. Proposed order exposure rule 11A-1. Release No. 19372, December 23.

Stoll, Hans R. 1985. Alternative views of market making. Paper presented at the Conference on Market Making and the Changing Structure of the Securities Industry. (Chapter 4.)

Appendix 5A
The Queueing Model with Reneging

Assumptions

1. Customers arrive from a single, infinite source with an interarrival time density function $a(t) = \lambda e^{-\lambda t}$.
2. An arriving customer always joins the queue.
3. After joining the queue, each customer will wait a certain length of time. If service is not completed by then, he departs. This is a random variable whose density is $d(t) = \alpha e^{-\alpha t}$.
4. Customers are served in order of arrival by a single server facility. Once service commences, it always proceeds to completion. The service time density function is $s(t) = \mu e^{-\mu t}$.

The State Probabilities

Since any of the n customers in the queue may renege, we need the density function of the minimum of n selected from $d(t)$. This is $d_n(t) = n\alpha e^{-n\alpha t}$.

If $P_n(t)$ is the transient probability of n in the system, the balance equations, derived in the usual manner, are

$$dP_0(t)/dt = -\lambda P_0(t) + \mu P_1(t)$$

$$dP_n(t)/dt = -[\lambda + \mu + n\alpha]P_n(t) + \lambda P_{n-1}(t) + [\mu + (n+1)\alpha] P_{n+1}(t) \quad (5A.1)$$

If P_n is the steady-state probability of n in the system, then the steady-state equations are

$$0 = -\lambda P_0 + (\mu + \alpha)P_1$$

and

$$0 = -[\lambda + \mu + \alpha n]P_n + \lambda P_{n-1} + [\mu + \alpha(n+1)]P_{n+1} \quad (5A.2)$$

From the steady-state equations

$$P_{n+1} = \left[\frac{\lambda + \mu + \alpha n}{\mu + \alpha(n+1)} \right] P_n - \left[\frac{\lambda}{\mu + \alpha(n+1)} \right] P_{n-1}$$

$$P_1 = \frac{\lambda}{\mu + \alpha} P_0 \qquad (5A.3)$$

the recursive relationship for P_n is

$$P_n = \left[\frac{\lambda^n}{\prod\limits_{i=1}^{n} (\mu + \alpha i)} \right] P_0 \qquad (5A.4)$$

Noting that $P_0 = 1 - \sum\limits_{n=1}^{\infty} P_n$ yields

$$P_0 = 1 / \left[1 + \sum\limits_{n=1}^{\infty} \frac{\lambda^n}{\prod\limits_{n=1}^{n} (\mu + \alpha i)} \right] \qquad (5A.5)$$

or

$$P_0 = 1 / \left[1 + \sum\limits_{n=1}^{\infty} \frac{\lambda^n}{\mu^n} \cdot \frac{1}{\prod\limits_{i=1}^{n} (1 + \frac{\alpha}{\mu}) i} \right] \qquad (5A.6)$$

If $\alpha = 0$, then P_0 reduces to the well-known result $P_0 = 1 - (\lambda/\mu)$. In the case with reneging, the probability the queue is empty is

$$P_0'' = 1 / \left[1 + \sum\limits_{n=1}^{\infty} \left(\frac{\lambda}{\mu} \right)^n \frac{1}{\prod\limits_{i=1}^{n} (1 + \frac{\alpha}{\mu} i)} \right] \qquad (5A.7)$$

Define $\rho = \lambda/\mu$. Comparing P_0'' with the probability of being empty without reneging, P_0, depends on

$$\sum\limits_{n=1}^{\infty} \rho^n > \sum\limits_{n=1}^{\infty} \rho^n \left[\frac{1}{\prod\limits_{i=1}^{n} (1 + \frac{\alpha}{\mu} i)} \right]$$

and $P_0'' > P_0$. The queue is more likely to be empty with reneging. The construction of the remaining results discussed in the chapter follow a similar line of reasoning.

6
The View from the Trading Floor

Donald Stone

A s a specialist on the New York Stock Exchange (NYSE), I am a continuous participant in the trading mechanism. When I consider the panorama of opportunity and trading in this country—the many different types of markets, including the options exchanges, the over-the-counter markets, the highly volatile government bond market—I take special pride in the agency auction markets, which have been more stable than any others.

When the institutional investor study chaired by John Whitehead took place in 1970,[1] he commented that the basic market structure should be retained, but that it should be flexible, allowing for appropriate change. Fourteen years later we see that the markets have changed dramatically. But this change did not arise from a sudden mandate to make all markets look like one another. Laws, SEC mandates, and Congressional interest have been catalysts; but the principal change has been the markets' tendency to become more efficient.

The introduction of electronic equipment, the bunching of orders, and earlier openings have enabled the markets to handle twice as much volume as in previous eras. Electronic systems designed for automatic executions, such as MAX, SCOREX, INSTINET, PACE, SUPERDOT, and CAES, have been and will continue to be competitive. The future will lead to ever more advanced systems. Those systems that provide the investing public and institutions with the most efficient, fastest, and least expensive execution will survive. But it is important to note also that other systems may survive as alternatives to existing markets.

Regional exchanges, offering tremendous competition to the NYSE, will thrive. I foresee a possibility that the Pacific Coast Stock Exchange will open, perhaps, an hour before the NYSE closes, and remain open for another five hours. In the longer term, we will achieve twenty-four-hour trading, which will provide investors with more fluid, continuous markets. Additional competition will result from the development of the international markets.

Today, less than 4 percent of NYSE transactions account for over 50 percent of NYSE volume. This small percentage of transactions is composed of institutional blocks of more than 10,000 shares each. Fifteen years ago, the average transaction was for 333 shares. Recently this average has been over 1,700 shares, and it is expected to increase substantially over the next ten years.

A major threat to agency auction markets is the growing influence of dealer markets.[2] These markets have benefited from the large volume accounted for by the growth of institutional block trading. Commission-oriented dealer trading is expected to increase as institutions continue to dominate the markets, and as the member firms themselves increase their market-making activity.

On the other hand, however, dealer markets may *decline* as institutions increasingly desire instant liquidity and, as a result, load up the block traders. For instance, consider a market decline that is sustained over a period of several months; at some point, senior partners turn to the managers of their block trading departments and say, "Enough! Cut our losses and liquidate the position." Consequently, the demand for liquidity changes, and the market and stocks quickly decline to new equilibrium values. If the demand for liquidity is open-ended, however, the result may be wide price fluctuations, even from one trade to the next. Even though the member-firm block trading community, in competing for the order flow, has provided institutions with more liquidity than was ever available before, they alone may not be able to provide enough. Then the efficiency of the auction markets will be more important than ever.

A topic receiving much attention is whether an acceptable proportion of limit orders are being executed in national markets. One recent study indicated that an average of only four public limit orders per day were not executed under a new block policy rule. This, and other Exchange studies indicate excellent limit order protection. This protection is due, in part, to the block policy transaction rule, which has been extended from the NYSE to the ITS.

The ITS system, considered a spoof by many at its inception, traded only a few hundred thousand shares in its first year of existence. Last year it traded over a billion shares, and it now is a major market participant. The fact that I am able from New York to consummate a trade on the Pacific Coast within 26 seconds implies tremendous market liquidity and electronic capability. Because of this liquidity, the markets will continue to attract capital; as additional capital is attracted, the auction markets will continue to improve.

I have always been and will remain a supporter of the agency auction market. This unique mechanism, which permits trades without dealers, has proved its efficiency. This is evidenced by the fact that over 50 percent of all trades occur at no price change from previous trades, and over 99.4 percent occur at a change of 25 cents or less. Electronic execution of trades at a price within one-eighth of the previous trade will allow for an even more efficient trading mechanism.

In brief, the exchange auction markets will continue to prosper. Moreover, as participants debate and continually challenge their structures, they will become even better. The public and the nation are well served trading in this highly visible, open, and accessible environment. This agency auction market is the backbone of capitalism and the model for the free world.

Notes

1. U.S. Securities and Exchange Commission (SEC), *Institutional Investor Study Report*, (Washington, D.C.: U.S. Government Printing Office), 1971.
2. Dealer markets are markets where customers buy from the dealer on the offer and sell to the dealer on the bid. Agency auction markets are markets where the customer has an agent acting on his or her behalf trying to buy or sell at the best price, oftimes trading with other customers between the bid and offer without a dealer interceding. In a dealer market (42–42½) if a buy and sell order arrive simultaneously, the buyer will pay the offer price (42½) and the seller will sell at the bid price (42). In an agency-auction market, the trade would probably take place between the bid and offer (42¼) as the agents acted on behalf of their customer's best interest.

Part II
Market and Regulatory Structure

7

An Era of Opportunity and Challenge for The Securities Industry

John J. Phelan, Jr.

There was a time when the New York Stock Exchange was not comfortable with the academic environment, nor with anyone who expressed new ideas about our business. One of the things that clearly marks the Exchange's progress from a membership organization to a quasi-public institution is a dramatic change in that attitude. We have really opened up. We have established a good working relationship with the academic community, not just here in New York, but throughout the country and worldwide. We hope our ongoing series of seminars for leading professors of economics, finance, and securities law—among others—has been useful to the academic community. Certainly these seminars have been very valuable to us as we have changed from an institution that avoided new ideas to one that both solicits them and tries to develop some of its own as well.

An old story about Albert Einstein illustrates how people used to think about the securities industry. According to this story, Einstein was having a terrible time getting along with people, and he consulted a psychiatrist. After a few sessions, the psychiatrist said: "Albert, your problem is that you're too introverted. You're a brilliant man, but you just don't know how to communicate with people."

Einstein replied, "I know. But I just can't meet strangers and talk to them."

"Try it. Go sit on a park bench and start a conversation with the first person who comes along. Then do the same thing with the next person. And the next. You'll find that it gets easier each time."

So Einstein agreed, and next morning, he went out to the park at nine o'clock. Soon a fellow came down the path.

"Excuse me, my name is Albert Einstein, and I'd like to talk with you." The fellow recognized him and was very flattered. "I'd be delighted," he said.

"Before we begin," Einstein said, "could you tell me your IQ?"

"Yes, 190."

"Wonderful. I'd like to discuss metaphysics with you. And space and time relationships, and mathematical formulas."

They chatted for about an hour and a half, and then the fellow said he had to get to his office. Einstein was feeling pretty good about how easy it had been when an attractive young woman came down the path.

"Excuse me, my name is Albert Einstein, and I wonder whether you'd have time for some conversation."

"Oh, that would be very nice."

When Einstein learned that her IQ was 140, they discussed government, politics, and world affairs—until she, too, had to leave.

A third fellow came along, and Einstein went through the same routine. When he came to the question about IQ, the fellow answered, "Sixty." Einstein smiled and said, "Hmm, how do you think the stock market will do today?"

My point is, of course, that the academic world once regarded most of us in the financial services industries as nonintellectuals who might know our own businesses, but not much else. What has happened over the past ten years or so is that those same people—in brokerage, banking, insurance—have turned the financial world upside down and brought on a national and international revolution in which everybody is both learning and getting into everybody else's business.

Americans like everything to happen quickly. We like instant tea and fast-food service, and we especially like overnight success. When things take longer than we think they should, we get impatient. We start feeling frustrated and complain about change taking too long. We overlook the fact that ten or fifteen or twenty years is really a short time when you're looking for the results of revolutionary change—especially when it happens to be someone else's revolution.

The modern age of competition among financial services institutions really dates back to the 1920s. At that time, banks and brokerage firms competed on essentially equal terms—underwriting issues, taking positions in them, and so on. In the wake of the so-called technical correction of 1929, we had the 1933 bank holiday. All the unpleasant experiences of depositors whose savings disappeared triggered demands to shore up the credibility of the banking system by devising new forms of protection for depositors. In that process, Congress returned to the old English system of commercial banking, taking underwriting and other high-risk activities out of the banking business. Congress did allow banks to continue in the government—and, to some extent, the municipal—bond business, for the simple reason that government continually has to raise money, and banks—not securities firms—had the funds to lend.

On the securities side, Congress emphasized the importance of protecting the customer—not the institutions—and that thrust created the Securities Act of 1933, the Securities Exchange Act of 1934, and a continuing succession of related legislation. World War II put the financial services industries in limbo, but Congress returned to socially oriented economic legislation almost immediately afterward: the G.I. Bill of Rights, which guaranteed nearly everyone an opportunity for higher education; the Full Employment Act of 1946; the Pension Act of 1949; and so on. All these measures brought on tremendous structural changes in our national economy that were destined to have a powerful impact on the capital-raising system and on the nation's financial institutions.

Most people tend to date the major changes that have modernized the securities business from 1967–1968, when market activity soared to what were then unprecedented levels. In retrospect, of course, that activity seems puny.

In 1968, for example, rising stock prices sent average daily volume on the NYSE up to nearly 13 million shares. On the busiest day that year, some 21 million shares changed hands. Volume for the full year set a new record of a little over 2.9 billion shares—nearly triple the volume of a few years earlier—and that represented a turnover rate of about 24 percent. Although the Exchange was able to process that volume without too much stress, most of our member firms could not. In the thick of the ensuing paperwork crunch, the industry had to restrict trading to four hours a day—and then to four days a week—while the firms, with help from the Exchange, struggled to clear up their back-office problems.

By 1970 most of the operational problems were yielding to corrective measures, reinforced by heavy investments in automation and people, when stock prices started dropping, volume declined, and scores of firms found themselves in deep financial trouble. The Exchange and its member-firm community put up some $140 million to make sure the customers of failing firms did not lose their accounts. By the time the smoke cleared, some 160 member firms—roughly one-third of our membership, including some of the best-known names in the business—had vanished forever, most of them through orderly self-liquidation and mergers with stronger firms.

The upshot of stretching our financial commitment almost to the limit for the relative handful that desperately needed help in staving off financial disaster for their customers was the creation, in the closing days of 1970, of SIPC—the government-backed, industry-funded Securities Investor Protection Corporation, our industry's version of the FDIC.

That was only thirteen years ago. Today we have one of the most highly automated and most intensely competitive industries in the country or in the world. Many firms, including most of the biggest ones, are publicly owned—something the Exchange did not permit in 1970. At the NYSE alone, we handle 100 to 150 million shares in a single day as a matter of routine, and we're gearing up for 250 million shares a day. Volume last year was 21.6 billion shares—more than seven times what it was in 1968—and the turnover rate had more than doubled, to 51 percent.

Along the way, we have survived the elimination of fixed commission rates, adjusted to heavy institutional participation in the market, built a smoothly functioning national market system, launched a series of attractive and important new products, and greatly strengthened our self-regulatory capabilities. We have also weathered a couple of serious recessions, double-digit inflation, challenges to the validity of our entire private-enterprise system, and the rise of OPEC. If anyone had predicted, even five years earlier, the explosion of market activity that burst on the securities industry in 1982 and 1983—and that the industry would be able to handle it without any real difficulty—he or she would have been hustled off to the nearest funny farm without delay.

Despite some recent price and volume declines, we have a strong industry and high levels of investor confidence. To be sure, the turnaround has been aided by more realistic government attitudes toward productive investment in our basic economic system, but it also reflects historic changes in the industry's own attitude toward itself and toward its role in our national economy. Nevertheless, people still complain that "things sure go awfully slow in this industry."

A lot depends on how you define *slow*.

In 1975 the SEC stood the securities industry on its ear by deregulating commission rates. If nothing else had happened, that one action alone would have changed the entire conduct of the securities business. The Cassandras predicted that the demise of fixed commission rates would send investors' costs spiraling upward, but that view entirely overlooked the historical fact that competitive forces bring rates down. Sure enough, commission rates on institutional orders plummeted by as much as 70 or 80 percent.

The firms tried to compensate for that lost revenue by raising individual rates, and people reacted sharply. They said, "Look what you did, you nasty government—you deregulated rates, the institutions benefit, and the poor individual investor gets stuck with the bill." Within a year or two, those complaints petered out as discount firms sprang into existence and started bringing retail rates down. Discounting was a naughty word, at first; but before long, several major firms began clearing for discounters, and their niche has become secure.

At least one established firm reacted pretty quickly. As early as the mid-1970s, Merrill Lynch came to a startling conclusion. At least, they acknowledged a fact that other firms did not. They recognized that they were not primarily in the securities business or the futures business or the options business or the commodities business. They were really in the depository business, and what they did with the funds in their custody—whether and how they made money on them—was what really counted. At that time, everyone in the industry thought they were going to lose customers' free credit balances. Faced with that prospect, Merrill Lynch came up with a brand new concept: the cash management account—CMA.

As with most truly innovative ideas, the concept of this one was really quite simple: Bring the funds inside, develop a plan and capability for managing them, and then provide a variety of peripheral services to use them that customers will find attractive. Once the idea took hold, Merrill Lynch did not move slowly—and that one new product completely revolutionized the business.

In effect, Merrill Lynch leapfrogged over the banks, which thought that credit cards and similar instruments gave them a permanent monopoly in the consumer credit business. Merrill did not create a major new product simply because they thought that would be nice, but because they felt they had to take the lead and get into other businesses at a time when their traditional lines of business looked less promising. Other firms were not slow to get on that bandwagon once it began to roll, nor were the banks slow to take some initiatives of their own.

By 1980 the financial services environment more and more resembled the environment of the twenties. Much of the structure that had existed for half a century was coming undone. The Federal Reserve was shaking up the banking industry; and, on the theory that the best defense is a strong offense, everybody—banks, insurance companies, securities firms—began moving quickly into new areas of financial services and stepping on one another's toes. Although there have been some casualties, the basic thrust of deregulation and intensifying competition has been to present great new opportunities—and great new challenges and risks—to anyone and everyone who is willing and able to innovate and compete creatively.

There has never been greater opportunity in the securities business than there is today. The number of NYSE member organizations has mushroomed from a low of 473 in 1977 to nearly 650 today. Many people are entering the business at the low end, which is not very capital-intensive—particularly in such areas as marketing and customer service.

An ironic incident that occurred at a recent dinner held by the Regional Firms Advisory Committee to the NYSE Board of Directors points up just how the business mix, and attitudes as well, are changing. The chairman of the committee, which keeps our board informed about the needs and concerns of regionally based member firms throughout the country, led off the discussion with a question: "How do we keep the banks out of our business?" He looked at me, and I said, "Don't look at me, talk to the group."

They began to talk and, within five minutes the committee member sitting next to him said: "Wait a minute, that's not my problem. My problem is how do we get into the banking business!"

That could not have happened as recently as three years ago. Then everyone at the table would have agreed vehemently not only that the banks should stay out of their business, but also that they did not want to compete in banking, either.

It is not clear what banks expect to do in our business. Many of them have more than enough problems now, just as some securities firms have some problems with the new businesses they are now in.

Overall, what we have today is a proliferation of new products and pro-liferating competition. We can certainly hope that out of this will come still greater liquidity for the markets, higher levels of business, and better service for our customers.

At the Exchange, we have come a long way from the old trade-association or membership-organization mentality to a not-for-profit—and not-for-loss, either—corporation that is truly a quasi-public institution with a broad range of constituencies extending far beyond our members and member firms. Those constituencies include, most prominently, the listed companies that provide the products traded in our marketplace and that are the underlying reason for our existence. Basically, it is the secondary market for listed securities that enables listed companies to raise the money they must have to grow and expand, invest in new plants and equipment, and develop the new products and services that create new jobs and prosperity and an expanding economy. The Exchange stands at the heart of that process, as an integral part of the capital-raising mechanism that fuels our national economic growth.

Other obvious constituencies are the institutional and individual in-vestors who use our marketplace, day in and day out. Another constituency, whether we like it or not, is government. Government is a partner of ours. It is sometimes—though less frequently than in the past—an adversary. I am not just talking about government at the federal level, also about state and local governments. Yet although we have these diverse constituencies to serve, we must also—somehow—manage to remain flexible enough to func-tion as strong competitors in our business.

We are, in fact, in a number of businesses—stocks, bonds, futures, op-tions. Another business that has become increasingly important to us and to our constituents is the business of dealing with major national economic con-cerns and issues. Those issues range from shareholder protection, to cor-porate mergers and acquisitions, to the crucial importance of maintaining a strong capital-raising mechanism, to the U.S. role in an international economic environment that is becoming more intensely competitive every day. We have been confronting some of these issues for a long time, and we think we have developed expertise in a number of areas. Others seem to think so, too, because they seek our advice on some of their own problems.

Right now, for example, the London Stock Exchange is facing many of the fears and questions that wracked our industry a decade ago. Some of our British counterparts are terrified about the prospect of unfixed commission rates. They have come over here in a steady stream, asking about our ex-perience in 1975, taking notes, going back home, and sending more col-leagues over to ask many of the same questions and a few new ones as they think them up. Our best advice, based on our own experience, has been very simple: "Don't try to play God. Let the fixed rates go and see what happens. You'll get it all sorted out soon enough." That's what happened in this coun-try, and it has worked out pretty well.

Our environment is continuing to change. The environment for our major product—equities—has become competitive to a degree that no one would have believed possible a decade ago. The second major catalyst for that—after we scrapped fixed commission rates—was the mandate to create a national market system, which also exploded in our industry's midst in 1975. Many in the industry sat and wrung their hands over that until we all picked ourselves up and started working on the assignment Congress gave us. Once we got into it, we discovered that it was not nearly as bad as everyone had feared. In fact, it was pretty good. Of course, there were problems and disagreements at first, but we found we could deal with them and overcome them. The task of linking all the markets in which listed stocks were traded offers a classic example. By 1978 all the competing major exchanges in the country agreed to cooperate in developing the Intermarket Trading System (ITS). The idea was to create an electronic linkage that would enable anyone entering an order on the floor of one exchange to get the best price that was available on any of the other floors on which a particular stock was traded. That would give every customer access to systemwide liquidity. Many people laughed and said the idea couldn't possibly work.

From mid-April 1978 through the end of that first year, the list of stocks eligible to be traded in ITS grew from 11 to 300. Daily average volume for that eight-and-a-half-month period was only 235,000 shares, however, and it took about two and a half minutes to get an execution. The scoffers had a field day, saying, "I told you so!"

By the end of 1983, however, some 1,100 stocks were being traded in the system. Volume for the year was more than 1 billion shares, and the average execution time was down to about 30 seconds. In many cases today our specialists must vie for order flow with six competitors on as many as six other exchanges. Most people now agree that ITS is, in fact, the heart of the national market system. Although it is impossible to be precise, we estimate that the opportunity to get a better price in another market may have saved investors as much as $150–$170 million since 1980.

The competitive impact has been considerable. Other exchanges have developed automated execution systems to compete with the NYSE and AMEX. All of us have created automated delivery systems that transmit customers' orders from member firms' offices to our trading floors at electronic speeds. At the NYSE, as we have become more expert in the technology that makes these things possible, we have steadily built on that technology to create additional trading support systems and facilities that have greatly increased our competitiveness, our order-processing capabilities, and our overall operational efficiency. These systems now enable us to handle smoothly trading volume loads that would have swamped us just a few years ago.

Today, with new products emerging all the time, the older markets are searching out more effective competitive techniques, and new markets are trying to plug into the system as efficiently as they can. Less than ten years ago, we were all worried about government putting us out of business. Today the main challenge is the challenge of competition, and most of us find ourselves thriving on it.

A very important element of that competition is competition for listings. In recent years the National Association of Securities Dealers (NASD) has come up with something called the NASDAQ national market system that provides a last-sale quote stream and end-of-the-day volume figures for stocks that are traded over the counter. They began the system with the stocks of 40 companies that are fairly active and that might be eligible for listing on the NYSE. Naturally, many of the 4,000 or so other over-the-counter (OTC) companies wanted to hook into that system, so they have been expanding it toward a new goal of including some 2,000 companies.

At the NYSE we are often asked, "Aren't you worried about how rapidly the over-the-counter market is growing?"

In fact, I think it's just fine. For one thing, it shows how successful some of the recent changes in national economic policy have been in encouraging the formation and growth of new enterprises. When most of those new companies go public, they simply do not have the capitalization, shareholder base, or widespread investor interest to qualify for listing on an exchange. They need a dealer-sponsor, and they need an over-the-counter market where their securities can be traded. That market serves a very useful function. The more over-the-counter stocks, the better. The OTC market also serves as a nursery for the exchanges, where companies can mature, gain wider recognition, and eventually qualify for exchange listing.

You have probably heard some talk about how the NASD today poses a big threat to new listings for the Exchange—that new companies are not really coming to us anymore. The fact is that last year we had a near-record number of new listings—89 in all, including 18 that were technically new because of new entities that were formed chiefly through mergers and acquisitions by existing companies, and 71 that were entirely new additions to our roster. The total number of shares listed for trading on the Exchange increased by a record 5.6 billion shares—to more than 45 billion. I should add that these figures do not include some 1.5 billion shares of the new companies formed in connection with the AT&T divestiture. Those issues began trading in November 1983 but were not formally listed until after the January 1, 1984, effective date of the divestiture. At the end of April 1984, the total number of shares listed had risen to well over 47 billion.

Were it not for the negative impact of mergers and acquisitions on our list, it would really be soaring, but we do not have any way to control what is happening in that area. As it is, we now list about 78 percent of all securities that are eligible for trading on the Exchange.

The NASD says that 600 over-the-counter companies are eligible for listing on the NYSE. We disagree with that figure; by our count, there are only about 465 such companies. Moreover, they include about 160 regional banks and insurance companies that technically meet our earnings and profitability requirements but that simply do not generate enough trading activity to make it worthwhile for them to list, because they still need that over-the-counter dealer sponsorship. Another 40 or so of those 465 companies are eligible to list on the AMEX but not on the NYSE, because we do not accept companies that issue nonvoting stock or that have certain other types of shareholder arrangements.

When you deduct all those companies, the real figure comes down to between 270 and 280, and we expect about 25 percent of them to come onto the NYSE this year. Thus, when you do all the appropriate arithmetic, we now list about 86 or 87 percent of the entire universe of securities that are eligible and appropriate for trading on the Exchange.

Certainly the NASD is becoming more efficient. It is a better market than it used to be. It serves a valid national economic purpose, just as we do. When it comes to competition for listings, however, the NYSE is doing very nicely and expects to continue to do very nicely. Significantly, companies often come to us and say, "One of the reasons we want to list is that we do business overseas. One of the first questions people ask us overseas is, 'Are you listed on the New York Stock Exchange?' So it's very important for us to be able to say, 'Yes, indeed, we are.' "

Someone asked me just the other day to explain the value of an NYSE listing. I answered with another question: "What is the value of that little star that juts up from the hood of a Mercedes?" I was not being facetious. A listing on the NYSE is really a recognizable and internationally accepted sign of quality, dependability, and reliability—both for the listed company and for the investors who want to buy and sell its stocks in what most people regard as the world's premier securities marketplace.

If that sounds a bit boastful, let me add that of course we see the NASD as a significant competitor for us today, and they are likely to be still more significant in the future. We think that is good for us as well as for them. It will help keep us on our toes. It will help make us harder and tougher, and we think it will make them better, too.

I said earlier that the Exchange today is in many businesses. We wanted to get into futures and options because, in a rapidly changing environment, you never know where the next challenge may come from. We have done that in a novel way, with products based on our NYSE Composite Index, that draws on our experience in trading the underlying equities. For all we know today, the derivative products may one day become more important than the underlying product itself. We hope that does not happen, but we want to be ready if it does.

The Exchange is also very much in the information business, through our Market Data System, as a member of the Consolidated Tape Association, and so on. What's more, we are in the regulation business, too—a business that many people think no one in his right mind would want to be in. On the other hand, polls and surveys of investors make it very clear that the public thinks that is one of our most important functions—and we agree. Of course, we cannot run the businesses of 650 member firms, and we wouldn't want to if we could. Self-regulation, like charity, begins at home—in this case, with each member firm's legal, compliance, and auditing people. With the structure of the industry changing every day, however, we feel we have an obligation to make certain they are conducting their financial, sales, and operational activities in a responsible manner. Similarly, the SEC watches us to make sure we are doing our job, just as Congress keeps an eye on the SEC. So we are all linked together in a strong self-regulatory chain that has accurately been called *cooperative regulation.*

After the disasters of the late 1920s and 1930s, most people thought government was the ideal regulator. It has taken half a century to discover that the ideal is, in fact, self-regulation with government oversight. That is what we have today.

Part of our job is to cooperate with our competitors at the same time that we vie with them for business. Another part is to keep a step ahead, if possible, of developments in all our businesses. At the Exchange, we have evolved a system of blue-ribbon constituent advisory committees to help us do that.

As the market environment continues to change—and as change continues to accelerate—there will be new challenges and new problems, perhaps bigger than any we have faced to date. We do not know when they may come—or where, how, or why. With market volatility increasing—not only domestically, but internationally as well—with competition becoming more and more intense, and with growing uncertainties about who is—or should be—in what business, there is likely to be a big structural problem. We hope we recognize it in time. We hope we will be smart enough to guide our member firms through any such crisis. If we have learned anything from the experiences of the past, it is the need to be ever more vigilant.

We see the markets growing and becoming more and more international in scope. We expect government to rely more and more on the individual to take care of his or her own needs—education, medical, retirement, and so on—and that will require more incentives for people to invest in their own futures. In 1975 some 25 million individual Americans owned shares of corporate stock and stock mutual funds. Today the shareowner ranks have swelled to more than 42 million, and we think the trend will continue upward—at the same time as financial institutions such as pension funds, life insurance companies, and mutual savings banks continue to pool and invest the savings of tens of millions of additional Americans.

All these people are our industry's customers. If we are to serve them effectively, we have to recognize and accept the fact that the times have changed and will continue to change. Competition and change make up the new order—the new way of life—in our business. We have to seek out new ideas and new opportunities for change, and both adapt them to our needs and adapt to them. We will need all the expert help and guidance we can get. I think we are heading for some very exciting times—times that may pose tremendous risks and dangers in the years ahead, but times that will bring tremendous opportunities, too.

8
The Competitive Environment of the Securities Market

John T. Wall

T he competitive environment of the U.S. and world securities markets has been drastically altered by the emergence in 1971 of the NASDAQ system—a facility that has completely transformed the nature of over-the-counter trading. NASDAQ is now the second-largest and fastest-growing U.S. stock market; its 1983 share volume was 74 percent of that of the NYSE and 7.5 times that of the AMEX. It is also the third-largest equity market in the world, after the New York and Tokyo stock exchanges.

Over the fourteen years of its existence, NASDAQ has captured an increasing share of the market—not only in terms of overall market volume but also in terms of number of companies. For example, more than 600 NASDAQ companies qualify for listing on the NYSE; more than 1,600 are eligible for listing on the AMEX. For various reasons, however, they remain with NASDAQ as the market of choice.

NASDAQ's competitive strengths include: state-of-the-art communications technology; the competitive multimarket maker system, and the NASDAQ National Market System, which provides issuers and investors with a combination of the best features of the OTC and the exchange markets.

To improve its competitive position, NASDAQ is developing a Small Order Execution System and other technological improvements, increasing the domestic visibility and recognition of NASDAQ securities, and further internationalizing the NASDAQ market.

The present and future competition is between two premier U.S. markets, NASDAQ and the NYSE. NASDAQ expects to make further gains in market share, particularly as artificial barriers to the voluntary exchange delisting of companies are removed in the competitive world of the 1980s and beyond.

The growth of the NASDAQ market has in recent years drastically transformed the traditional competitive pattern of the U.S. and international securities markets. Before the 1971 startup of the nationwide, computerized NASDAQ communications system for the over-the-counter (OTC) equity market, the old-line stock exchanges—the NYSE; the AMEX; and the regionals such as the Boston, Midwest, Pacific, and Philadelphia—dominated U.S. equity trading. The OTC market was mysterious, largely unrecognized, sometimes chaotic. In 1984, however, the NASDAQ market has become the second-largest securities market in the United States, exceeded in size only by the NYSE, and far larger than the AMEX and all the regional exchanges combined. The NASDAQ market has also become the third largest in the world, exceeded in dollar volume only by the New York and Tokyo stock exchanges, and far larger than the London Stock Exchange. Once the acknowledged spawning ground for stock exchanges, NASDAQ is no longer a junior market where little companies grow up until they are ready for an exchange listing. Today, NASDAQ's National Newspaper List of more than 2,600 securities is composed mostly of seasoned market performers—companies that stay on NASDAQ because they would rather have competitive market makers than a single exchange specialist.

U.S. Competitive Developments, 1983

In 1983, comparisons of the NASDAQ market with the NYSE and the AMEX showed the following:

1983 Share Volume

NASDAQ	15,908,547,000	36.3%
NASDAQ/OTC trading in listed securities	839,276,000	1.9%
AMEX	2,080,922,000	4.8%
REGIONALS	3,367,908,000	7.7%
NYSE	21,589,577,000	49.3%
Totals	43,786,230,000	100.0%

1983 Dollar Volume

NASDAQ	$188,284,596,000	16.8%
NASDAQ/OTC trading in listed securities	28,157,713,000	2.5%
AMEX	29,853,669,000	2.7%
REGIONALS	106,653,231,000	9.6%
NYSE	765,275,200,000	68.4%
Totals	$1,118,224,409,000	100.0%

The 1983 comparisons of the top ten volume leaders for NASDAQ, the NYSE, and the AMEX are as follows:

Comparisons of Top Ten Volume Leaders of
NASDAQ, NYSE, and AMEX
in 1983

NASDAQ

Security	Shares Traded	Price
MCI Communications	330,014,100	14 3/8
Apple Computer	200,967,900	24 3/8
Glaxo Holdings	122,413,600	10
Philips (NV)	106,614,100	14 3/8
Intel Corporation	100,014,800	42
Tandon Corporation	95,416,500	20
Convergent Technologies	89,013,000	23 3/4
Seagate Technology	88,659,800	14
Tandem Computers	82,265,900	35 1/8
Fuji Photo Film	59,070,300	16 7/8
Average	127,445,000	21.48

NYSE

Security	Shares Traded	Price
AT&T	388,532,400	61 1/2
IBM	222,837,400	122
Exxon	210,796,100	37 3/8
Chrysler	182,875,000	27 5/8
General Motors	151,676,300	74 3/8
Pan American	141,157,900	8 1/8
Merrill Lynch	140,927,300	32
Eastman Kodak	131,154,900	76 1/8
Citicorp	130,355,000	37 1/8
American Express	126,750,500	32 5/8
Average	182,706,280	50.89

AMEX

Security	Shares Traded	Price
Wang Labs	85,386,900	35 5/8
Dome Petroleum	78,958,600	3 3/8

Security	Shares Traded	Price
Cyprus Corporation	37,769,900	2 1/2
Champion Home	28,851,400	4 3/8
Instrument Systems	27,578,300	3
Amdahl	26,563,200	18 3/8
Texas Air	23,591,700	6 5/8
TIE Communications	23,529,000	27
Telesphere	18,859,800	5 1/4
Resorts International	18,778,900	38 1/4
Average	36,986,770	14.44

On seven days in 1983, NASDAQ volume surpassed NYSE volume:

Date	NASDAQ	NYSE	AMEX
May 27	79,747,800	76,290,000	13,880,000
June 24	85,200,400	80,810,000	10,590,300
June 27	74,283,100	69,360,000	10,280,000
July 12	72,131,800	70,220,000	9,552,000
August 23	66,909,000	66,800,000	6,713,000
August 29	55,679,450	53,030,000	5,307,000
December 30	78,761,700	71,840,000	10,593,000

U.S. Competitive Developments, 1979–1984

The competitive statistics for 1983 only accentuated a trend that had been building ever since the NASDAQ market came into being in 1971, and that has become especially pronounced in the last five years. The statistics for the period 1979–1984 show the following:

In 1979 NASDAQ volume was 3.7 billion shares. In 1983 it reached 15.9 billion shares, more than four and a half times what it was five years ago.

In 1979 NASDAQ share volume was 45 percent of NYSE volume. For 1983 NASDAQ share volume was almost 74 percent of that of the NYSE.

In 1979 NASDAQ share volume was less than three and a half times AMEX volume. In 1983 NASDAQ share volume was running at more than nine times AMEX volume. In the first quarter of 1984 the ratio went up to almost ten to one.

In 1979 there were 2,543 companies on NASDAQ; at the end of 1983 there were 3,901—a gain of 53 percent. Meanwhile, the number of companies on the NYSE declined by 1 percent while the number of companies on the AMEX declined by 12 percent. In the first quarter of 1984 NASDAQ added 124 companies.

In 1979 there were 2,670 securities traded on the NASDAQ market; at the end of 1983, there were 4,467—a gain of 67 percent. Meanwhile, the number of issues on the NYSE was up 5 percent and the number on the AMEX down 6 percent. In the first quarter of 1984, NASDAQ added 187 issues.

At the end of March 1984 there were 4,025 companies and 4,654 securities traded on the NASDAQ market:

Five-Year Comparisons of NASDAQ, NYSE, and AMEX,
1979–1983

NASDAQ

	Companies	Issues	Share Volume (billions)
1979	2,543	2,670	3.651
1980	2,894	3,050	6.692
1981	3,353	3,687	7.823
1982	3,264	3,664	8.432
1983	3,901	4,467	15.909

NYSE

	Companies	Issues	Share Volume (billions)
1979	1,565	2,192	8.156
1980	1,570	2,228	11.352
1981	1,565	2,220	11.854
1982	1,526	2,225	16.458
1983	1,550	2,307	21.590

AMEX

	Companies	Issues	Share Volume (billions)
1979	931	1,006	1.100
1980	892	973	1.626
1981	867	919	1.343
1982	834	944	1.338
1983	822	948	2.081

The International Picture, 1983

In addition to being the second-largest market in the U.S., NASDAQ in 1983 was the third-largest market in the world in terms of dollar volume of equity trading.

NYSE	Tokyo	NASDAQ
$765.3 billion	$235.1 billion	$188.3 billion

The 1983 dollar volume of equity trading in the NASDAQ market was larger than that of the London ($42 billion), Zurich ($38 billion), West German ($34 billion), American ($30 billion), and Paris ($12.4 billion) exchanges combined.

NASDAQ versus Listing

The competition between the NASDAQ market and the exchanges is qualitative as well as quantitative. Before NASDAQ, the over-the-counter (OTC) market was the seasoning and proving ground for small and startup companies; as such companies prospered and grew, they would often leave the OTC market and list on one of the stock exchanges, perhaps first on the AMEX and, if they grew and prospered some more, eventually on the NYSE. Today the traditional stream of listings from the OTC market to the exchanges is down to a very thin trickle. Out of NASDAQ's 4,000 companies, 600 could list their stocks on the NYSE, and 1,600 could list on the AMEX (see Appendix 7A).

These 600 to 1,600 companies stay on the NASDAQ market despite their eligibility for exchange listing and despite intense solicitation efforts directed at them by the NYSE and the AMEX. These companies are also some of the best-known enterprises in the country—MCI Communications Corporation, Apple Computer, Mack Trucks, People Express, American International Group, Kemper Corporation, Adolph Coors, Pabst Brewing, State Street Bank, and Tampax, among others.

Why do these companies prefer the NASDAQ market, and make it their market of choice?

Why NASDAQ Is Preferred

Companies stay on NASDAQ instead of listing for the following reasons, among others:

The competitive multiple market-maker system is preferred by many issuers to the single-specialist system of the exchanges. NASDAQ companies find these advantages in having competitive multimarket makers:

Sponsorship: Market makers conduct research into a company's performance and potential and continuously follow its stock. On the basis of their analysis, if it is favorable, market makers generate interest in the stock by discussing it with investors and recommending it to them. These efforts help to maintain marketability for OTC securities. They are efforts that exchange specialists, by the nature of the specialist system, do not and cannot undertake.

Competition: The competition among the multiple market makers in an OTC stock leads to its appropriate pricing in the light of the issuing company's performance and under prevailing market conditions. Market-maker competition also supports an appropriate level of trading volume in an OTC stock, as the market makers either respond to existing investor interest or try to create it where they think a security merits it.

Continuity of trading: Competition among market makers also assures investors that there are always dealers who will trade their stocks, and that investors can trade continuously and at any time. There are brief quotations halts in the NASDAQ market to permit the adequate dissemination of material news about a stock, but there are not the protracted trading halts that exchange specialists impose in uncertain circumstances.

Capital: Market makers support OTC securities by committing capital to them as they carry them in their inventories, and the combined capital of a number of market makers may well exceed the capital resources of a single exchange specialist trading a listed security. The market makers' capital commitment is always helpful, but it is particularly important in maintaining stability in an issue under adverse conditions.

The NASDAQ market is electronic and computerized, at state-of-the-art levels. Over the last several years, the NASD has invested more than $30 million in the most sophisticated central computers, market makers' and financial institutions' terminals, and network controls available, and has produced a nationwide communications system that is operating at 99 percent uptime.

The liquidity of NASDAQ securities is at least comparable, and often superior, to that of exchange-listed securities. A study prepared at Texas A&M University concludes: "OTC liquidity tends to dominate AMEX liquidity of stocks of the same size. . . . Moreover, for most size ranges short of very large companies, NYSE listing may imply a lower liquidity than had the firm remained OTC. That greater liquidity of OTC stocks probably results from the interest of multiple market makers in their stocks. . . . A small or even moderate size NYSE or AMEX stock has no such constituency, receiving the attention of a single specialist."

The cost of capital is no higher, and at times is lower, for NASDAQ companies than for exchange-listed companies. Susan M. Phillips, now chairman of the Commodity Futures Trading Commission, and S. Richard Zecher, now chief economist of the Chase Manhattan Bank, concluded in a 1982 study published by the SEC: "Listing stocks does not affect risk or cost of capital for companies of similar asset size, industry group and trading volume, and further, the decision to list does not appear to have any predictable effect on risk or on the cost of capital for the listing company." William G. McGowan, chairman and chief executive officer of MCI Communications Corporation, told 140 executives at the October 1983 NASD Conference for NASDAQ Companies: "MCI has raised in excess of $2 billion in the last 36 months; we measure our net cost of capital constantly; it is very important to us; and our experience is that our cost of capital would not be lowered by listing."

The NASDAQ National Market System offers issuers the best of the OTC market, combined with the attractive aspects of the exchange markets. The computerized NASDAQ NMS marketplace successfully provides qualifying NASDAQ companies, investors, and the securities industry with advantages available nowhere else: up-to-the-minute volume and last-sale information and competing multiple market makers. The NASDAQ National Market System (NMS) puts technology and competition to work together and represents, in dynamic operating form, the marketplace of the future.

NMS, two years old in 1984, is the second-largest continuous reporting market in the United States. Its 1983 share volume was 4.4 billion shares, 27.7 percent of total NASDAQ volume and well over double the volume of the AMEX. About 40 percent of the NMS volume consists of block volume of 10,000 shares or better, indicative of the strong institutional participation in the NASDAQ market. To issuers, NMS means that they can have the visibility that last-sale information provides, without giving up the advantages of the competitive, multimarket-maker system.

These various aspects of the NASDAQ market make it not only the second-largest and fastest-growing U.S. stock market, but also make NASDAQ very competitive with the exchanges in attracting and retaining high-quality companies, with broad investor interest.

The NASDAQ Market of Tomorrow

The NASD is well aware that in the competitive environment of the securities markets, it must continue to increase the quality and efficiency of the NASDAQ market in order to maintain its attractiveness to issuers, investors, and the securities industry. The market improvements that the NASD has under way include the following:

Expansion of the NASDAQ National Market System: At present there are around 1,000 securities trading in NMS. The NASD has pending before the SEC a proposal to make the financial criteria for the inclusion of securities in the NASDAQ National List also the criteria for the voluntary inclusion of securities in NMS. If the SEC approves, this could in time create a NASDAQ National Market of more than 2,500 quality securities, issued by very substantial companies. This would be a strong centerpiece of a further-expanding NASDAQ market.

SOES, a Small Order Execution System, for orders up to 300 shares: Such a system has been thoroughly discussed by the securities industry; we need it to keep up with the even greater NASDAQ volume that we expect in the coming years. At present, we are working on the technical design of the system and on its policy and operational rules. We expect to have the SOES in operation in late 1984. It is estimated that SOES will handle about 55 percent of orders between 1 and 300 shares.

More sophisticated NASDAQ terminals: Today, NASDAQ is the only market in the world with as much remote market-maker access—a feature recently noted by a prominent member of the British Parliament.

The NASDAQ terminals in the trading rooms are going to become more sophisticated and more versatile.

Short-term: Even before firms acquire the Small Order Execution capability, NASDAQ terminals will be able to use the new Trade Acceptance and Reconciliation Service (TARS), which will be extremely helpful in clearing up trouble trades, especially during periods of high-volume activity.

Long-term: In due course, the advances now being made in microcomputer technology will be reflected in NASDAQ system capabilities.

Options: The NASD will soon launch a NASDAQ options program, which will permit investors and market professionals to buy and sell standardized put and call options on qualified NASDAQ NMS securities and the NASDAQ family of indexes. Innovative second-generation options-trading concepts are being built into the proposed NASDAQ options program. These include a small-order automatic execution system patterned after SOES, and a locked-in trade feature for trade reporting, comparison, and clearance. The NASD's proposed NASDAQ options program represents a major step in the evolution of industry facilities and, when in place, will provide an options program superior to any existing today for two primary reasons:

1. The multiple, competitive dealer market allows for the making of bigger and better markets.
2. The trading of both options and their underlying securities in the same marketplace will result in a superior quality of surveillance, since a single regulator will oversee all aspects of trading.

It is anticipated that upwards of 100 NASDAQ NMS stocks will initially be eligible NASDAQ option stocks. SEC staff have recently advised that side-by-side trading, a k_ey feature of the Options Program, does not present philosophical problems in the context of a well monitored and highly competitive market.

Greater visibility: The visibility of NASDAQ securities and the NASDAQ market will certainly increase. We expect that NASDAQ data will be received on still more securities salesmen's quotations terminals and published in still more newspapers. We are also preparing for an era that is almost upon us, an era when NASDAQ data will be disseminated to personal computers in the homes and offices of investors, and to hand-held terminals, thereby permitting investors to follow the market and to trade, no matter where they are. This technological advance raises the not-too-distant prospect of greatly increased investment and trading interest in NASDAQ securities and thus gives rise to profound implications for the future.

Improvements in registration and transfer: The increasing NASDAQ volume will also require greater efficiencies in the areas of stock transfer and registration. We anticipate that greater efforts will be made in attempting to immobilize the stock certificate further by the book entry system via the various depositories and clearing facilities. These marketplace improvements will result in improved communications between companies and their shareholders.

Automatic marginability: Given the growing prestige of the NASDAQ market, we expect substantial streamlining in the marginability of NASDAQ securities. We are engaged in extensive discussions with the Federal Reserve Board in this area, and our goal is to make those NASDAQ securities that meet certain objective financial criteria automatically eligible for purchase in margin accounts. Also, we have been heartened by the interest expressed in this project by the Vice-President's Task Force.

Blue sky: Likewise, the growing prestige of the NASDAQ market should bring about the exemption of most NASDAQ securities from state registration. As indicated earlier, we have made major progress in this area in the last five years, and have reason to expect similar progress in the next five. We recently met with the officers of the North American Securities Administrators Association, who have expressed interest in pursuing this matter further.

Internationalization: Finally, although NASDAQ is already a world-class market, we expect that the visibility and the attractiveness of NASDAQ securities to overseas investors will grow substantially, and also that more foreign securities will be traded in the NASDAQ market. In 1983 the combined trading volume of the 78 American Depositary Receipts and 216 foreign securities on NASDAQ was 1.1 billion shares; the dollar volume of this trading exceeded $11.4 billion; and internationally known securities such as Glaxo Holdings, Philips Gloeilampen, Fuji Photo Film, Minerals and Resources, De Beers Consolidated Mines, and L.M. Ericsson Telephone were the six share volume leaders among foreign issues on NASDAQ. The growing importance of foreign issues and foreign investors in the NASDAQ market has led to the election of Alex Hammond-Chambers, joint deputy chairman of the firm of Ivory & Sime of Edinburgh, to the NASD's board of governors.

The Competitive Environment of Tomorrow

The time is virtually at hand in which U.S. and foreign issuers have a choice between two different but well-recognized markets, NASDAQ and the NYSE. The competition between these two markets will be healthy for everyone—investors, public-traded companies, and market professionals, even including stock exchange specialists.

One step must be taken to make that competition freer than it is today. That step has to do with the procedures for voluntary delisting from the NYSE. If a company is dissatisfied with the NASDAQ market, as determined by its board, it can leave—and that is as it should be in a free country. If, on the other hand, a company wishes to leave the NYSE, the rules of the exchange are that the shareholders must vote on the matter. What is more, for this issue, a quorum is not 50.1 percent but 66 2/3 percent; further, 10 percent of the stockholders are sufficient to block the voluntary delisting. If the proposal surmounts all these hurdles, it must still be published in the Federal Register for comment, and approved by the SEC.

This sort of anticompetitive regulation by the NYSE will not long stand up in the competitive environment of the 1980s.

The environment of the future will be characterized by broader and quicker dissemination of information, by changing technology, and by a much larger universe of participants. These factors will continue to shatter monopolies, to give issuers and investors greater freedom of choice, and to establish increasing competition—both between markets and within markets—as the norm of the financial services industry.

In that competitive environment, the NASDAQ market expects to continue to grow and to gain market share.

Appendix 8A

The number of NASDAQ companies that are considered eligible to list on the NYSE was derived by constructing a list of NASDAQ companies that meet *either* set of criteria listed here. That is, if a company meets the first set of criteria (set A) it is *not* subjected to the second set of criteria (set B). The financial data were tested against annual data and the securities data were tested against the most recent proxy data.

Criteria for Set A

1. Market value (float × price)	≥ 16,000,000
and	
2. Earnings Before Taxes (EBT)	
a. Most recent fiscal year end	≥ 2,500,000
and	
b. Second most recent year	≥ 2,000,000
and	
c. Third most recent year	≥ 2,000,000
and	
3. Public float	≥ 1,000,000

Criteria for Set B

Note: Only for companies that do *not* meet set A	
Public float	> 1,100,000
and	
Market value (float × price)	≥ 16,000,000
and	
Earnings test:	

1. a. Earnings before taxes most recent fiscal year   ≥ 4,500,000
     and
   b. Total earnings for last three fiscal years   ≥ 6,500,000
     or
2. a. Net income most recent fiscal year   ≥ 6,500,000
     and
   b. Net income second most recent fiscal year   > 0
     and
   c. Net income third most recent fiscal year   > 0

9
Arbitrage Trading

Samuel E. Hunter

One of the most basic laws in economics is the *law of one price*. In an efficient, frictionless market, where trades are carried out by rational agents, we should not observe different prices for the same commodity. If this law did not hold, the informational content of market prices would be much reduced; and market allocation, which depends on the price system, would be inefficient.

The study of capital-markets microstructure explores market mechanisms that reduce friction in trading and create an environment where market prices give as much information as possible about the true prices of assets. As a market mechanism, arbitrage trading fulfills an important role in capital markets. It is as if the arbitrageur were nominated by the exchange authorities and assigned the duty of ensuring that, net of transaction costs, the law of one price prevails. Arbitrageurs produce a public good for the benefit of all traders by increasing the information content of market prices.

The classic arbitrageur, much like the market maker, is not interested in the trend of market prices since he is not taking a position in the market. Rather, he is making his profit on price differences at a point in time across assets. Thus, by pursuing their own self-interest, arbitrageurs cause similar assets (asset combinations) to have—net of transaction costs—the same price at the same moment in time.

The recent development of markets for derivative products, such as options and futures, has increased the scope of arbitrage activity. Here, too, arbitrageurs provide an important function of tying markets together and thereby mitigating the fragmentation that may result from the development of the new markets. In this way, arbitrage helps to consolidate markets, thereby increasing their liquidity. In another way as well, arbitrage activity provides the market with greater depth: The ability of traders to hedge their position in one asset by taking opposite positions in other but similar instruments enables them to take larger positions.

Arbitrage is a complicated and highly sophisticated business. The classic case of arbitrage occurs when an investor, attempting to profit from price discrepancies, buys a security in one market where it is underpriced, and simultaneously sells the same security in another where it is overpriced. Usually these trades involve narrow spreads; therefore, profits depend on large volumes of activity.

The arbitrage business has developed well beyond the so-called classic case: Because of the large number of arbitrage participants and improved communications systems, markets have become too efficient for a substantial number of classic arbitrage trades to exist. Even more subtle cases of arbitrage eventually attract a large number of participants and, consequently, become relatively unprofitable. For example, several years ago, many brokerage firms were buying call options and selling short the underlying stock. They borrowed stock from their margin clients and used the receipts from the short sale in their business, thus reducing their overall interest costs. For example, suppose Merrill Lynch is selling at $24; a firm shorts the stock and purchases for $5 a $20 call option expiring in September. If Merrill Lynch falls below $19, the firm has an open-end short, or a synthetic put option, and increases its profit as the stock price drops.[1] As the number of firms involved in these transactions increased, the potential for arbitrage profit dissipated and simple trading judgment based on valuations became of increasing importance (that is, a firm had to make a trading judgment to leg—put one side of the trade on naked—in order to make any significant profit).

The opposite position to the synthetic put is the so-called covered-write side, which consists of buying the stock and writing a call option. This position can be protected fully be purchasing a put option. Given tax considerations, this can be a particularly effective transaction since 85 percent of the stock dividends received will be tax free if a put is not purchased. However, current variance tax acts under review in Congress may dampen these strategies.

Out of the once relatively simple options business has developed a proliferation of derivative products, both in futures markets and in the underlying options market. The most successful recent contract has been the OEX 100, an index of 100 stocks that replicates the market somewhat in higher capitalization stocks.

There still exist market inefficiencies that enable investors to set up intelligent spreads. Many creative arbitrageurs who initially spread in the trade option market are now creating proxy portfolios similar in volatility to the Standard & Poors (S&P) index. When the S&P future is low, they buy the future and short the proxy portfolio; when the S&P future is high, they buy the portfolio and short the future. This strategy requires substantial updated data and software and involves some execution risk: Forty to fifty stocks must each be sold short, quickly, and on an up-tick.

A less complicated but widely used spread involves the purchase of a convertible bond selling close to parity and the short sale of its underlying stock. For example, a $1,000 bond convertible into 40 shares of common stock currently selling for $30 would be worth a minimum of $1,200. Under the normal premium relationship existing in the market, the bond would probably sell for approximately $1,250, or between a 4 and a 5 percent premium. If an investor were to purchase 10 bonds and sell 400 shares of its underlying stock short at $30, and the stock subsequently drops to $22, the convertible bond will pick up significant premium as it moves closer to par. As the stock price continues to drop, the convertible bond price acts more like debt; and the spread widens favorably as the short sale becomes more profitable.[2]

An arbitrage strategy somewhat closer to the traditional strategy consists of trading when-issued stock and regular-way stock. The when-issued stock will generally sell at a modest premium over the regular-way stock, since many investors do not have to pay for the stock until it becomes a regular-way delivery contract.[3]

A corporation owning a security for sixteen days around the ex-dividend date qualifies for the 85 percent exemption.[4] A ninety-day holding period for the intercorporate dividend exemption is required when the paying corporation is clearing arrears. Although this strategy requires remaining at risk for ninety days to achieve the tax benefits, often those arrears are substantial, as with those paid by Chrysler last year. This strategy may lose its attractiveness if the 1984 tax bill is passed.

Risk arbitrage, currently receiving substantial publicity, is not for the faint-hearted. Participants in this business spend large sums of money for as much information as can be obtained legally. Major participants generally employ tax counsel, antitrust counsel, general counsel, and so forth. Once a deal has been announced, an investor can sell in the open market, passing the risk and modest profit to an arbitrageur, or assume the risk for himself by continuing to hold the stock. For example, when Mobil announced its purchase of Superior Oil of California, investors knew the terms of the front end for 51 percent;[5] however, they had to wait sixty days to discover the terms on the back end. Thus, not knowing the proration and eventual terms for the 49 percent interest put them at a significant risk. Investors must determine the arbitrage community's involvement and predict institutional activity. If the deal involves previously unissued paper, investors are at risk. There are ways to hedge this risk in part, although the paper cannot be sold until the SEC clears the registration statements and the deal is effective.

The time horizon is very important to arbitrageurs. They forecast the number of days before a deal is closed and carefully compute the potential risk versus their annualized return. Many investors will hedge against paper by purchasing various derivative products or shorting financial futures. These are not perfect hedges, but they do provide some protection.

Among the interesting developments in the international arena is the very sophisticated and fluid risk arbitrage market in London. Many brokerage companies have established close affiliations with British firms, employed counsel, and extended their participation in this market. There is a significant ordinary-share and American ADR market. (Ordinary shares are the underlying shares trading on the country's exchange; the ADR is the American Depository Receipt that has been created over the years.) In Britain, sometimes the ADR has higher trading volume than does the market for its underlying shares. Once a stock has been taken out of the ordinary market, the 1 percent British stamp does not apply, and the ADR can trade over and over without stamp duties, making them 1 percent less expensive than the underlying shares.

There is a significant market in Eurodollar convertibles. The European system of offering Eurodollar convertibles in Japanese, U.S., and other securities is considerably different from ours. They have low coupon rates and sell at very small premiums over the common stock because most of the underlying stocks pay virtually no dividends. Traditional U.S. offering terms involve higher coupon rates and higher conversion premiums than in the European system.

The arbitrage business has been closely examined by the SEC and other regulatory authorities. Even under close scrutiny, this business seems to lend liquidity to the market, enabling it to operate more efficiently. Many firms in the block business would not bid nearly as aggressively as they do if not for their ability to trade options, futures, and the like. At least, with some type of hedge, investors are not exposed completely in the event of dramatic news overnight.

The number of arbitrage business participants with sophisticated advisors has increased significantly in the past five years. During the same period, the number of amateurs entering the field has increased dramatically, and this has caused spreads to tighten considerably; that is, these amateurs are too aggressive in their open-market accumulation in the early stages of an announced deal.

At present, the antitrust climate is extremely probusiness. Very few major deals have aborted, although there have been a few minor antitrust skirmishes and some anxious moments, as when the bill putting a six-month hold on the Gulf Oil deal was introduced in Congress. Virtually no company, no matter how large, is immune from being taken over.

Retail participation in the arbitrage business has increased considerably. Oppenheimer and Bear Stearns both publish research and make recommendations in the arbitrage business to their clients. At the same time, they actively trade in the business. Although I believe that represents a difficult conflict of interest, I am sure Oppenheimer and Bear Stearns have excellent counsel and are able to handle this conflict properly. They have found a very interesting niche because many small institutions and wealthy individuals do want to participate in the arbitrage market.

The fixed-income arbitrage business is still in its infancy. I think Salomon has been most successful in this business, employing highly sophisticated strategies for hedging both its customers' portfolios and its own. Many fixed-income arbitrageurs are constantly setting up yield curve and interproduct spreads. In some cases, given enough time and volatility, they are able to profit on both sides of their straddles. Sophisticated participants are paying particular attention to this business because it enables them to profit considerably while facing limited exposure.

There are a wide variety of arbitrage participants, including most major brokerage firms such as Goldman, Morgan, Salomon, Bear Stearns, Drexel, L.F. Rothschild, and Merrill Lynch. Many of these are also investment banking firms, so they are restricted from participating in certain deals. There are also a number of very large specialty NYSE participants, such as Boesky & Company. Some activators, such as Icahn, in some cases create situations out of which deals arise, and corporations such as Loews and American Financial are also active participants. Private money pools, hedge funds, aggressive domestic institutional investors, and selective foreign institutions have all been attracted to the arbitrage business. A number of individual investors have also been attracted, many of them supported by companies such as Bear Stearns and Oppenheimer.

On the surface, the arbitrage business appears simple, but it is not. It requires hard work from some of the most dedicated people on Wall Street. The returns can be substantially higher than market returns, but so can the risks. Although the arbitrage business will continue to receive very little publicity, it will be a significant factor in increasing the breadth of the market and making it a more effective pricing mechanism.

Notes

1. The arbitrageur, having created a synthetic put option, can compare it to an actual put option for the same stock, with the same conditions, trading in the market. If there is a price disparity, he can go after the option with the better price, or he can fully hedge his position. See Copeland and Weston (1983, pp. 238–239) on put-call parity.

2. A purchase of a convertible bond resembles the purchase of a regular bond plus a call option on the corporation's equity. Buying the convertible bond and shorting the stock thus resembles the creation of a synthetic put option. See Ingersoll (1977).

3. Between the split announcement and the actual ex-split date, the stock is traded side by side with a when-issued security that reflects the expected ex-split price. However, there are usually arbitrage differences. See Choi and Strong (1983).

4. The drop in the ex-dividend stock price is usually smaller than the amount of the dividend distributed, the difference being greater for investors at a higher tax bracket. Because of the tax exemption on 85 percent of the dividend, the institution investing in a dividend-paying stock is expected to realize a gain at the ex-dividend date. See Copeland and Weston (1983, pp. 506–508).

5. In a front-end merger the bidder offers a higher price for a majority of the target's shares, and the remaining shares usually receive a lower price. Arbitrageurs then have an opportunity to buy the target's shares and enjoy the premium; however, they take the risk of having their tendered shares prorated (see, for example, Jensen and Ruback 1983).

References

Choi, Dosoung, and Strong, Robert A. 1983. The pricing of when-issued common *Journal of Finance* 38(September):1293–1298.

Copeland, Thomas E., and Weston, J. Fred. 1983. *Financial theory and corporate policy.* Reading, Mass.: Addison-Wesley.

Ingersoll, Jonathan E., Jr. 1977. A contingent-claims valuation of convertible securities. *Journal of Financial Economics* 4(May):289–322.

Jensen, Michael C. and Ruback, Richard S. 1983. The market for corporate control. *Journal of Financial Economics* 11, 5–50.

10
Upstairs Trading

Richard S. Falk

Within the past decade, upstairs trading has moved to center stage in the securities industry. To understand fully the current status and structure of upstairs trading and where it might be headed, we need to review briefly the events of the past decade.

In the early 1970s, demand in the institutional equity market was relationship-oriented. Research and information flows lead the customer to the firm. Since 1975 the institutional equity market has been moving toward a transactional model, as firms such as Paine Webber, Merrill Lynch, Morgan Stanley, and others have rapidly built trading expertise and have backed that expertise with large sums of capital. Trading capability and capital commitment now dominate. Research beyond a critical mass no longer differentiates the competition.

Why is this happening? Three factors are key: *economics* (external and internal), *technology,* and *regulation.*

Economic conditions over the past ten years have created considerable upheaval, putting pressure on both the financial-services industry and its clients. Inflation has reduced the real return on investments for clients and has increased the cost of servicing clients. High inflation and correspondingly high interest rates have also resulted in a greater volatility of returns on financial instruments. As countries have struggled to bring inflation under control, inefficient valuations have developed in various instruments and sectors. All this has led to greater volume and more emphasis on trading, as assets move from sector to sector to take advantage of these inefficiencies.

A further economic influence has been asset growth. Institutional cash flow creates a new Alliance Capital or Morgan Bank every eight or nine months. The difficulty of managing these huge pools of money (especially in a volatile environment) places greater emphasis on liquidity (that is, trading skills and capital). This trend has been accentuated by electronic technology.

Technological advances have increased the speed of information flow and the ability to process large quantities of data rapidly. New technologies also provide broader access to that information at continually lower costs. Because financial markets respond to information, as this information is provided to more people and is moved more quickly, *two* things happen: (1) Transactional volume increases, and (2) arbitrage takes place between various financial instruments as investors search for an edge.

Regulation has also played a big role. It has joined with electronic technology to further reduce costs. In the past decade, commissions have been deregulated, as have floor brokerage charges. Computerized linkages between exchanges (ITS) and upstairs-trading experiments, such as Rule 19c.3, have further sharpened competition and brought about a reduction in transaction costs. Lower transaction costs have in turn made trading more attractive as an investment strategy, thereby influencing volume.

This combination of technology and regulatory change has also served to eliminate barriers to arbitrage among various financial instruments. Likewise, influenced by the increasing worldwide availability of financial data, barriers to capital inflows and outflows are disappearing. Again, the result has been an increased importance for trading in the investment process.

It is not surprising, therefore, that the upstairs-trading room in 1984 is very different from what it was five to seven years ago. It has become the focal point for much of the new electronic hardware, from touch screen data phones and on-line inventory monitoring, to systems allowing constant updating of interproduct arbitrage.

Trading hours have expanded to twenty-four; settlements are in guilders, yen, and sterling as well as dollars. More important, there is a constant flow of new products—options, futures, indexes, and currencies—and crosses into other sectors such as financial futures. With each of these come new trading strategies—baskets of stocks versus futures, options versus convertibles, synthetics, dividend capture, reverse conversion, currency arbitrage, and so on.

Obviously, none of this has happened without change in staffing and capital commitment. Paine Webber, for example, has grown from two listed block traders in 1977 to fourteen in 1984. These block traders, moreover, are quite different then those of seven years ago. They all trade multiple vehicles; a couple of them are mathematical geniuses; several have been bond traders; two have been arbitrageurs; most are young; and many have MBAs. There is also a technical analyst and a number of computer jockeys. Capital commitment has gone from $5 million to $500 million.

With all this has come a dramatic change in spheres of influence. I would argue that much responsibility for performance has shifted to the clients' trading desk; likewise, much of the broker's profitability (or lack thereof) rests with the upstairs desk. A potential conflict is developing between clients' growing dependence on executions to improve performance and brokers' increasing dependence on their trading departments to produce a reasonable return on capital.

The current proliferation of outside services to be paid for with commission dollars is exacerbating this situation. Just as the loss of small, bread-and-butter orders to DOT, SCOREX, and the like drove specialists' capital off the floor to seek better returns, so the loss of relatively easy business (as opposed to capital-intensive bid/offer business) will likely send brokers' capital away from customer facilitation and toward proprietary trading, or away from equities altogether. Ultimately, transaction costs, which declined in the late 1970s, will rise (disguised as higher or lower prices).

Should this scenario develop fully, perhaps the equities business will begin to mirror the fixed-income business, where trading is done not to facilitate, but to profit. The implications for market structure and investment style are obvious, and represent profound change. The next few years will tell the tale; they should be very interesting.

11
Multiple Regulators: Their Constituencies and Policies

Ernest Bloch

he United States is the only developed country that has some 14,500 banks, many more thousands of other financial intermediaries, three different *federal* banking regulators, and fifty state regulatory agencies. Because the legislative process and recent market changes appear to be creating a similar multiple regulated system for broker-dealer firms (for example, the SEC and the CFTC), it is useful to review how and why the banks arrived at the complex setup that now prevails.

Many observers have argued that the main reason for the multiple supervisory arrangements in banking can be traced back to the several bureaucracies that wish to maintain their power and their jobs. Some have also suggested, however, that the banks being regulated also like the diffusion of regulatory power. This is the position supported in this chapter. It will be suggested that because the banks feel that multiple regulators provide them with an opportunity to maximize equity value, many efforts to simplify the regulatory system have been frustrated. The same argument may hold for broker-dealer firms. Thus attention should be paid now to structuring a simple, straightforward supervisory system, for soon the chance to keep the structure simple may be lost.

More than a decade ago, George Stigler, in a pathbreaking article, argued that an industry generally will acquire the regulation that ". . . is designed and operated for its benefit."[1] Since that writing, some industries have been deregulated, often against their will or even against their protest. These industries include the trucking industry, featured in Stigler's article.

The deregulatory process has been a feature of the financial services industry since the 1950s. For example, the Security Act Amendments of 1975, which deregulated equity brokerage commissions, and the associated lifting of Regulation Q ceilings on time deposits, represent a substantial easing in regulatory policies. Nonetheless, a multiple regulatory structure pervades U.S. financial industries. That multiple structure represents an aspect of regulatory policies that is not necessarily reflected in a Stigler-type *legislated* industry cartel, but it does reflect the interaction of industry participants and their manifold regulatory partners.

This chapter begins with a brief summary of the current regulatory, deregulatory, and multiple regulated relationships in the competitive banking and broker-dealer industries. The subsequent section discusses the behavioral relationships between regulatees and multiple regulators. The chapter then concludes with reflections on the relationship between banks and other financial-services firms. In view of the fact that the banks are by far the largest financial-services industry currently expanding into allied (for example, broker-dealer) activities, multiple regulators may well become the rule in most financial industries.

Regulation of Broker-Dealer Firms

Regulation pervades virtually every U.S. financial activity, including banks and other financial intermediaries, the securities markets, and their participants. Securities markets participants (like broker-dealers), are subject to both state and federal regulation through the so-called blue-sky laws that were generally put in place before World War I.[2] The term *blue sky* derives from a famous citation that refers to "speculative schemes which have no more basis than so many feet of blue sky." There is a good deal of variation among state statutes, but they generally prohibit fraud in security sales while requiring registration of brokers and dealers (as well as investment advisers) and the registration of (nonexempt) securities. Some degree of coordination among state statutes has been achieved, but only by those states that have passed (in part at least) the Uniform Securities Acts put forth in 1956 by the National Conference of Commissions of Uniform State Laws.

By far the most important pieces of legislation regulating the issuance and trading of securities came about in the aftermath of the crash of 1929 and during the Great Depression that followed. The Securities Act of 1933 was the first major federal legislation. The act requires the securities issuer to register new issues and to disclose all relevant information to a potential buyer; it also prohibits misrepresentation and fraud in security sales. The Securities Exchange Act of 1934 extends the same principles and prohibitions to secondary markets, and requires the registration of national securities exchanges and brokers and dealers. Since 1934 both acts have been administered by the Securities and Exchange Commission (SEC). Subsequently, the SEC was also charged with administrative responsibility for half a dozen pieces of additional legislation, almost all directed toward the oversight and regulation of particular components of the security industry.

In the same context the Glass-Steagall Act (or Banking Act of 1933) should also be mentioned. This act prohibited commercial banks from underwriting new corporate issues either directly or through affiliates, thereby leaving that area of the securities business to broker-dealer and investment banking firms, which were to be regulated by the SEC. Subsequently the SEC was given other responsibilities by the following acts, each addressed to a specific industry segment or financial activity:

1. The Public Utility Holding Company Act (1935).
2. The Bankruptcy Act of 1938.
3. The Trust Indenture Act of 1939.
4. The Investment Company Act of 1940.
5. The Investment Advisors Act of 1940.

In addition, the panoply of federal and state regulations (and regulators) relied heavily on the principle of *self-regulation* by self-regulating organizations (SROs). For example, the SEC has delegated to the stock exchanges— and to the National Association of Securities Dealers (NASD), which represents the over-the-counter (OTC) markets—the power to set policy, to control trading practices, and to implement their own regulations, including sanctions against transgressors of the rules. As if all this were not enough, the U.S. Congress also has oversight responsibility for the entire state-federal-SRO process; this occasionally results in reviews of the process, particularly when securities-market problems begin to surface. The most obvious example of this was the burst of legislative-regulatory activity of the 1930s. A more recent example is found in the technical dislocations in securities trading of the late 1960s and early 1970s, which were associated with the switch from stock market trading, through multiple exchanges of pieces of paper, to interlinked transactions via electronics. One product of that dislocation and of Congress's renewed interest in regulatory issues was the Security Act Amendments of 1975, which eliminated fixed brokerage commissions, mandated development of a national market system (NMS), and led to other deregulatory moves. As the discussion of the current state of financial (de)regulation will show next, the major changes that were instituted had the policy goal of removing barriers to competition.

The Current State of Financial Regulation and Deregulation

The longest-lasting cartel-type regulation in financial markets was not price regulation (although fixed minimum brokerage commissions lasted a long time) but, rather, structural, or market-limiting. In the most recent past, it is market limits that have been deregulated. For example, until the late 1970s banking and financial intermediary transactions were limited to banks and other financial intermediaries (such as savings and loans). Likewise, equity security trading was confined, essentially, to broker-dealer firms. Most market participants firmly believed that that state of affairs would continue, since it was enshrined in legislation by the Glass-Steagall Act and has been supported by case law for half a century.

This state of industrial regulation has been put under increasing pressure, however, by the process of financial innovation and by the advance of information technology. In early 1984 the House Committee on Government Operations held hearings and issued a report entitled "Confusion in Legal Framework of the American Financial System and Service Industry" (April 24, 1984).

To set the scene, it is useful to cite one example that led to that "confusion": In a speech made a year ago at the University of Maryland Law School, Stephen J. Friedman, a former SEC commissioner, suggested how financial innovation at the firm level can lead to a regulatory process that becomes duplicative or obsolete. He argued as follows:

> As we all know, the SEC regulates mutual funds—which are equity products—and the banking agencies regulate intermediaries that accept deposits and offer transaction accounts. Consider the brokerage firm version of the central asset management account. Although there is a bank in the picture, which is regulated as a financial intermediary, that bank really holds no funds. It performs operations functions and runs a zero balance checking account. The real "deposit" is in the money market fund or, on a more transitional basis, in the free credit balance held at the brokerage firm. There is a real intermediation function being performed here and it should be identified and regulated as such. But by which agency?
>
> To carry this one step further, suppose that the broker does not use a money market fund, but chooses instead to pay interest on free credit balances. And suppose those balances can be accessed through a zero balance checking service? The current touchstone to determine whether those funds are being held as a "deposit"—and are therefore subject to bank regulation— is whether the funds are only being held as an incident to being invested.

The Merrill Lynch Cash Management Account (CMA) innovation and its like have shown that any transaction could use this type of broker-dealer intermediation. The CMA has been very successful, even with the availability in *non*bank intermediary institutions of NOW accounts which, of course represented another breach in Glass-Steagall (namely, interest-bearing transaction balances). These additional transaction services meant more competition in more markets. Indeed, if broker-dealers got into the intermediation game, the banks would go into the brokerage and related businesses, often with the support of the particular regulator in charge of that sector of the financial industry. This in turn caused the regulatory arrangements in each market to become less tidy and more competitive.

The most significant recent regulatory changes in market structure that have dismantled industrial boundaries are what I call *tactical* deregulation policies. These were approved, first, by the Comptroller of the Currency, the regulator in charge of national banks, followed by the other regulators.

Deregulation and Multiple Regulators

To suggest the pervasiveness of the "me too" approach to deregulation, we will cite just a few recent examples to indicate the sequence followed by the several regulators (these moves are given in detail, by agency, in appendix 11A).

On August 26, 1982, the Comptroller of the Currency permitted Security Pacific National Bank to provide discount brokerage services (under Section 16 of the Glass-Steagall Act).[3] The Federal Reserve Board followed suit, albeit with its usual lag, by permitting, on January 7, 1983, Bank America Corporation (the holding company of the Bank of America) to acquire Chas. Schwab, the nation's largest discount brokerage firm. Further openings of bank activities into the broker-dealer business were permitted in 1983 by the Federal Deposit Insurance Corporation (FDIC), which, in effect, declared that small banks that were nonmembers of the Federal Reserve (but insured by FDIC) were *exempt* from the Glass-Steagall Act. Even savings and loans were permitted to operate brokerage subsidiaries by the Federal Home Loan Bank Board, though under some modest constraints.

As an illustration of how multiple regulators expand their responsibilities, consider the fact that in November 1983 the SEC proposed that it also get into the *bank* regulation game by registering banks as brokers-dealers to the extent that they publicly solicit brokerage business, receive transaction compensation, and deal in or underwrite securities other than exempted municipals.

The process discussed in this section only represents its most recent manifestation. It has been the nature of multiple regulators to follow the industrial organization changes of member firms (mostly banks) that wish to innovate or to keep up with the innovation of others. As a result, the nature of the financial business is changed, and the regulators have learned to follow suit. The Comptroller was generally the lead regulator in breaking cartel-type boundaries. Time and again, beginning with the turn of the century, it was that agency that permitted an easing of industry constraints to its membership (see table 11–1). Because the other agencies have followed policy changes with variable lags, regulatory complexity or confusion has been the outcome.

The regulatory process has undergone many changes in legislation, in agency policies, and in the decisions by individual banks to change their regulatory niches. Nevertheless, the current Depression-based structure of multiple regulators has survived for more than half a century. Why should such a confused situation show such survivability? We suggest the answer is that the member institutions like it that way. They have repeatedly shown how they can manage very well with that complex and confused structure.

Concepts of Regulation and Deregulation

Multiple regulators have persisted, if only for structural reasons. Each piece of legislation that established a new regulator simply layered the agency charged with administering the new rules on top of the existing structure. To be sure, some simplifying schemes have been offered, among which the Hunt Commission was one of the more ambitious of the 1970s. Currently a task force headed by Vice-President George Bush is engaged in developing still another simplifying scheme. So far, however, none of the simplifying proposals has been enacted. Why is this so?

If we consider regulation as a tax, and differences among multiple regulators as offering the equivalent of differential tax rates, it is not difficult to see why the regulated firm has often found it advantageous to improve its opportunities by switching its regulator. If a significant number of such switches occur and/or more are threatened, the equivalent of a class-action defection from a given regulator may take place. As will be indicated, there have been instances where the threat of class-action defections to another regulator has pressed a policy change upon the more reluctant regulator. The fact that some of the firms involved, by a mere threat to switch, got a free ride from the policy change suggests that the benefits (net of cost of regulatory change) may be even greater for nonswitchers than for switchers. From the regulator's point of view, the loss of some portion of his regulated clientele is more than a numbers game. The firms switching regulators may be the most active, progressive, or the largest, since those are the firms in the industry that expect the greatest benefit to equity value.

It is helpful to distinguish among the three different types of deregulatory processes:

1. Activist regulators may generate pressures on more conservative regulators by their own tactical policy changes, and attract more regulatees. We call this *tactical* deregulation.
2. Switches may be initiated by the regulated firms, we call this *homemade* deregulation.
3. As various financial industries (for example, S&Ls) were approaching financial distress in the periods of high interest rates of the late 1970s and 1980s, Congress opened some previously closed markets to disadvantaged competitors. We call this *legislative* deregulation.

Tactical deregulation by a regulator has given rise to what Ed Kane has called a "regulatory dialectic". Possibilities are opened up for added activities and hence for greater returns (that is, a lower tax) to those being regulated. The possible transfer to an easier regulatory environment implicit in home-made deregulation likewise suggests better returns to those considering, or doing, the switching. Accordingly, both sets of regulatory freedoms are likely to be capitalized into equity values by those being regulated. Greater freedom to switch thus may be associated with expectations of greater rates of (after-tax) returns.

There would appear to be a chance for regulatory simplification if one of the beneficiaries of multiple regulator choices does not see much benefit in that multiplicity—namely, when the aforementioned equity benefits appear to be nil or small. This typically occurs in periods of financial crisis. At that point, when the very existence of many firms is at risk, incremental benefits to firm equity of regulatory choice are likely to be minimal.

With regard to legislative deregulation, many well-intentioned pieces of legislation have broken down previously set cartel-type price fixing (Regulation Q) or restrictions of entry (for example, NOW accounts, consumer loans, and the like). None of the legislation, however, deals with the regulatory policy conflicts that arise *because* now two or more regulators are simultaneously active in a field that previously was separated by a market barrier.

The conventional view is that the complex regulatory structure that exists today has persisted because it maintains a power structure and, in the most cynical view, a large set of substantial jobs. This is no doubt true, but it is doubtful that this alone could sustain the present complex regulatory structure. The interest of the regulated firms in retaining a multiplicity of regulators appears to offer a much stronger motive. In that view, a simplification of the regulatory system would not be supported by the regulated industry because its members are aware of value added to equity of past tactical deregulatory incidents, or homemade deregulation possibilities. Even the most skillful attempts to simplify regulatory structure may be frustrated by a membership that is very concerned even about a perceived loss of flexibility—that is, loss of *perceived potential equity value.*

We will describe how we arrived at the excessively complex structure we now have. When the structure was first organized, Congress did not review the costs of merely superimposing regulator on regulator. Nor did Congress assess that problem when regulatory market barriers were dropped. As a result, we lumped together a regulatory structure higgledy piggledy. Now the institutionalized regulatory duplication may not be amenable to reorganization or even renovation because of the benefits it offers to the regulated firms.

A Case Study of Early Regulatory Competition:
State Branching

The U.S. history of conflict among regulators is almost as old as the country, and the conflicts in a federal system between central and state authorities have been played out in several scenarios. For example, the landmark decision by the U.S. Supreme Court in 1819 (*McCulloch* vs. *Maryland*) upheld the constitutionality of the Second Bank of the United States as the "necessary and proper" exercise by the Congress in its constitutional power to "coin money and regulate the value thereof." Nevertheless, President Jackson vetoed the charter renewal of that bank, thereby institutionalizing state sovereignty over bank regulation. A century later, when, in the Great Depression of the 1930s, the foundations of another level of the regulatory structure were laid down, the maintenance of state sovereignty in chartering and supervision was retained even after its weakness had been clearly illustrated. The implicit federal-state duality of U.S. regulatory systems has been used to illustrate: (1) the emotive context and political fears with which notions of a single *national* regulator are regarded; and (2) the assertiveness of political power and independence by state regulators and their presumptive charges, the state-chartered banks.[4]

State control over branching is a useful touchstone for a review of bank regulation. From the point of view of the branching bank, geographical dispersion is a reasonable approach to diversifying risk. From the point of view of the bank's customers, competition by several banks or branches in a local banking market is likely to provide better services at a market-determined price.

From the viewpoint of the local banker running a bank, however, any competitive entry into *his* market is equivalent to a foreign invasion and necessarily evidence of "overbanking." Indeed, elements of the rhetoric that ended the life of the Second Bank of the United States in 1836 still color populist attitudes and the financial xenophobia of some parts of the country. The fear of dominance of an eastern (or western) seaboard financial octopus can be found among states (mostly in the Midwest) that are the last bastions of unit banking. Even through the so-called free-banking period in the nineteenth century, and after the establishment of a national banking system in 1864, the tradition of state sovereignty over branching was maintained. It was one of the Comptroller's earliest decisions that national banks should be *unit* banks. Thus was established the cartel-type constraint on bank-market structure that is slowly being dismantled today.

Through the nineteenth century most states in the center of the country prohibited branching. By the end of the nineteenth century, however, branching had become an increasingly attractive option in the coastal states, where state-chartered units could take advantage of growing urbanization. In other states, where the laws were not totally restrictive, national banks acquired equity interests in other state-chartered banks, thereby setting up chain banking systems. In some cases, state-chartered banks likewise set up chains of banks.

Another substitute for branching was the multibank holding company, or the bank-affiliate system. Because none of these substitutes was as efficient as branching directly, some national banks began to convert to state charters. The Comptroller, who was losing his clientele quickly, got the message. As a result, he recommended repeal of the national unit banking rule to prevent further losses of membership. Even during the century of the so-called free-banking period, from the end of the Second Bank of the United States until the Great Depression (1836–1932), the fact that multiple regulators could be played against each other was known to bankers. The 1913 Federal Reserve Act granted the right to branch to national banks, as long as they did their branching outside the United States. State-chartered banks fought domestic branching to protect their own equity values in many political rear-guard actions reminiscent of the debates of nearly a century earlier that raised the specter of big-city and eastern domination related to the charter renewal of the Second Bank of the United States. It was the important resolution of these debates that resulted in the complex chartering/supervisory network shown in figure 11–1.

Breaches in the regulatory wall against branching on the part of national banks occurred after World War I and in the early 1920s. However, the right to develop de novo branches by national banks came only with the McFadden Act of 1927. Like most other pieces of financial legislation, that act was a compromise between the state-oriented interests against branching, on the one hand, and those who feared that safety and stability of the banking system were at risk, on the other. The failure of hundreds of banks in the West and South in the 1920s had reduced opposition to branching locally.[5] At the national level, the defection of banks with national charters to state charters as a way of obtaining branching capability induced an interest by the Comptroller's bureaucracy in the branching issue. Similarly, because such defections also meant a loss of Federal Reserve membership in many cases, the Fed approved proposals for improved branching for nationally chartered banks. The McFadden Act, then, provided for the national banks' branching powers within their headquarters city if state-chartered banks had similar powers.[6]

Innovation as a Force in Generating Conflicts among Regulators: Homemade Deregulation

Table 11–1 summarizes a lot of historical development. What is impressive about the historical record is the regulatory response that is repeated a number of times by financial deregulation through innovation in the banking markets.

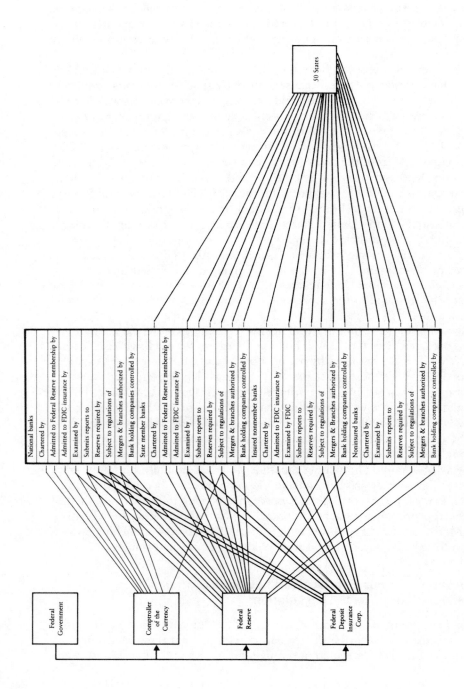

Source: Hearings on Financial Structure and Regulation before the Subcommittee on Financial Institutions of the Senate Committee on Banking, Housing and Urban Affairs, 93d Congress, 1st Session, 1973, p. 619.

Figure 11–1. The Tangled Web of Bank Regulations

Innovation by Trust Companies

In the early years of the twentieth century, Federal Reserve legislation was developed in relation to the English or real-bills theory of banking. Concurrently, the U.S. financial system was moving toward what became known as the German system through development of state-chartered trust companies. These institutions were given broad incorporation documents that permitted them to engage in virtually any type of financial business.

At first the trust companies managed estates and wills of wealthy individuals. Service to the dead, however, led naturally to financial services to the living, including the solicitation of deposits. This put them in competition with commercial banks. In addition, broad counseling and financial assistance was made available to business (users of funds) as a natural counterpart to investment advice to wealthholders. In some cases trust companies acted as mere selling agents for new-money issues of corporations. In other cases, the trust companies gave the securities their approval and even promoted them with potential investors. At times, securities were purchased with funds held in trust, or with the trust company's own funds.

By the beginning of the twentieth century, the trust companies were widely recognized as the department stores of finance. Clay Herrick, one of the early students of trust companies, suggested that such organizations appeared to "travel ahead of statute law." In his opinion, laws such as the National Banking Act (1864) were meant to apply strictly to "established businesses" and not to innovative firms. It would be "unfortunate," Herrick felt, if new demands for regulation prevented developments so "in harmony with the changing conditions of American life."[7] The absence of federal regulation of trust companies or state-chartered banks and the broad freedoms granted by state incorporation laws permitted these firms to expand simultaneously into commercial and investment banking.

In order to compete with the trust companies, state banks demanded and received from state legislatures a broadened set of powers. By the turn of the century, these banks and trust companies could offer customers a similar set of diversified services, although "the precise legal distinction was not the same in any two states."[8] It is possible that diversification by output category was used by some of these institutions as a substitute for branching: Both types of diversification imply a reduction in risk and, by extension, an improvement in equity value. The national banks failed to prevent these gains by state-chartered units. As a means of regaining competitive parity, many made plans to enter the investment banking field directly, and many subsequently did so.

Competitive Retaliation: Investment Bankers and National Banks

In the early decades of the twentieth century, the firms that had originally been involved mainly with investment banking functions began to broaden

Table 11–1
Multiple Regulators and the Evolution of Bank Regulation

Periods	Institutions	Original Regulator	Second Regulator	Policy Change
Early Days				
1864	National banks	Comptroller	States	New legislation
1927	National banks: McFadden Act	Comptroller	States	Branching
1900–1914	Trust companies and state-chartered commercial banks	States		Diversified investment banking
1900–1914	Investment bankers	None	States: Commercial bank subsidiaries	Diversification into commercial banking
1900–1914	National banks	Comptroller	States	Diversification into IB through state-chartered affiliates
1913–	Federal Reserve member banks	States comptroller	Fed	Grandfathered earlier powers
Post–World War I	National banks	Comptroller	States, Fed, etc.	Comptroller refuses to enforce restrictions against securities activities.
Depression				
1933	All member banks	All regulators	All regulators	Glass-Steagall results in *dropping* security affiliates
1933				Securities Act
1934				Securities Exchange Act affect broker-dealers now segregated from banks.
1963	National banks	Comptroller	Fed	Underwrite revenue bonds (state and local)
1966	National banks	Comptroller	Fed	Court upholds Fed's constraint *against* revenue bond underwriting.

Year	Constituency			Policy
1967	National banks	Comptroller		Fed rescinds rule against revenue bond underwriting.
1970s	National banks	Comptroller	Fed	Merger policy
Recent Past				
1980	Member banks	Fed		DIDMC Act: Deregulation of Regulation Q.
1982	Member banks, S&L's	Fed FHLBB		Garn–St. Germain Act Deregulation of loan constraints "extraordinary" mergers interstate inter-industry for failing institutions.
1982	Security Pacific National Bank	Comptroller	Fed	Established discount brokerage
	Other national banks	Comptroller	Fed	Discount brokerage direct, or through affiliates
1983	All of above	Comptroller	Fed	District court approves discount brokerage (11/2/83).
1983	All of above	Comptroller	Fed	Permits "collective investment" program for IRAs, Keoghs (reverses *ICI* vs. *Camp*).
1983	All of above	Comptroller	Fed	Approves NB affiliation with mutual fund sponsor and advisor; advisor charters nonbank banks.

their activities. The private investment bankers that had been prominently involved in the development of the railroads and in the huge industrial concentrations late in the nineteenth century entered deposit banking as follows: Because of their needs for increasingly large financial resources to underwrite the new securities, and to participate in their marketing, they used the device of developing subsidiary state-chartered banks and trust companies as tools in the market. By the beginning of World War I, there "were no effective market barriers in law or custom" to prohibit *any* financial institution from participation in *any* form of banking or investment banking activity.[9]

Toward the end of the nineteenth century, in order to achieve comparable treatment with state-chartered banks, court interpretations of the implied powers of (federally chartered) *national* banks permitted them to invest in state, municipal, and corporate bonds. The U.S. Comptroller of the Currency, which was in charge of the federally chartered banks, subsequently followed suit. As investment in all types of securities was permitted in secondary markets, it became impossible to prohibit the underwriting of such securities at new issue. When the Comptroller ruled that national banks should stop their underwriting of equities (stocks), the national banks began in 1908 to create security affiliates chartered under *state* law.[10] These affiliates were thus removed from the constraints of federal law and regulation, but were perceived as a significant factor in improving the equity value of the parent bank. This is the first example of homemade deregulation under multiple regulators.

In the aftermath of World War I, after state-chartered commercial banks and trust companies had shifted from flotation of government securities to flotation of industrial bonds and stocks, the Comptroller of the Currency (in his position as administrator of the national bank system) felt the pressures from his constituency:

> Because of competition with state banks and trust companies and the fear of driving banks out of the National Banking System, the Comptroller did not enforce the existing restrictions on the powers of national banks and suggested leniency in the national banking laws. From 1923 to 1927 the Office of the Comptroller was the driving force behind the legislation which conferred on national banks the power to engage in a modified securities business.[11]

The foregoing illustrates the power of financial innovation to demonstrate to the more constrained competitors the way to maximize returns. Clearly, those being regulated away from higher returns will escape the constraints by homemade deregulation or by putting pressure on the constraining regulator to recognize that higher returns are better than lower ones. As the example cited here indicates, the Comptroller understood the game early on. We shall soon see that the Federal Reserve acquired the knowledge a bit later.

Tactical Deregulation

Ten years ago, in a famous address to the American Bankers Association, Arthur F. Burns, then chairman of the Federal Reserve Board, criticized "the diffusion of authority and account-liability that characterizes the present regulatory system. . . ." He argued that ". . . the present regulatory system fosters what has sometimes been called 'competition in laxity'. . . . I need not explain to bankers the well-understood fact that regulatory agencies are sometimes played off against one another."[12]

Burns was reflecting on a number of policy controversies and differences in statute interpretation that had pitted the Federal Reserve against (mainly) the Comptroller of the Currency, with the FDIC representing the swing vote. The major players in that game were the member banks, which had been pressuring the supervisory agencies to loosen regulatory reins by threatening to escape from federal supervision to *state* membership. Let us review this case of homemade deregulation in more detail.

Competition among Regulators

The interaction between a regulatory agency and its membership involves a sometimes subtle, sometimes bluntly expressed calculus of gains and/or losses expected by a bank from the decision to accept a particular regulator. The tactical game must be played by the regulators as well since a switch of banks will leave them with a larger—or smaller—membership. The postwar competition between regulators began in 1963 when James Saxon, then Comptroller of the Currency, opened up for national banks the underwriting of state and local revenue bonds. The Fed, by insisting on a narrow interpretation of the Glass-Steagall Act, argued that the Comptroller's interpretation was invalid. A suit by investment bankers in 1966 to uphold the Fed's interpretation was sustained.[13] By 1967, however, the Fed reversed itself, now *supporting* the capability of member banks to underwrite revenue bonds, which was subsequently voted by Congress into one section of the Housing Act of 1968.

Why did the Fed change its mind? It was forced by the increasingly rapid switching away from Fed membership of state-chartered banks, as well as by switches to *national* charters by some large-state member banks. The politics of membership could overcome stubborn adherence to policy. Further, the same pressures developed in bank merger cases.[14] Congress purposely had sought in the Bank Merger Act of 1960 to get a more uniform evaluation of competitive elements in bank mergers. To do so, it specified that the Justice Department and supervisory agencies were to comment on seven "factors" before a given agency could approve a merger under its jurisdiction as "being in the public interest." In the actual application of that criterion, and in the methodology cited, the general rule appeared to be that the Comptroller saw a merger approval if it improved competitive characteristics among the larger group into which the newly merged bank had moved. In contrast, the Fed saw a diminution by merger of the number of smaller, local banks as anticompetitive. The FDIC became the unpredictable swing vote as it changed policy during the 1960s. Later in the decade, it moved from a policy closer to the Comptroller's, to one closer to the Fed's. This took place despite a clear Congressional intent, in passing the 1960 Bank Merger Act and the 1966 amendments, that uniform standards were to be established among the agencies.

The extent to which diversity prevailed was borne out in a 1975 study that indicated that the Comptroller viewed most adversely those merger cases under Fed jurisdiction, whereas the Fed viewed the Comptroller's cases most adversely.[15] The study concluded that "if the intent of Congress was to establish procedures to insure uniformity in the treatment of bank mergers, then clearly this goal has not been achieved under the present regulatory scheme." Worse yet, these multiple criteria have been explored and employed by the banks. The capacity to shift among regulators to suit a bank's policy preference may be summed up in the following quote from a letter written by a former governor of the Federal Reserve Board to Senator Proxmire:

> Recently a bank in a southern state switched to the jurisdiction of a particular supervisor which it thought would approve a proposed merger, and then, the merger having been approved, returned to its original supervisory authority where the merged operation could be conducted on a more economical basis for the bank.[16]

When one examines the asset size of banks converting to a national organization, it becomes clear that the conservative Fed was the significant loser as a regulator—about 1 percent of the assets of the banking system shifted away from its jurisdiction in each of the Saxon years. By itself, that does not appear to be a very large proportion of the total banking system; in its impact on regulatory attitudes, however, it represents a powerful pressure point. The subsequent slowdown in the conversion rate to nationals may have been brought on by the Fed's accommodation to policy changes desired by member banks (as in the Glass-Steagall policy switch), as well as by the pressure from another interested set of participants—namely, state banking supervisors. The latter met with the Fed following the 1968 changes to national charters from state charters of Wells Fargo Bank ($5 billion assets) and Wachovia Bank ($1.6 billion assets) that, in turn, had followed the 1965 conversion to national charter of Chase Manhattan ($13 billion assets). According to Howard Hackley, then chief counsel to the Fed, on August 14, 1968, following a meeting with state supervisors, the Fed reversed its policy orientation completely. It permitted a bank (1) to establish and invest its funds in a subsidiary corporation to carry on part of its banking business and (2) to set up a loan production office without (as previously) qualifying that office on the same basis as a bank branch. In Hackley's words, "not surprisingly, the board's action was promptly and profusely applauded by banks and state bank superintendents."[17]

Deregulation by the States: Delaware and Others

Even in the 1980s, with major advances in information technology and the sharp reduction in cost of the transmission of assets and other transactions, federal law constrains federally chartered units to the extent each state chooses to set. Although the states have, albeit reluctantly, moved branching policy beyond horse-and-buggy technology, not until the early 1980s did states such as Nebraska, Oklahoma, Pennsylvania, West Virginia, and Illinois pass legislation allowing banks to expand beyond a single location. Other states, such as Connecticut, Massachusetts, Maine, Alaska, North and South Dakota, and Delaware, have permitted out-of-state banks to acquire banks within their borders.

Of the latter, the cases of South Dakota and Delaware are the most interesting in that both states have recently *encouraged* out-of-state banks (or holding companies) to acquire a de novo bank under the Douglas Amendment of the Bank Holding Company Act of 1956. The Delaware action involved the passage in 1981 of the Financial Center Development Act (FCDA), a statute purposely designed to imitate the effect of Delaware's liberal incorporation law, which has made it the corporate enfranchisement capital of the United States. Accordingly, FCDA has invited *large* out-of-state banking companies to enter Delaware by providing three types of incentives. Two of the three are familiar: They provide for deregulation of credit terms (set between lender and borrower) and elimination of usury limits. The third, and probably the most innovative, is a state *tax* incentive with purposely *regressive* rates; the rate falls as taxable income rises, with the highest income levels paying rates of about one-third of the lowest.[18] To the extent that large banks pay state taxes, that incentive will become greater the larger and the more profitable the bank. (Here is an instance where regulation *directly* affects after-tax income.) And to the extent that banks can benefit by moving income to Delaware, that particular set of incentives will, of course, be capitalized into equity value. Table 11–2 shows the effectiveness of FCDA by detailing the moves to Delaware by some well-known financial firms from New York, Maryland, and Pennsylvania up to spring 1983. Finally, it indicates that the imaginative use of state sovereignty *today* can also generate incentives for homemade regulatory shifts between the states that raise after-tax incomes and, thereby, necessarily improve equity values.

Table 11–2
Out-of-State Bank Holding Companies Establish Delaware Subsidiaries

Parent Bank Holding Company	Delaware Subsidiary (Date Opened for Business)	Type of Business	As of March 31, 1983	
			Dollar Assets (millions)	Number of Employees
New York				
J.P. Morgan & Co., Inc.	Morgan Bank Delaware (12/21/81)	Wholesale banking	$1,853	126
Chase Manhattan Corp.	Chase Manhattan Bank (USA), N.A. (2/11/82)	Consumer lending on a national basis	409	206
Chemical New York Corp.	Chemical Bank (Delaware) (10/1/82)	Wholesale and commercial lending	857	68
Citicorp	Citibank (Delaware) (10/6/82)	Full range of cash management services to institutional customers nationally	54	35
Manufacturers Hanover Corp.	Manufacturers Hanover Bank (Delaware) (1/3/83)	Wholesale commercial banking and trust business, domestic and international	231	40
Bank of New York Co., Inc.[a]	Bank of New York (Delaware) (forthcoming)	Commercial banking and trust business, domestic and international, credit card operations	100	25
Maryland				
E.F. Hutton[b]	E.F. Hutton Trust Co. (7/9/82)	Limited-purpose trust company	27	5
Maryland National Corp.	Maryland Bank, N.A. (3/15/82)	Credit card operations	209	223
First Maryland Bancorp	First Omni Bank, N.A. (5/7/82)	Bank debit and credit card services	100	133
Equitable Bancorp.	Equitable Bank of Delaware, N.A. (6/11/82)	Bank debit and credit card services	119	98
Suburban Bancorp	Suburban Bank/Delaware (9/15/82)	Retail banking and consumer credit operations	70	74

PNC Financial Corp	Provident of Delaware Bank (3/10/82)	Investors' services wholesale and consumer lending, international business	202	87
Pennsylvania				
Philadelphia National Corp.	Philadelphia Bank (Delaware) (6/1/82)	Credit card services	166	113
Mellon National Corp.[c]	Girard Bank Delaware (12/30/81)	Full range of services	401	492

Source: J.M. Moulton, "Delaware Moves Toward Interstate Banking," *Federal Reserve Bank of Philadelphia Business Review*, July–August 1983, p. 21.

[a]They plan to begin operations with 25 employees and to expand to 125 within one year.

[b]Special legislation enabled E.F. Hutton, an investment banking firm, to set up a subsidiary that is exempt from FCDA requirements.

[c]Special legislation enabled Girard Company to acquire the troubled, state-assisted Farmers Bank.

Legislative Deregulation

The surge in interest rates to all-time highs in the late 1970s and 1980s led to crisis-type disintermediation among a number of financial industries. Accordingly, Congress passed the Deregulation and Monetary Control Act of 1980, and the Garn–St. Germain Act of 1982—two major pieces of legislative deregulation. In part, the 1980 act was passed at the request of the Federal Reserve to eliminate the further loss of member banks. The quid pro quo to member banks involved promises of further deregulation of rate constraints (Regulation Q) so as to avoid future disintermediation.

The Garn–St. Germain Act of 1982 further deregulated some liabilities of savings and loans and lifted asset constraints (following the liability deregulation of the 1980 act). Perhaps the most interesting change instituted by Garn–St. Germain is the permission to federally chartered savings and loans to make the equivalent of business loans, either on an overdraft basis or in the form of straight commercial loans. This process not only takes funds from the formerly sacrosanct area of housing finance, but also moves one industry's previously constrained asset pattern over into another industry's turf.

There are other boundary-breaking openings for these institutions. New opportunities cover consumer and educational lending, and variable-rate mortgages. In addition, state rules regarding borrower protection from due-on-sale provision in mortgage contracts are preempted, thereby improving future rates of return on assets. Further, the act provides for easier switching of charters (if state laws permit) from state to federal (or the reverse); between stock and mutual; and between a savings bank and a savings and loan. In short, homemade deregulation has now been institutionalized.

Finally, some emergency powers were added to the FDIC and FSLIC, including purchase and acquisition powers; capacity to make loans and deposits in troubled units; as well as capacity to approve so-called extraordinary mergers, discussed later. Indeed, the new act provides for interstate banking arrangements on a de jure basis that followed approvals in 1982 (prior to the act's passage) by the Federal Reserve Board and Federal Home Loan Bank Board of *interindustry* and *interstate* mergers. The most notable of these was Citicorp's acquisition of Fidelity Federal Savings and Loan Association of Oakland, California. The new law permits authorization by the FDIC of the acquisition of any large, closed commercial bank, or a closed (or endangered) mutual savings bank (more than $500 million in assets) by another federally insured unit, whether in state or out of state. Failing thrift institutions may be taken over by another unit (in or out of state) if FSLIC permits. Finally, any qualified purchaser may make bids, "including out-of-state banks, holding companies, other insured institutions or *any* acceptable company."[19]

Once again, we see that opening up regulatory barriers or breaking prior rules can be done when the equity value being deregulated is near zero. Under those conditions, even the breakthrough to an *inter*state system can be rationalized: In crisis there is power.

Conclusions

We have argued that the process of financial deregulation has had the effect that previously separate financial services industries are now competing in the same market(s). Necessarily, if each of the previously separate markets had its own regulator, we now have multiple regulators in the same market(s) to the extent that intermarket competition has been stimulated.

We have argued further that in the presence of multiple regulators, the regulated firm will do what comes naturally; namely, it will switch, or threaten to switch, to maximize its own equity value. From the point of view of that firm, the decision to engage in homemade deregulation requires only the continuing availability of choice. For the more thoughtful managers of these firms, that choice will provide a potential for future increments in equity value. One might argue that the unpredictability of that benefit may give it relatively little value. We have shown that, when equity values are depressed, any legislative body with regulatory oversight was able to trade off a rescue operation for a change in future regulatory freedoms. By the same token, when equity values are secure, those being regulated will have small interest in eliminating even unpredictable potential benefits to positive net worth. The clinching argument must be one of cost: To the regulated firm, having the availability of a second (or third) regulator beyond the current one carries absolutely no current expense whatsoever.

This brings us to an interesting conclusion: For the innovative and competitive financial services firms that are well managed, the regulatory constraints imposed on all to protect against bad firms, bad trades and/or loans, and financial crisis are basically unnecessary. For well-managed firms, the best world would be an unregulated one. The second best world, however, is one of multiple regulators to give the good firms a mechanism by which to minimize the loss to equity value from regulation. In that world, we perceive a heretofore undiscussed aspect of Stigler's theory of regulation: In his 1971 article, he argued that the government will provide the supply, and industry the demand, for regulation to benefit the industry involved. The multiple regulatory process we have discussed suggests we have moved to a further stage of regulatory development. We now have a market for regulation in which those being regulated select the regulator that maximizes regulatory utility: Multiple regulators represent a secondary market in regulation, whereas the legislative bodies represent the primary market.

The choice is made by regulated firms through the process of what we have called homemade deregulation. The transaction medium in that market is the regulator's membership roster, and the value given in exchange is a more satisfactory policy for the membership. Because of these externalities, an induced policy change gives all other industry members a free ride with respect to these changes. This suggests that if administrators or legislators expect support for regulatory simplification from the regulated industries, they may continue to be disappointed. Who, then, is in favor? Certainly not the regulators about to lose power. But perhaps the foregoing may help explain why so many well-reasoned proposals of the past have remained just that.

Notes

1. G.J. Stigler, "The Theory of Economic Regulation," *Bell Journal*, Spring 1971, pp. 3–21.

2. *Hall* vs. *Geiger-Jones Co.*, 242 U.S.539 (1917).

3. Subsequently, other banks were given the same authority, and these moves were approved by a Federal District Court, District of Columbia, November 2, 1983.

4. For a recent discussion of the historical background of state versus federal regulation issues and on problems of instability implicit in local banking monopolies, see T.F. Huertas, "The Regulation of Financial Institutions: A Historical Perspective on Current Issues," in G. Benston, ed., *Financial Services, The American Assembly* (Englewood Cliffs, N.J.: Prentice-Hall, 1983), pp. 6–27.

5. It is often forgotten that a very large number of bank suspensions took place in the 1920s: Between 1921 and 1929 more than 5,700 banks suspended operations. This number was exceeded only during the Great Depression: Between 1930 and 1933 there were about 9,100 bank suspensions.

6. To most present-day observers the McFadden Act represents *not* a positive improvement in bank market structure, but a negative constraint on expansion *across* state lines.

7. Citations from Herrick, *Trust Companies: Their Organization, Growth and Management* (New York, 1909), p. 53, in Perkins, op. cit., p. 488.

8. Ibid.

9. Perkins, p. 490.

10. In this device the pioneer was the First National Bank of New York, which, prior to 1908, had been involved directly in investment banking. In that year, following government criticisms of the bank's buying and selling of common stock, it created one of the first security affiliates for a national bank, called the First Security Company. That firm was incorporated under New York State law and thus was free to engage in investment banking or any other business. W.N. Peach, *The Security Affiliates of National Banks* (Baltimore: 1941), p. 61.

11. Peach, *Security Affiliates*, p. 150, cited in Treasury study, Appendix, p. 7.

12. Address to American Bankers Association, October 21, 1974.

13. *Baker, Watts & Co.* vs. *Saxon*, 261 F Supp. 247 (DDC 1966).

14. The following is based on E. Bloch, "Regulation and Deregulation in Financial Institutions," in Jules Backman, ed., *Regulation and Deregulation* (Bobbs-Merrill, 1981), pp. 149–174.

15. Robert Eisenbeis, "Differences in Federal Regulatory Agencies' Bank Merger Policies," *Journal of Money, Credit and Banking*, February 1975, p. 104. At the time of writing, Dr. Eisenbeis was chief of the economic research unit of the FDIC.

16. Letter to Senator William Proxmire, December 23, 1974. Reprinted from U.S. Congress, Senate Committee on Banking, Housing, and Urban Affairs, *Compendium of Major Issues in Bank Regulation*, 94th Cong., 1st Sess., Committee Print No. 2, August 1975, pp. 903–909.

17. See Howard H. Hackley, "Our Discriminatory Banking Structure," *Virginia Law Review*, December 1969, p. 1444. The preceding owes much to Mr. Hackley's article.

18. The tax rate is 8.7 percent for the first $20 million of net income; 6.7 percent for income from $20 to $25 million; 4.7 percent for income from $25 to $30 million; and 2.7 percent on income above that amount. All Delaware home state banks currently have incomes of less than $20 million, and will not benefit. For the large *out-of-state* banks, a shift of income will raise *both* the large banks' after-tax incomes, and Delaware's total tax take. For a more general discussion of interstate competition for corporate charters, see P. Dodd and R. Leftwich, "The Market for Corporate Charters: Unhealthy Competition versus Federal Regulation," *Journal of Business* vol. 53, no. 3, pt. 1 (1980), pp. 299–283.

19. This is quoted from "The Main Features of the Act," *Economic Perspectives* (Federal Reserve Bank of Chicago), March–April 1983, p. 9. Much of the preceding discussion was based on that useful issue. More recently still, the Fed further deregulated interstate banking possibilities. Indeed, the rate of change has accelerated even in this area to the point where, at the end of March 1984, the Federal Reserve Board ruled that the U.S. Trust Corporation of New York *could* make consumer loans and *could* accept consumer deposits in Florida. Since that time, several other banks (Mellon National, First Interstate) have proposed development of interstate consumer banking branches.

Appendix 11A

The following outline provides details of the present situation regarding the opening up of broker-dealer activities for various financial industries.

Comptroller of the Currency

1. a. On August 26, 1982, the Comptroller permitted Security Pacific National Bank to establish discount brokerage (under Section 16, Glass-Steagall).
   b. Subsequently, approvals were given for discount brokerage to other banks directly, or operating through subsidiaries.
   c. These moves were approved by District Court, District of Columbia, November 2, 1983.
2. a. Operation by national banks of collective investment programs for IRAs and Keogh plans in effect reversed the *ICI* vs. *Camp* decision (1971) because the current program was *not* considered to be an open-end mutual fund.
3. Approved national bank affiliation with mutual fund sponsor and advisor (J & W Seligman and Dreyfus Corp.): The investment advisor charters a nonbank bank.
4. National bank affiliates itself with investment advisor and discount broker—September 6, 1983 (American National Bank of Austin, Texas). Whereas bank's *original* application was for discount brokerage subsidiary, bank was then authorized to provide brokerage services *and* investment advice through two *related* subs.

Federal Reserve

As in earlier periods (see below) the *Federal Reserve System*, the second Federal regulator, followed suit with a lag in its regulation of bank holding companies.

1. Acquisition of Discount broker by Bank Holding Co.:
   a. On January 7, 1983, Bank America Corp. received Fed approval to acquire Chas. Schwab. The reason given was that Bank America was acting as agent under Section 20 of Glass-Steagall. According to the 1983 view by the Fed, this does *not* constitute a "public sale of securities" prohibited to bank affiliates under Glass-Steagall. The decision was upheld by Second Circuit court of appeals (SIA vs. Board of Governors, July 15, 1983).
   b. Feb. 22, 1983: the Federal Reserve Board (FRB) proposed an amendment to Regulation Y adding discount brokerage agency *provided* this is done without securities advice (The Comptroller's approval of Austin National Bank scheme *includes* advice).
   c. Bank Holding Company (BHC) affiliation with Futures Commission merchant: On July 1, 1982 the Federal Reserve Board approved an acquisition by J.P. Morgan & Co.; subsequently Bankers Trust Co. got similar ruling. These futures contracts would be limited to contracts for bullion, foreign exchange, U.S. Governments and some other money market instruments.
   d. BHC *underwriting* of Government Securities and some Money Market Instruments: On March 2, 1982, the FRB approved an application by Citicorp (BHCo) to set up a subsidiary to underwrite deals in some government securities and money market instruments; the government securities are limited to U.S. and general obligations of states and political subdivisions. The money market securities are limited to Bankers Acceptances (B.A.s) and CDs. The rule was made because Glass-Steagall Section 16 *permits* government underwriting by banks, and that BAs and CDs are *not* considered "securities." Finally in May 1983 the FRB proposed a *general revision* of Regulation Y. That revision would permit banks to engage in "securities activities" as "closely related" to banking. This would include discount brokerage, underwriting and dealing in governments and money market instruments, and acting (with some restrictions) as a futures commission merchant.

FDIC

The third major Federal regulator is the Federal Deposit Insurance Corporation (FDIC). Perhaps the most direct break with Glass-Steagall—although limited to small banks—came with the application to the SEC by Boston Five Cents Savings Bank (an insured *non*member bank) to engage in what I call "homemade" deregulation, as follows:

1. form a mutual fund;
2. establish two subsidiary corporations:

a. to underwrite and distribute shares in the fund and
b. to provide advice to the fund.

The SEC requested advice from the FDIC as to the legality under Glass-Steagall of a *non*member to engage in such operations. On August 23, 1982 the FDIC stated that restrictions in Glass-Steagall (Sec. 20) against a bank affiliating with a securities firm and (in Sec. 32) against interlocking directorates between bank and securities firms do *not* apply to *non*member banks. In a policy statement issued Aug. 23, 1983, FDIC concluded that insured *non*member banks may legally affiliate with securities firms; the securities activities that subsidiaries could conduct would, however, be limited to those *not* restricted by Glass-Steagall and "best efforts" underwriting of top rated debt issues, or money market type mutual fund shares. In addition, some other operating constraints were retained on activity of subsidiaries as well as on the bank and/or its trust department.

FHLBB

There are actions by Federal Home Loan Bank Board (FHLBB) for S & L brokerage subsidiaries and S & L service corporations or, its converse, the application by broker-dealers to acquire S & L's as well as the SEC's issue of no-action letters regarding S & L's conducting broker-dealer activities. No-action SEC letters indicated that S & L's would *not* have to register as broker-dealers so long as brokerage service on the S & L's premises registers as a broker-dealer and conducts its activities in a segregated area of the institution, and makes clear that services are offered by B-D, and *not* the S & L.

SEC

But—and this is a large but—on Nov. 8, 1983, the SEC issued a proposed amendment that would give SEC regulatory power over banks, even though the banks are *not* being considered as brokers or dealers. Under the November 8, 1983 amendment banks would be subject to SEC's B-D registration requirement to the extent that banks:

1. publicly solicit brokerage business
2. receive transaction compensation for brokerage for trust, agency or other accounts (advice)
3. deal in, or underwrite, securities other than exempted municipals.

Banks which use subsidiaries that *are* registered by the SEC would not have to register. The SEC's legal authority was based on several sections of the 1934 Securities Exchange Act including the definitional section of the preface of the Act. In addition, the SEC called attention to changes in the nature of the bank's security activities.

12

The Securities and Commodities Markets: A Case Study in Product Convergence and Regulatory Disparity

Douglas Scarff

D uring the 1970s the marketplace witnessed accelerating product convergence between derivative instruments traded on securities exchanges and those traded on commodities exchanges. The exchange trading of standardized options on individual corporate stocks began in 1973 at the Chicago Board Options Exchange, Incorporated (CBOE). Starting about the same time, the commodities exchanges began to introduce futures contracts on a variety of financial instruments, including foreign currencies and government debt securities. By the early 1980s, both futures and options were traded on foreign currencies, government debt instruments, and stock indexes. The increasing overlap between these markets created concern and confusion over which federal agency—the Securities and Exchange Commission (SEC), the Commodity Futures Trading Commission (CFTC), or both— did or should have regulatory jurisdiction over these new products. The confusion was generated by broad statutory grants of jurisdiction allowing conflicting claims of jurisdiction by the SEC and the CFTC. The concern was largely due to the acknowledged disparity in regulatory regimes governing futures markets and securities markets.

In late 1981 the agencies acted decisively to address the jurisdictional uncertainty by reaching an unprecedented interagency accord, which was subsequently codified in amendments to both the securities and commodities laws. By restraining product convergence, the agencies acted out of a belief that it was contrary to the public interest to frustrate the development of many new financial products pending congressional resolution of the fundamental regulatory disparities issues. On the other hand, as the securities and commodities

The author acknowledges substantial assistance in the preparation of this paper by Alden S. Adkins, staff attorney in the Division of Market Regulation.

The Securities and Exchange Commission, as a matter of policy, disclaims responsibility for any private publication by any of its employees. The views expressed herein are those of the author and do not necessarily reflect the views of the Commission or of the author's colleagues on the staff of the Commission.

exchanges were freed to introduce some functionally similar products, the very notable success in removing jurisdictional uncertainty has itself served to highlight the lack of progress in addressing differences in the regulatory schemes governing the two industries.

This chapter chronicles the history of the jurisdictional dispute between the CFTC and the SEC and its resolution through enactment of the Shad-Johnson Accord and the recently published guidelines regarding nondiversified stock index futures. Because the existence of substantial regulatory disparities is widely conceded, the specific nature of those disparities is not discussed here. I have, however, attached an appendix detailing those disparities. Nor is it the purpose of this chapter to argue whether futures and options on financial instruments are indeed similar in economic purpose or function; that point too is not disputed.[1] Rather, the purpose of this chapter is to explain what the accord has accomplished and to examine what it leaves to be resolved in light of the similarity between certain futures and options products and the disparity in their regulation.

The Accord

The Legislation

In 1974 the definition of *commodity* in the Commodity Exchange Act (CEA) was amended to include any "services, rights and interests which contracts for future delivery are or in the future may be dealt in."[2] The purpose of this amendment was to bring within the scope of the CEA futures contracts in a growing number of commodities, such as coffee and foreign currency, that were being traded on commodities exchanges but were not subject to regulation under the CEA.[3] In addition, this amendment was intended to assure CFTC jurisdiction over new futures contracts, such as ones on government-guaranteed mortgage-backed securities, that were contemplated at the time but not yet traded.[4] This all-inclusive definition appeared to allow the CFTC to approve the trading of futures on almost anything, possibly including traditional securities.[5]

In addition, the CFTC Act provided that the CFTC would have "exclusive jurisdiction with respect to accounts, agreements (including . . . options) and transactions involving contracts of sale of a commodity for future delivery; traded . . . on an exchange."[6] This amendment was intended to give the CFTC control over not only futures contracts but also "commodities options," meaning—depending on whom you asked—options either on futures contracts or on the new broadly defined class of actual commodities. At the same time, a savings provision was enacted, providing that "except as herein-above provided, nothing in this section shall supersede or limit the jurisdiction at any time conferred on the Securities and Exchange Commission."[7] Read together, these amendments could be interpreted as giving the CFTC exclusive jurisdiction over futures on securities and, arguably, even over options on corporate securities.

This broad statutory language soon led to an open dispute between the SEC and the CFTC regarding its intended meaning. In 1975 CFTC approval of a Chicago Board of Trade (CBT) application for designation as a contract market in the trading of futures contracts on Government National Mortgage Association (GNMA) certificates precipitated an exchange of letters between the SEC and the CFTC. The SEC asserted that futures on GNMAs were securities, within the SEC's jurisdiction; the CFTC responded that these instruments were within the exclusive jurisdiction of the CFTC.[8]

This dispute was next aired in Congress during the CFTC's reauthorization hearings in 1978. Chairman Williams of the SEC argued that the SEC's interest in the securities underlying futures contracts, and its more extensive experience in the trading of options, warranted SEC regulation of futures and options on securities instruments.[9] Others testified in support of amending the grant of exclusive jurisdiction to the CFTC to limit it to futures on traditional commodities, with the SEC being given jurisdiction over futures and options on securities.[10]

The commodities industry, on the other hand, argued that the key regulatory distinction was the derivative instrument, not the underlying property, so that the CFTC should continue to have jurisdiction over all futures products.[11] The result of this debate was that the statutory language conferring the CFTC's grant of exclusive jurisdiction was left unchanged.

The jurisdictional dispute again arose in early 1981, when the SEC approved a proposal by the CBOE to trade options on GNMA certificates.[12] The CBT challenged the SEC's approval,[13] and the Seventh Circuit stayed the CBOE from trading GNMA options until it rendered its decision. At this point, the chairmen of the SEC and CFTC—Chairmen Shad and Johnson—entered into a jurisdictional agreement, often referred to as the Shad-Johnson Accord (the Accord).[14] Under the Accord, the SEC was to regulate options on securities, certificates of deposit, foreign currency (traded on a national securities exchange), exempted securities such as GNMA certificates, and stock groups or indexes. The CFTC was to regulate over futures (and options on futures) on exempted securities (except municipal securities), certificates of deposit and on broad-based groups or indexes of securities,[15] as well as options on foreign currency not traded on a national securities exchange.[16] It was agreed that futures (or options on futures) on individual nonexempt securities and municipal securities would not be allowed. The Seventh Circuit, however, concluded that the CEA granted to the CFTC exclusive jurisdiction over GNMA options and that the Accord was not effective to change this legislatively mandated jurisdictional grant.[17]

Subsequently, Congress enacted the Accord into law in substantially the form of the agreement by the two agencies.[18] The principal addition to the Accord was a provision requiring SEC concurrence in stock index futures contracts submitted to the CFTC after December 9, 1982. For stock index future contracts submitted before December 9, 1982, the legislation provided the SEC with a special consultative role.

By its codification of the Accord, the Congress has made express the CFTC's exclusive jurisdiction over futures and options on futures on Treasury securities, stock indexes and other financial instruments. At the same time, Congress has clarified SEC jurisdiction over options on these financial instruments and prohibited futures (or options on futures) on individual nonexempt securities and municipal securities.[19]

The Joint Agency Guidelines: Stock Index Futures

Under the Accord as codified, if an application for designation as a contract market for a stock index future was submitted before December 9, 1982, the SEC may review and comment on the application and is given the right to obtain judicial review of the CFTC's decision on the application. If the application is submitted after December 9, 1982, the SEC has a so-called veto authority.[20] The statute sets forth three basic criteria a stock index future must meet regardless of when an application for contract designation was submitted to the CFTC:

1. The futures contract must be cash-settled.
2. It must not be readily susceptible to manipulation.
3. The underlying index must reflect the market for all or a substantial segment of publicly traded equity or debt securities.[21]

In November 1983, in applying these criteria to a Chicago Mercantile Exchange (CME) application for designation as a market for futures contracts on an Energy Index, the SEC took the position that an index composed of securities exclusively in a single industry could not satisfy the third Accord criterion.[22] The SEC based this determination largely on the belief that the third criterion (the "substantial segment" standard) was intended to prevent futures contracts from disrupting the securities markets or serving as surrogates for security products. In the SEC's view, futures on a single-industry index could lead to trading on inside information or could otherwise disrupt the securities markets. The SEC viewed the possibility of surrogate trading as inappropriate in light of the continuing differences in the regulatory schemes applied to trading in securities and futures.[23] The CFTC, though not denying the surrogate trading purpose of the substantial segment criterion, disputed what types of indexes could serve as useful surrogates.[24]

After further consultation and deliberation,[25] the two agencies were able to agree on an interpretation of this statutory provision. On January 18, 1984,[26] the two agencies published the following interpretive guidelines for futures on nondiversified stock indexes:[27] the index should (1) include 25 or more stocks; (2) have a total capitalization of at least $75 billion dollars and be maintained at over $50 billion; and (3) have no one stock that constitutes more than 25 percent of the weighted value of the index, and no three stocks that together constitute more than 45 percent of the index value.[28] The agencies agreed to reexamine these guidelines one year from their publication.

Subsequent to the publication of the guidelines, the CBT filed a lawsuit alleging that the guidelines were illegally promulgated rules that exceeded the agencies' authority. The CBT's suit was dismissed recently on the grounds of failure to exhaust administrative remedies and ripeness.[29] The CBT's motion for reconsideration of the district court's decision is pending.

Discussion

One way to view the Accord is as a pragmatic acceptance of those currently traded or contemplated futures and options products whose concurrent trading under differing regulatory regimes presented an acceptably low level of danger of disrupting those respective regulatory regimes.[30] The Accord did ensure that futures products that could act as surrogates to either trading in a stock or its related option would not be permitted. The Accord left unaddressed, however, the issue of regulatory disparities for new futures and options products—presumably because Congress, the SEC, and the CFTC felt that allowing the development of these select new products to proceed did not pose serious regulatory risks and, at any rate, was preferable to the delay that would be necessitated by attempting to resolve the regulatory disparities prior to approval of these products.

The Accord legislation authorized trading under the respective jurisdiction of the SEC and CFTC of products that already were trading under their oversight. Thus futures and options on exempt securities and certificates of deposit were permitted because futures on these products existed at the time;[31] because it would have been unfair and would have served little regulatory purpose to prohibit options on these products; and because the simultaneous trading of these futures and options products did not appear to threaten any undue damage to the SEC's regulatory scheme (the underlying products not being subject to SEC regulation).[32] Similarly, futures and options on broad-based stock indexes were permitted because futures on these products existed at the time;[33] because it would have been unfair and unnecessary to prohibit options on the products; and because the "substantial segment requirement" assured that the simultaneous trading of these futures and options products did not threaten any undue damage to the scheme of SEC securities regulation.[34]

Conversely, futures on individual nonexempt securities and narrow-based stock indexes were not traded at the time and, more important, threatened to disrupt seriously the regulation of the securities markets. Futures on nonexempt securities may act as substitutes for the securities themselves. Thus trading of futures on nonexempt securities, absent harmonization of the regulation of the futures and the underlying securities, could threaten to disrupt and provide clear opportunities to avoid the carefully constructed regulatory scheme for securities. This same concern underlies Congress's limitation of stock index futures to ones that relate to indexes that represent a "substantial segment of the market." This requirement seeks to assure that a stock index future will not represent a useful substitute for any of the individual securities that make up the index—a result that would be unacceptable for the same reason as would the trading of a future on an individual nonexempt security.

Although the jurisdictional accommodation has permitted the introduction of new products and has cleared up the confusion that affected this area before the Accord, it has, by its very design, left us with the issue of regulatory disparities. If anything, that question has been exacerbated because similar products now are actually trading (for example, futures and options on Treasury bills and stock indexes) subject to different regulatory treatment. As Appendix 12A indicates, these disparities are substantial.

Some hope may be offered by the ongoing study of the Futures and Options Markets.[35] Other than that study—which is examining a number of fundamental issues beyond questions of regulatory disparities—there is no ongoing effort to resolve these regulatory disparities.[36] I believe this is a subject that cannot be deferred indefinitely. On the basis of interviews the SEC staff has conducted with a number of broker-dealers in connection with the Study of the Futures and Options Markets, it is clear that increasing numbers of securities firms have expanded, have opened, or currently plan to open commodities departments. Securities firms are qualifying substantial numbers of their account executives to handle customers' futures transactions. With the extraordinary success of stock index futures and options, the rationalization of existing regulatory differences is becoming crucial to the securities and commodities industries as well as to public investors. Although the solutions lie not in simply drawing lines such as those embodied in the Accord, the agencies can build on their recent record of cooperation to begin this task.

Conclusion

For now, we live under the terms of an uneasy detente, one that, by settling jurisdictional squabbling, allows the converging commodities and securities industries to proceed with some innovative and potentially useful new products. At the same time, we are left with similar products trading under vastly different regulatory regimes, for which a day of regulation reckoning is inevitable.

Notes

1. For an interesting discussion of the similarities and dissimilarities between options and futures, see the submissions of the SEC and CFTC made in response to questions posed by Representative Timothy Wirth during hearings on the Accord. The SEC's response is contained in a letter dated May 12, 1982, from then SEC General Counsel Edward Greene; and the CFTC response is contained in a letter dated May 20, 1982, from Philip McBride Johnson, then chairman of the CFTC.

2. Section 2 of the Commodity Futures Trading Commission Act (CFTC Act), P.L. No. 93-463, 88 Stat. 1389 (1974) (codified at 7 U.S.C. §2 [Supp. V. 1981]).

3. See S. Rep. No. 1131, 93d Cong., 2d Sess., 19 (1974); and H.R. Rep. No. 975, 93d Cong., 2d Sess., 41–42 (1974).

4. Id.

5. The potential expansiveness of this definition is manifested in recent proposals that have surfaced for futures on, among other things, freight insurance rates, the consumer price index, the prime rate, and indexes of commodity prices.

6. Section 2 of the Commodity Futures Trading Commission Act (CFTC Act), P.L. No. 93-463, 88 Stat. 1389 (1974) (codified at 7 U.S.C. §2 [Supp. V. 1981]).

7. Id.

8. Securities Exchange Commission–Commodity Futures Trading Commission Jurisdictional Correspondence [1975–1977 Transfer Binder], CCH ¶ 20, 117, consisting of a letter to the CFTC from SEC Chairman Roderick W. Hills (November 13, 1975) and a memorandum in response prepared by the CFTC Office of General Counsel (December 3, 1975).

9. Extend Commodity Exchange Act: Hearings on H.R. 10285 Before the House Subcommittee of Conservation and Credit of the House Committee on Agriculture, 95th Cong., 2d Sess. 189-91 (1978) (1978 House Hearings) (statement of Harold M. Williams).

10. Reauthorization of the Commodity Futures Trading Commission: Hearings Before the Subcommittee on Agricultural Research and General Legislation of the Senate Committee on Agriculture, Nutrition and Forestry, 95th Cong., 2d Sess. 467 (1978) (1978 Senate Hearings) (statement of Joseph Sullivan, president, CBOE), and 1978 House Hearings, supra note 9, at 32–34 (GAO).

11. 1978 Senate Hearings, at 171–172, (testimony of Robert H. Wilmouth, president of the CBOT).

12. Securities Exchange Act Release No. 17577 (February 26, 1981).

13. The CBT's argument proceeded as follows: Under the CEA a *commodity* is defined as anything on which futures are traded. The CEA grants the CFTC "exclusive jurisdiction" over accounts, agreements (including options), and transactions involving contracts of sale of a commodity for future delivery. Since GNMAs were the subject of futures trading, they are commodities; and options on that commodity come

within the CFTC's exclusive jurisdiction. The CBT also argued that neither the definition of *security* contained in Section 3(a)(10) nor the explicit authority over options trading contained in Section 9 of the Exchange Act provided the SEC with jurisdiction over options on exempt securities. Brief of Petitioner Board of Trade of City of Chicago, *Board of Trade* v. *SEC*, July 13, 1981.

14. Joint Explanatory Statement of the Securities and Exchange Commission and the Commodity Futures Trading Commission reprinted in [1980–1982, Transfer Binder] Comm. Fut. Rep. (CCH) ¶ 21,332 (February 2, 1982).

15. The Accord's definition of *broad-based* indexes is described later.

16. At the time the Accord was announced, the CFTC had approved futures contracts on government securities (CME, T-bills, CFTC Release No. 92-75, November 26, 1975; CBT, T-bonds, CFTC Release No. 323-77, August 2, 1977; COMEX, T-bills, CFTC Advisory, June 20, 1979; and NYFE, T-bonds and bills, CFTC Release No. 611-80, July 15, 1980); and certificates of deposit (NYFE, CFTC Release No. 773-81, July 1, 1981). Futures contracts on foreign currency had been traded even prior to the 1974 amendments to the CEA. *See* S. Rep. No. 1131, 93d Cong., 2d Sess., at 19 (1974) and H.R. Rep. No. 975, 93d Cong., 2d Sess., at 41–42 (1974).

17. *CBT* v. *SEC*, 677 F2d 1137 (7th Cir.), *vacated as moot* 103 S. Ct. 434 (1982).

18. The amendments to the securities laws were adopted in the Securities Acts Amendments of 1982, (P.L. No. 97-303, 96 Stat. 1409 (1982); and the amendments to the commodities laws were adopted in the Futures Trading Act of 1982, P.L. No. 97-444, 96 Stat. 2294 (1983).

19. After the enactment of the Accord, the Supreme Court vacated the Seventh Circuit's decision as moot: *CBT* v. *SEC,* 103 S. Ct. 434 (1982).

20. Under this so-called veto authority, the SEC must review and approve an application for designation as a contract market in a stock index future before trading in the futures contract may occur. The CFTC, of course, must also review and approve such applications; thus the SEC's authority to disapprove a designation has been termed by some a *veto authority.*

21. Section 2(a)(1)(B)(ii) of the CEA as amended by the Futures Trading Act of 1982, 7 U.S.C. 2a(i). The precise language of this provision is as follows:

> (I) Settlement of or delivery on such contract (or option on such contract) shall be effected in cash or by means other than the transfer or receipt of any security, except an exempted security under section 3 of the Securities Act of 1933 or section 3(a)(12) of the Securities Exchange Act of 1934 as in effect on the date of enactment of the Futures Trading Act of 1982 (other than any municipal security, as defined in section 3(a)(29) of the Securities Exchange Act of 1934 on the date of enactment of the Futures Trading Act of 1982) ["cash settlement standard"];
> (II) Trading in such contract (or option on such contract) shall not be readily susceptible to manipulation of the price of such contract (or option on such contract), nor to causing or being used in the manipulation of the price of any underlying security, option on such security or option on a group or index including such securities ["antimanipulation standard"]; and
> (III) Such group or index of securities shall be predominately composed of the securities of unaffiliated issuers and shall be a widely published measure of, and shall reflect, the market for all publicly traded equity or debt securities or a substantial segment thereof, or shall be comparable to such measure ["substantial segment standard"].

22. See letter dated November 29, 1983, from George A. Fitzsimmons, secretary, SEC, to David Horner, acting director, Division of Economics and Education, CFTC.

23. Id.

24. See Memorandum to the CFTC regarding CME's proposed contract on the S&P Energy Index from Kenneth M. Raisler, general counsel, CFTC, December 23, 1983; and Memorandum to the CFTC regarding CME's proposed contract on the S&P Energy Index from the Division of Economics and Education, CFTC, January 6, 1984.

25. Because the CME contracts in question were submitted to the CFTC prior to December 9, 1982, the SEC's only recourse in the event the CFTC approved these contracts over the SEC's objections would have been a judicial challenge. See Section 2(c)(1)(B)(iv)(I) of the CEA, 7 U.S.C. 2(a)(1)(B)(iv)(I).

26. Interpretation and Statement of General Policy of the CFTC and SEC, Securities Exchange Act Release No. 20578 (January 18, 1984), 49 Fed. Reg. 2884 (January 24, 1984). The CME Energy Index contract, which the CFTC had approved prior to the publication of the guidelines, satisfied the interpretative criteria contained in those guidelines.

27. In the policy statement, *nondiversified* indexes are described as those composed of equity securities of United States issues in the same or a similar industry. The SEC thus has revised its single industry interpretation of the Accord's third criterion.

28. The guidelines also indicate that a stock's weighted share of a noncapitalization weighted index should not exceed three times its share of the total capitalization of the index.

29. Decision of Judge Kocoras, N.D. Ill., No. 84 C 1141, March 30, 1984.

30. The CFTC has suggested that the Accord as codified has three principal objectives:

> (1) to eliminate the jurisidictional issues between the agencies and provide a level of certainty to the futures and securities industries; (2) to avoid upsetting the status quo in the marketplace; and (3) to maintain the traditional rules of the [SEC and the CFTC] by ensuring that the CFTC would continue to regulate instruments and markets that serve as hedging and price discovery mechanisms while the SEC would regulate instruments and markets that have an underlying investment purpose.

Memorandum of CFTC in opposition to Motion for Preliminary Injunction and Summary Judgment and In Support of Motion to Dismiss or, in the Alternative, for Summary Judgment, *CBT* v. *CFTC and SEC,* No. 84, C 1141 N.D. Ill., March 2, 1984).

31. As indicated in note 16, futures on government securities and certificates of deposit had been approved by the CFTC prior to announcement of the Accord.

32. Exempt securities are, of course, subject to the antifraud provisions found in both the 1933 and the 1934 acts; except for municipal securities, they are not, however, subject to the other regulatory restrictions and requirements of those acts. Certificates of deposit have been held to be not securities in some circumstances, and thus are not in those circumstances subject even to the antifraud prohibitions. See *Marine Bank* v. *Weaver,* 455 U.S. 551 (1982).

33. Between the date of announcement of the Accord and its enactment by Congress, the CFTC approved futures on several stock indexes. (The Kansas City Board

of Trade's Value Line Average Contract, approved on February 16, 1982, was the first such contract approved by the CFTC.

34. See, e.g., S. Rep. No. 390, 97th Cong., 2d Sess., at 6 (1982). Accord criteria are designed to "assur[e] that future trading is limited to broad-based securities groups on indices that are not conducive to manipulation or disruption of the market for the underlying securities."

35. This study was mandated by Section 236 of the Futures Trading Act of 1982, P.L. No. 97-444, 96 Stat. 2294 (1983); 7 U.S.C. §26 (1983).

36. On a somewhat related matter, the agencies have issued joint releases seeking input from the public on ways in which they might coordinate and simplify the regulation of entities subject to both SEC and CFTC jurisdiction. Securities Exchange Act Release No. 19706 (April 28, 1983). Although this undertaking has attempted to address matters (such as the registration of firms and their associated persons) in which the agencies regulate the same subjects in somewhat different or uncoordinated ways, it did not attempt to address matters where the agencies imposed markedly different substantive regulations (such as in the customer protection and sales practice areas).

Appendix 12A
Regulation of Options and Futures

The following chart summarizes several of the principal rules and regulations governing securities options and futures (and options on futures).

Options	*Futures*

I. Customer Protection Rules

    A. *Threshold costs (Margin)*

        1. *Authority*

Options	*Futures*
The Federal Reserve Board and SEC have pervasive authority to establish and enforce margin standards for securities options.	Under the Commodity Exchange Act, the CFTC is not permitted to review the futures margin requirements of the boards of trade. The CFTC does have authority, however, to establish "temporary emergency margin levels" for any futures contract. The Federal Reserve Board generally does not have authority to establish margin requirements for futures. However, it has asserted that it possesses such authority with respect to futures on securities indexes (although it has not yet sought to exercise that authority). Although the CFTC has asserted that it has authority to review and approve exchange rules relating to commodity option margin, it has not yet required the exchanges to submit to it for approval commodity options margin rules. The CFTC does review, however, exchange rules relating to the payment of commodity option premiums.

Options	Futures

2. Initial Margin

Purchasers must pay 100% of premium (i.e., options have no loan value in a customer's margin account, although market maker's clearing firms may give credit for the market maker's position). Uncovered writers (analogous to both futures sellers and purchasers) must post the following margin:

Stock options—30% of market value of underlying securities.

Debt security options—Since the margin is premium-based, precise percentage levels cannot be stated. However, as a general matter, this will put margin for debt securities roughly in the range from 5% for Treasury bond and GNMA options to 0.5% for 13-week Treasury bill options.

GNMA options—130% of options premium plus $1,500 minus the amount the contract is out-of-the-money.

Treasury bond options—100% of premium plus $3,500.

Treasury note options—100% of premium plus $2,000–$3,000.

Treasury bill options—100% of premium plus $3,500–$7,500.

Broad-based index options—100% of premium plus 10% of contract value minus amount the contract is out-of-the-money; minimum of 2% of contract value.

Narrow-based index options—30% of contract value, plus or minus in- or out-of-the-money amounts; minimum of $250 contract.

Purchasers and sellers are subject to the same margin. Futures margin deposits generally range from 2% to 10% of the contract, with margin for hedgers somewhat less than margin for speculators. The following are margin requirements for the principal financial futures contracts:

GNMA and Treasury bill, note, and bond futures—$2,000 (speculators), $1,500 (hedgers). (Thus speculative margin would range from 2% for Treasury bond and GNMA futures to 0.2% for Treasury bill futures.)

Stock index futures—initially established with speculative margin of approximately 10%, hedger margins of approximately 5%; the margin has generally not been adjusted upward, however, as the value of the underlying indexes rises and margins currently range from 3.2% to 4.0% of hedgers and 6.5% to 8.0% for speculators.

Foreign currency futures—between $900 and $2,000 (for speculators), depending on the particular currency underlying the futures contract.

With respect to options on futures, purchasers may pay 100% of premium. Persons with short positions must post premiums plus margin for underlying short futures position.

Options	*Futures*

Foreign currency options—130% of premium plus $750 minus the amount the contract is out-of-the-money.

3. *Maintenance margin*

Open options positions are marked-to-the-market daily. Federal Reserve Board Regulation T provides that additional margin must be deposited with the customer's broker within seven business days.

Open futures positions are marked-to-the-market daily. Persons with open positions that have moved away from the market are required to post additional margin the following business day.

B. *Suitability*

The rules of the options exchanges, NYSE and NASD (options SROs) prohibit member firms from recommending to any customer *any* options transaction unless they have reasonable grounds to believe that the entire recommended transaction is not unsuitable for the customer on the basis of information furnished after reasonable inquiry concerning the customer's investment objectives, financial situation and needs.

There are no provisions in the CFTC or board of trade rules governing the suitability of recommended futures transactions. Although there also are no securities-type suitability rules governing commodity options, as noted in part D, FCMs must provide oral disclosures concerning commodity options at the time they open a customer's account that are tailored to the personal circumstances of the customer.

They also prohibit broker-dealers from recommending *opening* transactions unless they have a reasonable basis for believing that the customer has such knowledge and financial experience that he can be expected to be capable of evaluating, and financially can bear, the risks of the transaction.

C. *Account opening*

The rules of the options SROs require that in order to engage in options trading, a customer's account must be specifically approved for options trading. Before opening the customer's account, a broker-dealer must exercise due diligence to learn the essential facts as to the customer, his investment objectives, and

The CFTC and commodity exchanges do not impose restrictions on the opening of futures accounts, although, as Chairman Johnson has noted in previous testimony, some firms may impose voluntary requirements as to net worth and other matters.

Options	*Futures*

his financial situation. In particular, the broker-dealer must seek to obtain and verify from natural person customers 15 specific categories of information, such as investment objectives, income, net worth, and investment experience. Account approval must be in writing and and can only be made by a qualified branch office manager or other supervisor. Exchange rules also require separate account approval before a customer may trade debt security and foreign currency options (whether or not the customer's account already is approved for stock options trading).

As noted earlier and discussed in part D, an FCM, before opening a commodity options account, must make certain disclosures to a customer and make an investigation of the customer's financial condition, objectives and sophistication. The record of the information obtained must be reviewed and approved by an officer or other supervisor of the FCM before the account may be opened.

D. *Disclosure*

The federal securities laws and the options SRO rules require that options investors receive at or before the time their accounts are approved for trading a basic options disclosure document which describes in detail the terms, mechanics, risks, and uses of options. In addition, detailed disclosures about new options products (such as options on debt securities, foreign currencies and stock indexes) is required to be provided in separate supplemental disclosure documents.

Disclosure about futures is provided to customers in a risk disclosure statement that discusses generically the risks and characteristics of futures. The futures risk disclosure statement does not provide customers information concerning particular futures contracts, such as financial futures. The text of the risk disclosure statement is set forth in the CFTC's rules.

For commodity options, CFTC rules require that FCMs provide to customers a commodity options risk disclosure statement. Like the futures statement, this statement discusses commodity options generically and the text of the statement is set forth in the CFTC's rules. The commodity options disclosure statement includes a description of commodity options and discussions of the mechanics of options trading, margin requirements, the profit potential of an options position, and the risks of options trading.

In addition to dissemination of the risk disclosure statement, the CFTC's

Options	*Futures*

| | commodity options rules prohibit an FCM from opening a commodity options account for a customer unless the FCM has provided the customer "with a degree of disclosure and explanation concerning the risks inherent in options trading appropriate to the personal circumstances of the customer." The FCM is required to use due diligence to inquire, consider, and make a record of the customer's financial conditions, investment objectives, and market sophistication. |

E. *Advertisements and sales literature*

| The rules of the options SROs establish detailed standards concerning the content and manner or presentation of options advertisements and sales literature. All advertisements and sales literature (except completed worksheets) must be approved in advance by a firm's Compliance Registered Options Principal. Broker-dealers also are required to submit advertisements to options SROs for approval or review prior to use. | The CFTC relies on its general anti-fraud rules to regulate futures advertisements by FCMs. CFTC regulations for commodity pool operators and commodity trading advisers specifically prohibit them from advertising in a manner that is false, misleading, or deceptive; and the CFTC has issued a release providing guidance as to the types of advertisements prohibited by this rule. Some boards of trade specifically regulate advertisements, although none require prior approval or review of advertisements by a firm officer or supervisor, nor do they regulate sales literature. |

| | The CFTC's commodity options rules contain more rigorous provisions governing commodity options "promotional materials," including a provision that boards of trade require that all promotional materials be submitted by member FCMs to the boards of trade and promptly reviewed by them. The commodity options rules also prohibit fraudulent or "high-pressure" sales communications by FCMs. |

F. *Testing*

| The options SROs require that all registered representatives pass a general | The CFTC does not require associated persons of FCMs to pass qualifying |

Options	*Futures*

securities examination that includes options questions. Options supervisors must pass a general principal examination plus a separate options principal examination. Persons selling, or supervising the sale of, options on debt securities or foreign currency must pass a separate interest rate options or foreign currency options examination.

examinations relating either to futures or options on futures in order to market those instruments to the public. Several boards of trade do require associated persons of member firms to pass a general futures examination administered by the Futures Industry Association. In addition, the National Futures Association is expected to institute an examination for associated persons of FCMs and other members. Additional examination requirements are not imposed on supervisory personnel, or on persons marketing financial futures.

G. *Supervision*

The options SROs require (i) that member firms develop and implement a written program for the supervision of their options business; (ii) that those options programs be under the overall supervision of a designated senior registered options principal; and (iii) that compliance responsibilities be under the supervision of a designated compliance registered options principal; and (iv) that all branch offices (except those with fewer than three options representatives) be supervised by a principal-qualified branch office manager.

CFTC rules impose a general requirement that FCMs must diligently supervise the handling of all firm futures activities. Although this provision does not impose any specific supervisory requirements, the CFTC's rules require that FCMs trading commodity options must adopt and enforce written supervisory procedures enabling them to supervise adequately each public customer's options account.

Exchange rules on debt and foreign currency options essentially require the adoption of a parallel supervisory structure, with the responsibility for supervising trading in those options resting with persons specifically qualified with respect to those options.

H. *Performance fees*

The rules of several securities SROs prohibit member firms and their associated persons from receiving "performance

Neither the rules of the CFTC nor those of the boards of trade prohibit the charging of performance fees on com-

Options	*Futures*

fees," i.e., sharing in customer profits or losses, except to the extent they contribute capital to the account. Section 205(1) of the Investment Advisers Act also prohibits investment advisers from receiving performance-based compensation, although the Commission has recently published a rule proposal that would substantially liberalize the current exemptions from the Section 205(1) prohibition.

modity options. For commodity pool operators and commodity trading advisers, the CFTC has adopted rules requiring the disclosure of their fee structures, including possible conflicts of interest.

I. *Protection against broker insolvency*

In the securities market, the Securities Investor Protection Act (SIPA) provides protection of broker-dealers that are forced to liquidate. Currently, the limits of protection are $500,000 per customer, of which $100,000 may be claims for cash. Options customers are entitled to SIPA protection.

Customers trading futures and options on futures are not entitled to SIPA or any similar protection even if the FCM is also a registered broker-dealer. Before enactment of the legislation creating the CFTC in 1974, Congress considered commodity account "insurance," but instead directed the CFTC to study the matter. In 1976 the CFTC concluded the need for insurance was low because (1) public confidence in the safety of customer funds was high, and (2) insurance would not be cost-effective. Private insurance for commodity customers accounts is available but not commonly used.

J. *Investor remedies*

Several provisions of the federal securities laws grant investors express causes of action against securities professionals and others. In addition, rights of action also have been implied by the courts under other provisions, particularly Section 10(b) of the Securities Exchange Act and Rule 10b.5 thereunder, although implied causes of action have been held not to exist under other provisions of the federal securities laws. Investors may also pursue remedies under

Purchasers and sellers of futures contracts have explicit, statutory rights of action under several sections of the Commodity Exchange Act, including the antifraud provisions. In addition, some courts have held that futures customers may have remedies under the antifraud provisions of the federal securities laws. Investors may pursue remedies under general state antifraud laws, but not blue-sky laws or other laws relating specifically to futures. In addition, the CFTC

Options	*Futures*

state general antifraud statutes as well as state blue-sky laws. In addition, the securities SROs have established uniform arbitration procedures for the handling of investor grievances against broker-dealers. There is no reparation procedure under the federal securities laws similar to that established under the Commodity Exchange Act.

has a unique reparations procedure, in which aggrieved futures customers may file claims for damages against FCMs based on violations of the Commodity Exchange Act.

K. *Civil penalties*

The Commission may enjoin, suspend, or impose similar sanctions on broker-dealers and their associated persons and securities exchanges. The Commission lacks the power, however, to impose fines against such persons. The securities exchanges possess the power to fine member firms and their associated persons, as well as to pursue injunctive actions, for violations of the federal securities laws and exchange rules.

In addition to injunctive power, the CFTC has the power to levy fines of up to $100,000 against any person, including FCMs, their associated persons, and boards of trade. The boards of trade may fine or enjoin member firms and their associated persons.

L. *Minimum financial requirements*

Since 1979, with the exception of certain minor differences, the Commission and the CFTC have imposed substantially identical net capital requirements on dually registered broker-dealer/FCMs.

Net capital requirements, with some minor exceptions (related primarily to FCMs that are not registered as broker-dealers) are uniform for FCMs and broker-dealers.

M. *Safekeeping of customer funds*

Commission rules require that funds deposited by customers must be segregated from a broker-dealer's own funds. Margin deposits made by one customer, however, may be loaned out by a broker-dealer to other customers.

The Commodity Exchange Act requires FCMs to "separately account for" (or segregate) the funds deposited by each customer. Those funds cannot be commingled with the funds of the FCM, and may not be used for any purpose other than to cover the trading obligations of the particular customer for whom they were deposited.

Options	*Futures*

II. Trading Rules

A. *Dual trading*

The options exchanges prohibit floor traders (with the exception of the specialist on the two options exchanges employing a specialist system) from acting as both broker and dealer in the same options class on the same day. The purpose of this rule is to avoid self-preferment or other conflicts of interest on the part of floor traders.

The CFTC and commodities exchanges do not prohibit floor traders from trading for both their own account and the accounts of customers, although CFTC rules prohibit a member firm from trading for its own account while holding a customer order executable at the current market price.

B. *Time stamping*

The options exchanges require that all order tickets state the time of execution of the order (to the nearest minute). Transactions also must be reported immediately to floor reporters for entry into the exchanges' transaction reporting system.

The CFTC has proposed, but never adopted, to-the-minute reporting requirements for futures transactions. Instead, it requires that futures transactions be reported within 30-minute segments. Only the New York Futures Exchange requires timely reporting of individual trades. CFTC rules require that customer orders be time-stamped to the nearest minute upon receipt on the floor by a floor broker and again to the nearest minute when they are reported back as executed.

Similar 30-minute bracket rules have been instituted for commodity options transactions. For customer orders, in addition to recording the time an order is received and reported back as executed, FCMs must record the time to the nearest minute an order is transmitted for execution.

C. *Transaction reporting*

The options exchanges disseminate on a timely basis (through the Options Price Reporting Authority) reports of the price and size of all options trades,

The commodity exchanges report only changes in prices, not each transaction, on a timely basis, and are not required to disseminate size or cumulative

Options	*Futures*
both in options on equity securities and in new options products.	volume information. Similar rules will apply to commodity options trading. The New York Futures Exchange voluntarily captures timely price and size information on each transaction effected on the exchange.

D. *Audit trail*

The options exchanges have been required by the Commission, and have in place, audit trails designed to permit the exchange to ascertain complete information about each options transaction effected on the exchange, including the time, price, and size of the transaction and the floor broker and clearing firms on each side of the trade.	Since reporting of each transaction is not required by the CFTC or boards of trade (with the one exception noted earlier), the boards of trade lack the data necessary to construct a complete audit trail. Since to-the-minute information is received concerning the time customer orders are sent to and returned from the trading floor, it may be possible under limited circumstances to determine the relative time customer and firm orders were executed.

III. Insider Trading

Insider trading of stock based on material nonpublic information is illegal. In addition, at least one court has held that a private right of action exists under both Rule 10b.5 and Rule 14e.3 for options writers when the purchasers of the options bought on the basis of material, nonpublic information about a tender offer. *O'Connor & Associates* v. *Dean Witter Reynolds Inc.,* 529 F. Supp. 1179 (S.D.N.Y. 1981). But see *Moss* v. *Morgan Stanley,* 719 F2d. 5 (2d Cir. 1983). One court, however, has dismissed a suit by an option purchaser against the issuer of the underlying security where the issuer traded its own security but not options. *Laventhall* v. *General Dynamics Corp.*; 704 F2d 407 (8th Cir. 1983). The same rationale was applied in dismissing an action by options traders against a corporation for nondisclosure	The commodities laws do not prohibit insider trading. As required by Section 236(b) of the 1982 Futures Trading Act Amendments, the CFTC is currently studying futures trading by persons possessing material nonpublic information regarding present or anticipated cash or futures transaction of others. The CFTC is required to report the results of its insider trading study by September 30, 1984.

Options	*Futures*

of material information. *In re McDonnell Douglas Corp.*, CCH ¶ 99,437 (E.D. Mo. 1983).

IV. Tax Treatment

Under current tax law, a holder or writer of any option (put or call and regardless of the underlying security) must recognize short-term (no options currently exist with terms in excess of nine months) capital (assuming the option is held as a capital asset) gain or loss when the option position expires or is closed out by entry into an offsetting transaction. Writers of calls and holders of puts also must recognize gain or loss if the option is exercised, with the premium received added to the purchase price of the underlying security sold (writer of call) or subtracted from that purchase price (holder of a put). Under pending legislative proposals, all market maker gains and losses on options on individual securities would receive capital gain or loss treatment, 60% long-term and 40% short-term. In addition, all unrealized gains and losses would have to be recognized. Individual investors would continue to receive short-term capital gain or loss treatment, but would be subject to loss deferral for positions offset by the underlying or another option. The treatment of options on stock and indexes differs between the two major pending proposals, with broad-based index options receiving 60/40 treatment under one version but not under another.

Profits and losses on futures contracts are traded at 60% long-term and 40% short-term rates. All unrealized gains or losses are marked-to-market and must be recognized as of year end.

The tax treatment of commodity options is unclear. Legislation has been introduced that would tax commodity options in the same manner as futures contracts are taxed.

13
Regulation and the Futures Markets

Susan M. Phillips

The various chapters of this book not only represent a variety of issues related to the changing structure of the financial markets, but also raise a number of questions regarding the appropriate regulatory environment of these markets. There is clearly a divergence of viewpoints on how regulatory authorities might best adapt to a rapidly changing market structure for the trading of securities and other financial instruments. My comments will be addressed to the regulatory issues involved.

Because the securities industry itself is expanding into new areas of endeavor, the regulatory issues addressed here might best not be confined to securities regulation only. The authors of several chapters have appropriately expanded the inquiries; I will focus my discussion around the themes presented in papers by Stigler (1971), Peltzman (1976), Bloch (chapter 11), Scarff (chapter 12), and Schreiber and Schwartz (chapter 2). I hope readers will forgive my use of futures markets for purposes of illustration.

Schreiber and Schwartz in chapter 2 present a good illustration of the adaptation of the economic concepts of one market to another. Price discovery in the trading of securities is a concept that is not widely discussed in the academic literature. It is, however, integral to futures trading, depending in large part on the active participation in the competitive auction process of various cash market users—from producers to processors to distributors to consumers. The bids and offers of all these participants allow the futures pit to discover prices that better reflect underlying supply and demand conditions.

Perhaps the notions of price discovery, price efficiency, or even manipulation are more easily identified with futures trading because the futures price does relate in some consistent way to the cash price. Thus if the futures price is out of line with the cash price, it may be artificial or manipulated. The same is true with options. But how can one recognize an inefficient stock price? Securities regulators' concentration on competition and the cost of trading rather than on the quality of prices is understandable.

The views contained in this chapter are those of the author and do not reflect those of the Commodity Futures Trading Commission.

If, on the other hand, securities regulators do concentrate more on price efficiency or price discovery, the issues of insider trading, monopoly specialist systems, volatility, and off-board trading must be addressed differently than they are in current practice. These not only are very troubling issues, but also represent long-standing traditions of securities regulation that may be at odds with efficient price discovery.

The comparison of the economic functions of different markets inevitably leads to the comparison of their respective regulators. Yet such a comparison need not conclude that regulatory disparity is something that needs to be fixed. To the contrary, Bloch (1985) in chapter 11 concludes that multiple regulators may have constructive outcomes. The author's recognition of certain benefits to regulation by competing entities centers around the pressures to change the regulatory approach that result from the presence of another regulator (which may have different regulatory requirements because of different statutory requirements). This competition may be healthy and force some regulatory flexibility, but the traditional argument concerning multiple regulators is the concept of "competition in laxity." This concept is often accepted without analysis as a truism among regulators. It is refreshing to see the argument made that checks and balances have a place not only in government in general, but also in regulation in particular.

This competitive pressure can operate through what Bloch calls "homemade deregulation." Of course, such pressure can also lead to regulatory changes or shifts that strengthen regulation. There is no doubt that actions in one regulatory sphere put pressure on other regulators. When the Securities and Exchange Commission (SEC) permitted the development of exchange-traded options, it was only a matter of time before the fifty-year ban on agricultural options was lifted. Deregulatory initiatives can occur for a variety of reasons—to accommodate growth in healthy industries, to reflect changing market conditions, or to alleviate financial pressures in the industry. For example, when the equity values of the regulated entity are zero, the regulator likely will be motivated to change regulations, particularly if regulatory restrictions are part of the problem. Regulatory initiatives, on the other hand, generally seem to be made to protect either industry participants or consumers.

A useful theoretical framework for explaining regulation has been developed by Stigler (1971) and more generally formalized by Peltzman (1976). The Stigler-Peltzman theory views regulation as a transfer of wealth to a politically dominant interest group; that is, some are taxed and others gain or even are subsidized. The theory specifies characteristics of a dominant group but does not require that the dominant group necessarily be the regulated industry.

Depending on the number and types of interest groups, there may, in fact, develop coalitions among various groups; ultimately, regulatory structure may reflect the interests of a variety of groups. In this vein, an analysis of the broker-dealer industry and its choice of regulatory forum would not necessarily totally describe the development of the financial regulatory system. There are surely other groups that have influenced financial regulation; investors or speculators and commercial hedgers come to mind immediately (particularly with the tradition of securities laws to protect investors, and the commodities law to protect the integrity of the markets as risk-shifting mechanisms). In addition, exchanges—to the extent they have developed as entrepreneurs creating new products (as opposed to service-type member organizations only)—also would be expected to influence regulation.

The increased competition among various types of financial services by different financial institutions has resulted in less reliance on industry to determine regulatory forum. Recognizing the phenomenon, the Vice-President's Task Group on Regulation of Financial Services, composed of the heads of all financial regulatory agencies and chaired by Vice-President Bush and Treasury Secretary Donald Regan, quickly abandoned the concept of industry regulation, opting instead for functional regulation. Even within the framework of their recommendations, however, the concept of regulator choice remains. The staff of the Task Group estimate that any meaningful legislation in this area would take five years to complete, which indicates projected resistance to regulatory change. Apparently, both regulators and regulatees grow comfortable with a particular regulatory environment.

Although the support for multiple regulators is not generally verbalized, silence on that subject may speak just as loudly. In the Stigler tradition, regulation is a market process: Only when the costs of duplicative regulatory structures outweigh the benefits of regulatory competition will change occur.

There is, of course, a demand side to this market process; someone or some group wants regulation, so it may not be realistic to even entertain the prospect of a regulationless environment.

Scarff in chapter 12 presents a case study of the securities and commodities markets where there has been some convergence in instruments traded, although they are regulated by different federal agencies. Although there have been market developments, the regulation of futures and securities under different statutes and separate agencies (the Commodity Futures Trading Commission [CFTC] and the SEC) is not a bureaucratic or Congressional accident but, rather, reflects differences in the regulated instruments, their economic functions, and their trading environments. Futures are predominantly risk-shifting contracts (as opposed to securities, which are capital-formation financial assets), traded in a competitive pit auction market. If a futures contract is economically viable and successfully performs its price-basing and hedging functions, it is likely a deep and liquid market. Approximately 70 percent of the volume of futures markets represents member transactions—those of professional risk takers (speculators) or hedgers—and the markets continue to be dominated by commercials.

The regulatory structure for futures markets is the same, regardless of the underlying commodity or the industry from which the market participant comes. The basic mission of the CFTC is to protect the financial integrity of the markets by preventing corners, squeezes, other manipulations, and fraud and financial improprieties by market professionals. All futures trading is subject to the financial protections of clearinghouses and mark-to-market margining, and exchanges are the required trading forum (that is, there is no over-the-counter trading of futures). There is no assigned market maker or specialist. Liquidity in futures depends on participation in the market by members and commercial interest. By contrast, the SEC's mission is investor protection while facilitating capital formation, and the SEC's regulatory philosophy relies heavily on disclosure.

The difference in the functions of the instruments, their trading environments, and the types of market participants has meant that the regulatory structures for futures and securities have evolved quite differently. The customer protections offered by the futures markets may not be appropriate for securities markets, although the options markets are beginning to adopt several futures-type protections. Futures protections, which generally have no counterpart in securities regulation, include an economic purpose test for contract designation (commercial hedging or price basing), speculative limits, daily price limits, market surveillance, segregation of customer funds, uniform disclosure statements, reparations, CFTC emergency powers, clearinghouse guarantees, competitive pits, large-trader reporting requirements, broad availability of private rights of action, and CFTC authority to assess civil penalties up to $100,000 per offense. Again, these protections are designed and have evolved around the particular nature of futures markets.

Scarff's focus is on the multiple regulatory structures for stock index products. The argument generally is made that industry-specific or substantial segment indexes are surrogates for stock trading, thus posing dangers to securities laws' insider trading rules. In view of the antimanipulative protections built into the futures regulatory structure, this concern may be somewhat overstated. Nevertheless, I am convinced that these markets are yet developing. After all the various experiments and pilots in indexes and options are tried in the market, we may find that the economic purposes of futures and securities remain fundamentally different, again allowing different functionally based regulatory structures.

The lack of market acceptance of stock subindex instruments to date may be early evidence that the gray area between stock and commodities trading may not be of great significance. The further development of the markets and the congressionally mandated studies of financial futures and options markets and insider trading in futures markets should provide a broader understanding of whether or not any regulatory changes are appropriate.

Based on the current stage of index options and futures market development, however, it is simply too soon to make a judgment that regulatory disparity is a problem that needs to be solved, one way or the other. While the market for these new products is yet developing, so too are their regulatory structures. It is not at all clear that the ultimate regulatory configuration will result in less regulation: To the contrary, more, less or simply different rules may characterize the final regulatory environment. The market for regulation is no different from any other market process; as always, free lunches are hard to find.

References

Bloch, Ernest. 1985. Multiple regulators: Their constituencies and policies. (Chapter 11.)

Peltzman, Samuel. 1976. Toward a more general theory of regulation. *Journal of Law and Economics* 19 (2):211–240.

Scarff, Douglas. 1985. The securities and commodities markets: A case study in product convergence and regulatory disparity. (Chapter 12.)

Schreiber, Paul S., and Schwartz, Robert A. 1985. Efficient price discovery in a securities market: The objective of a trading system. (Chapter 2.)

Stigler, George. 1971. Theory of regulation. *Bell Journal of Economics*, Spring.

14
Reflections on Securities Regulation

Lawrence J. White

Thischapter offers a discussion of the goals and structure of regulation of the securities industry.

Regulatory Goals

As set forth in Schreiber and Schwartz (chapter 2), there are three separate policy goals that concern regulators in the securities area:

1. Promoting fairness.
2. Promoting efficiency with respect to broker and dealer services (for example, through encouraging competition in brokerage fees).
3. Promoting efficiency with respect to the quality of securities prices (for example, enhancing the process of price discovery and being concerned with questions of liquidity, thinness, and variability).

Schreiber and Schwartz discuss these goals and remind us that there may well be trade-offs among them. For example, the question of insider trading involves trade-offs between goals (1) and (3); that is, allowing insider trading may hasten the adjustment of prices to proper levels, but it seems to contravene many individuals' notions of fairness. Further, encouraging more competition among market makers may involve trade-offs between goals (2) and (3); more competition may fragment the markets, creating thinness and greater variability (although I am skeptical that this trade-off is a serious one).

There may be another possible trade-off between goals (1) and (2): If the notion of fairness applies not only to equality of access to information and to trading priority rules, but also to equality of access to brokerage services (for example, equality of fees), then competition in brokerage services represents a trade-off between fairness and brokerage efficiency.

Contemplation of this last trade-off should lead one to think again about the fairness issue in general. Is fairness in access to information substantially different from fairness in access to brokerage services? If we think that the competition that has followed the unfixing of commission rates in the early

1970s provided the proper solution to the trade-off between brokerage efficiency and equality of access to services, then perhaps we should also think harder about allowing competition (in the discovery and revelation of information) to provide the solution to the trade-off between fairness in access to information and pricing efficiency.

The Regulatory Structure

The current structure of regulation of the securities industry is of a dual or multiple form, similar to the structure that has existed for a long time in banking (see Bloch, chapter 11). It is not surprising that the banking institutions that have been regulated have largely welcomed this structure, since it has offered them alternative possibilities—places to retreat or migrate to—when their existing regulatory environment became unfavorable or the alternative environment became more favorable.

As new technological opportunities and the discovery of legal loopholes allow commercial banks and securities firms to invade each other's turf, a new dual regulatory structure in this area of overlap is becoming a reality. Migration from one regulatory regime to the other is difficult for entire firms, however. Instead, we are likely to hear, still more frequently, calls for a level playing field by *both* sets of players, as each side sees only the relative disadvantages of its form of regulation.

This multiple regulation structure raises an important issue in the realm of normative or welfare economics: Does dual regulation lead to greater social efficiency or to less? This issue can be analyzed in the following framework. Let us assume (for the purposes of argument) that the regulation in question is unnecessarily onerous and is generating social costs. In this case, we can liken the regulatory requirements to the imposition of a sales tax.

Consequently, dual regulation will tend to have the welfare effects of a system of different taxes placed on similar items. If two products have similar costs of production and would otherwise be expected to sell for similar prices, the product that is subject to the lower tax will ultimately prevail. This outcome is efficient. But if the products have different costs and the higher-cost product is subject to the lower tax (and the lower-cost product cannot migrate to the lower-tax category), then the higher-cost product may prevail. This outcome may well be inefficient.[1]

The analogies in dual regulation are easy to draw. If banking services offered by state-chartered banks are identical to banking services offered by federally chartered banks, those banks located in the least onerous regime will prevail. Given the foregoing assumption, that is an efficient outcome. If, however, banks offer a checking account service and securities firms offer a checking account service that is similar, and the two have different costs and are subject to differing regulatory regimes, the more efficient service may not prevail.

Another important issue in the area of multiple regulation is that of *market allocation*: In the early 1980s, new developments in the financial markets brought forth new products that were substitutes both for each other and for traditional securities. The regulatory responsibilities and boundaries of the Securities and Exchange Commission (SEC) and the Commodities Futures Trading Commission (CFTC) for the new products were initially unclear. After a period of uncertainty, the regulators colluded and divided the market. As Scarff (chapter 12) points out, however, the division was not perfect. Some close substitutes continue to extend across the two regulatory regimes. And the regulators agreed that one set of products—futures in nonexempt securities (that is, normal corporate stocks and bonds)—will not be provided.

Why did the regulators agree to divide their turf and ban some products? Here we can refer to the first regulatory goal outlined earlier: promoting fairness. The SEC is very much concerned with insider trading; the CFTC is much less so. To preserve its control over insider trading, the SEC needed to gain or maintain jurisdiction over anything that might be affected seriously by insider trading; in return, the SEC was prepared to give up jurisdiction over items that are not affected by insider trading.

The ban on futures on specific stocks and bonds is also consistent with this pattern. Futures on specific stocks and bonds clearly could be affected by insider trading. The SEC, however, is not accustomed to regulating futures markets and would probably be suspicious of the CFTC's ability to police insider trading in these futures. Simultaneously, the CFTC would probably be reluctant to have the SEC acquire the expertise and precedent in regulating futures markets. Agreeing to a ban on the product was an easy, risk-averse solution for both agencies.

Of course, an efficiency loss has accompanied this solution. Some individuals or institutions who might find futures contracts on IBM stocks or GMAC bonds to be useful complements to their portfolios are being deprived of this opportunity. Perhaps futures contracts on individual stocks and bonds would be superior vehicles for hedging and laying off risk (and for speculation) than the option products that have mushroomed in the last decade. Unfortunately, there is no easy way to estimate the efficiency loss from this ban. It may be small, or it may be large.

Finally, let us remember that there are a few competing interest-rate instruments that are subject to the two differing regulatory regimes. It will be interesting to see whether one type of instrument prevails. Even then, we will not easily be able to determine whether its success is due to its inherent superior efficiency or to a differentially favorable regulatory environment.

Note

1. An alternative analytical framework to that offered in the text would be to treat the regulatory requirements as having the effects of effluent fees, set at the socially appropriate levels to counteract externalities or spillovers. In that case, the taxation is not socially onerous, and the success of any financial instrument would reflect its overall social efficiency, including the externalities.

Part III
Trading Systems and Automation

15
An Integrated Computerized Trading System

Yakov Amihud
Haim Mendelson

The propagation of information systems technology in various industries has followed remarkably similar patterns. In the first stage, the computer is used to replace or improve existing clerical functions. The emphasis at this stage is on the cost-reduction potential of the machine in applications such as payroll, check processing, and accounts receivable. As users become more familiar with the computer, its potential in a variety of other application areas is recognized. This gives rise to a second stage, characterized by a proliferation of computer-based applications. The potential benefits of new computer systems are recognized, and the emphasis shifts from efficiency to effectiveness, from cost-reduction to the generation of new benefits. A variety of problems and ideas lead to computerized solutions, and diverse systems are developed at a high rate. Although the cumulative effect of the systems developed through this stage is impressive, the computer system is still viewed as an auxiliary tool which is used to facilitate existing functions in diverse ways without fundamentally changing the general approach to doing business.

In many industries—especially service industries—the use of modern information systems technologies not only facilitates various business functions, but also completely revolutionizes the fundamental business philosophy. This is especially true when the activities of the industry revolve around the dissemination and processing of information, as in the case of the securities industry. Such industries advance to a third stage, characterized by a complete restructuring of the basic business procedures to take full advantage of the capabilities of modern information technologies. This costly and sometimes painful stage is further complicated by the need to provide services continuously over a transition period and by uncertainties regarding the future course of both the industry and the technology. At this stage, there is no substitute for a long-range plan that provides a sense of direction and reduces the natural tendency to emphasize the pressing problems of the present while sacrificing the vital issues of the future.

Focusing on the development of information systems in the securities industry, the first stage of automation has naturally involved high-volume clerical and accounting operations—classical cases of substantial cost reduction by the use of data-processing technology; in fact, the processing volumes were so high that there was no substitute for automation. The establishment of the Securities Industry Automation Corporation in 1972 has marked the beginning of the second stage, characterized by the proliferation of automated aids designed to support the prevailing trading philosophy. Systems such as the Designated Order Turnaround (DOT) the Opening Automated Reporting Systems (OARS) on the New York Stock Exchange, or the Securities Communication Order Routing and Execution system (SCOREX) on the Pacific Stock Exchange represent a transition from the second stage toward the third stage: Rather than facilitate existing activities, such systems will ultimately revolutionize the operations of the exchanges. It is difficult, however, to view these systems as the outcome of a coherent plan; and it is virtually impossible to predict where they will lead the securities industry in the next decade.

This chapter presents the conceptual framework of an integrated approach to the problem of exchange automation, which, we believe, could serve as a basis for the planned development of information systems in the securities industry. Our approach is based on the integration of subsystems and capabilities and the development of interfaces that will enable the industry as a whole (and, consequently, the ultimate consumers—the transactors) to take full advantage of modern information systems technologies.

An important principle that has guided us in the design of the system is that market forces can do a better job of selecting trading mechanisms than systems designers or economists can. Thus our design must be flexible enough to allow for competition among various forms of exchange. This flexibility implies that traders will have the freedom to choose among alternative forms of exchange; thus market forces will determine the correct mix of trading mechanisms for each security at any point in time to the benefit of investors.

Our approach is not based on the application of any innovative hardware features, but software development for the proposed systems, as well as their initiation, would require substantial resources. At this point, the systems are rather tentative; the purpose of this chapter is to present our underlying approach as a basis for further discussion. We hope this discussion will lead to a conceptual view of the exchange of the future that will provide guidance for planning the next automated subsystems as interfaced components of an overall integrated system.

Finally, we expect that the greater liquidity generated by our proposed system will contribute to economic welfare by reducing the required returns on traded securities (see Amihud and Mendelson, 1984a, 1984b).

The plan of the chapter is as follows. The next section discusses trading mechanisms in securities exchanges and presents our basic trading procedures. The third section describes the data elements of our integrated system. The fourth discusses order handling by our integrated system, and the fifth describes how traders interact with the system. The final section discusses some implementation issues.

Trading Mechanisms

The first step in the design of a computer-based information system is an analysis of the existing functions and procedures: A prerequisite for studying the trading mechanisms of the future is an understanding of the trading practices of the present. Current trading procedures have survived the market test and hence must possess some attributes that are desirable to transactors. Therefore, it is instructive to categorize existing trading practices in a way that will identify the relevant alternatives for the future.

Numerous trading procedures can be identified in securities exchanges around the world (see, for example, Whitcomb, chapter 16). Abstracting from actual implementation details, however, we can identify three broad categories, or models, of trade:

1. the dealer market,
2. the clearing-house, and
3. the open auction.

The dealer market is a market that is dominated by a dealer, or specialist, who has an affirmative obligation to continuously quote bid and ask prices at which he is willing to trade. Traders react to these quotes and buy from the specialist at the ask or sell to the specialist at the bid. The specialist updates his bid and ask quotations in response to the public demand and supply, inferring on prevailing market conditions by observing his inventory position as well as by employing additional relevant information. The dealer market system prevails in many of the U.S. securities exchanges and has received considerable attention in the market microstructure literature (for a review, see Cohen, Maier, Schwartz, and Whitcomb 1979).

The clearing house (Mendelson 1982) is a periodic market-clearing procedure under which traders submit orders to buy or sell specified quantities of the traded security either at the market price or subject to a limit price qualification. These orders accumulate and remain sealed until clearing time. At clearing time, sell orders are sorted according to the type of order (market or limit, with market orders sorted first), and limit orders are further sorted by increasing price sequence; buy orders are sorted by type of order (market orders first) and by decreasing price sequence. The sorted schedules are exactly the supply and demand schedule, respectively, constructed from the orders submitted to the market. These schedules are then intersected at a market-clearing price. A clearing-house procedure is employed extensively by European stock exchanges, where the market is cleared periodically (see Mendelson 1982, 1984a, 1984b; Whitcomb, chapter 16; Spray 1964; Doron 1960; Noyes 1973); the automated exchange procedure employed by the Tel Aviv Stock Exchange for low-volume securities is also a generalized version of the clearing-house organization.[1]

The open auction is a continuous market-clearing procedure under which traders continuously submit buy or sell orders to the market. Orders may be communicated electronically or by open outcry, and may be recorded manually or on computerized storage media. When orders cross, they are executed on the basis of price and time priority.

All three trading procedures are widely used by securities exchanges. Even on the New York Stock Exchange alone, we can find combinations of all three methods: Trading in the opening, while controlled by the specialist, resembles the mode of operation of the clearing house, whereas trading on the floor over the day is a combination of the dealer market and the open auction market. The survival of all three modes of exchange over time suggests that all three have economic viability, and that computerized trading need not necessarily eliminate any of them. In fact, we argue that a computerized exchange is likely to benefit from potential competition among these forms of exchange. The role of competition in market design has been emphasized by economists in studies of prevailing institutional arrangements (see Smidt 1971; U.S. SEC Study 1971); we suggest that, in the context of a computer-based exchange, the relevant dimension for competition is competition among alternative *forms* of exchange. We shall show that a combination of competing mechanisms will enable transactors efficiently to trade off immediacy, flexibility, and price. Even if some of the mechanisms may ultimately be eliminated for some securities, this should occur through natural market forces rather than by design.

We now evaluate the role of each of the trading mechanisms in the context of a computerized exchange. The open auction has been suggested as a leading candidate for automated exchange, in the form of a "hard CLOB" (Consolidated Limit Order Book). The best known and most comprehensive proposal along these lines is the Peake-Mendelson-Williams proposal for a National Book System (see Mendelson et al. 1979). In this system, any qualified broker may enter bids or offers, which are recorded in the CLOB. A summary of the number of shares bid or offered at each price could be viewed on CRT screens at any member firm. Crossing orders will be executed instantaneously, and the CLOB will be updated to reflect the new status of the system. Price priority is achieved automatically; time priority is preserved easily by recording the time at which each order was placed.

The hard-CLOB approach may be attractive for some investors, but not necessarily for all. This results from two characteristics of this approach:

1. When a trader places an order on the CLOB, the order is likely to be executed at its limit price without leaving a surplus between the quoted price and the execution price.
2. Since orders are conditional on price only, they cannot adjust dynamically to the state of the market. Any such adjustment requires continuous

attention to the state of the market, accompanied by cancellation and reissuing of orders to the Book.

The first characteristic follows from the disclosure of the CLOB to all transactors. Clearly, traders will prefer to hit the limit prices of existing orders on the CLOB if they are about to submit an order that will be executed. Thus in this system traders may be able to increase their trading profits by withholding their orders from the CLOB while monitoring it continuously; they will require significant compensation (measured by the difference between the *quoted* limit price placed on the Book and their *actual* reservation price) for placing on the Book an order that is a sitting duck for all practical purposes. The inevitable result is an increase in the bid-asked spreads. See also Ho, Schwartz, and Whitcomb (1984) for a discussion of the difference between limit price and reservation price and its implications.

The inability of limit orders on the Book to adjust dynamically to market conditions may become a severe problem when trading is performed electronically rather than on the exchange floor. A trader in the crowd is exposed to numerous informal pieces of useful information. The smiles of traders in the crowd, the loudness of their voices, or an occasional chat provide information that is difficult to display on a CRT terminal. Traders' desire to keep abreast of the market is clearly demonstrated by the variety of order types currently available in the exchanges. Many of these order types cannot effectively be recorded on the CLOB, and must be emulated by a broker monitoring the activity in the market.

Thus the execution of some types of orders may require continuous monitoring of the state of the market, and possibly following various forms of gaming and order-placement strategies, rather than straightforward placement of orders on the Book. Furthermore, various forms of qualification and conditioning that are implicit when trading is performed in the auditory crowd must become explicit and well defined in an electronic trading system. This does not imply that a CRT terminal is an inferior medium for order placement and monitoring; it does imply that orders in an effective automated trading system are likely to be quite different from the existing types of orders, and that provision of additional support functions by the trading system may be necessary.

The clearing-house trading procedure allows traders to overcome some of these shortcomings. Orders submitted to a market which is organized as a clearing-house enjoy dual protection:

1. The price at which an order is executed is usually different from, and better than its limit price, since the execution price is determined by the intersection of the demand and supply schedules constructed by batching many orders. Thus there will in general exist a gain, equal to the difference between the limit price of an executed order and its execution price. In particular, a relatively small order is unlikely to be the marginal order that de-

termines the execution price, and execution prices are more likely to reflect the underlying market demand and supply schedules.

2. The limit price of an order is not disclosed to the rest of the market. Thus, even if a trader submits an order that could be exploited in an open-CLOB system, other traders are unlikely to be able to take advantage of such an order under the clearing-house operating procedure. Furthermore, the incentive to follow sophisticated gaming strategies to affect the execution of a straightforward order is eliminated, or at least reduced. This implies that traders will not have to expend significant real resources to achieve execution at a fair price, and the batching feature of the clearing-house reduces their ability to manipulate the market price.

The main shortcoming of the clearing-house trading procedure is its timing: The market is cleared periodically rather than continuously, and some traders may find it bothersome to wait for an hour or so until their orders are executed. Shortening the inter-clearing time interval may alleviate this problem somewhat, but then the number of orders per clearing will go down, and consequently the market will become less liquid and the aforementioned advantages less prominent.

An important difference between the open auction mechanism and the clearing-house is that the former is asynchronous, and the latter is synchronous. That is, the market is cleared under the clearing-house trading procedure at predetermined points in time, whereas, under the open auction mechanism, trading may occur at any point in time. This difference affects both the capabilities and the technical implementation aspects of the two trading procedures. An order submitted to the open auction market remains frozen on the book until it is executed or canceled, whereas an order submitted to the clearing-house may include floating parameters such as cash available, market indexes, and interest rates. Since clearing-house orders are executed periodically in a synchronous fashion, computation of such parameters may be performed at the market clearing epoch. In contrast, the terms of orders on the open auction Book are fixed and binding. To enhance the flexibility of open auction orders, our system will include an automatic enable/disable mechanism that may be used to sweep orders between the Book (which will contain only effective, or enabled, orders) and a file of disabled, or potential, orders. When an order is submitted to the open auction market, it may contain optional enable/disable conditions which will automatically control this sweeping operation. In subsequent sections we further specify the various forms of order conditioning.

The role of the specialist in an automated trading system is quite controversial. Rather than indulge in the arguments for or against designated market makers, we note that specialists exist in the prevailing trading systems in the United States and are likely to remain, at least through a substantial transition period. This implies that, at least for the sake of continuity, an integrated trading system has to support the participation of the specialist. The ultimate role of the specialist would then evolve with the development of the market; if the specialist has no viable role, this will be reflected in his profits (or losses), and the specialist function will then be eliminated by competition with the other mechanisms. We do suspect that specialists will continue to play an important role at least in some cases; market forces, however, should make the final determination.

The specialist feature is a simple extension of our integrated trading system. Although it could be built as an integral part of the open auction procedure, there are some advantages in maintaining it as a separate component that could also serve as a backup continuous trading subsystem. There is little doubt that such backup would prove useful (and profitable), at least during a transition period. Specialists' quotes will be highlighted or displayed separately on investors' CRT terminals; other than a few support functions, such as inventory management and quotation-support systems (see Amihud and Mendelson 1980, 1982), and possibly higher priority when interacting with the system, incorporating the specialist function as part of our system is quite straightforward. In fact, for most practical purposes specialists' quotes may be regarded as part of the open auction procedure, and we shall treat them as such in the sequel.

Our automated system will allow transactors to choose between trading via an open auction procedure (including the specialist) and trading via an automated clearing-house. Traders willing to pay the price for immediacy of execution are likely to choose the open auction procedure; traders who find the price of immediacy too high, or who value the added flexibility of orders submitted to the clearing-house, will opt for the latter. Traders' freedom to choose between the two options is the best way to regulate the bid-asked spread. If, for some traded securities, one of the options dominates, it will naturally attract most of the order flow and will consequently provide higher liquidity. For example, it may well be that the high volume of trading in a security such as IBM will mitigate the potential problems of trading via the open auction procedure, whereas the clearing-house trading procedure will often be chosen for some of the less liquid securities. This choice is clearly affected by variables such as volume, inherent price volatility, the degree of insider trading, and the like. It is worth reemphasizing our view that rather than make a judgment (which, necessarily, will be somewhat arbitrary) about the best trading procedure, we believe market forces should determine the correct mix of trading mechanisms for each traded security.

Our system is presented in the next two sections. The next section discusses the data elements supporting the integrated system, and the subsequent section describes how orders are handled by the automated system.

The Integrated System

One of the important advantages of automation results from the ability to integrate subsystems that were previously managed separately. Distributed database technology, which is expected to reach maturity long before the implementation of our integrated trading system, provides the ability to access geographically dispersed data systems as if they were stored on a single centralized database. The result is that system components that were treated as unrelated and independent may be integrated. Furthermore, from a design point of view, we can abstract from the question of database location—which can be treated separately at the implementation level—and focus on the fundamental issues.

We view the trading system as consisting of three related subsystems:

1. the order execution subsystem;
2. the clearing and settlement subsystem; and
3. the portfolio subsystem.

Discussions of automated trading systems usually focus on the order execution subsystem. After all, securities exchanges automated their clearing and settlement procedures long ago, and portfolio management is outside the scope of operations of the exchanges. Yet there is a clear feedback relationship between these three subsystems. Traders submit orders to the exchange for the purpose of revising their portfolios; thus orders, which serve as inputs to the order execution subsystem, are the outputs of the portfolio subsystem. The output of the order execution subsystem is transactions, usually in the form of prices and quantities. These transactions form the input to the clearing and settlement subsystem. The output of the clearing and settlement subsystem is in the form of settlements—that is, modifications to investors' portfolios—which in turn serve to update the portfolio subsystem. We thus obtain a feedback loop connecting the portfolio, order execution, and clearing subsystems. Traders' orders are certainly conditional on the state of their portfolios; however this conditioning is currently implicit in the orders they submit to the exchange. As long as the portfolio subsystem is completely separate from the order execution subsystem, this form of conditioning cannot be made explicit.

We suggest an integration of the order execution subsystem, the clearing and settlement subsystem, and the investors' portfolio subsystem into a comprehensive integrated trading system. When an investor's order is executed, it will immediately update the state of his portfolio, which may trigger the cancellation of existing orders and/or the submission of new orders. Furthermore, the parameters of orders submitted to the clearing-house trading procedure may involve variable portfolio or market data; these data will be automatically updated by the system, thus allowing investors to keep abreast of market developments as well as changes in their portfolios without requiring continuous monitoring, cancellation, and reissuing of orders. The important advantage is that the translation of traders' preferences into orders may become more meaningful and less time-consuming than it is today.

It is worth pointing out that we do not view integration as a process whereby brokerage houses disappear and all trading is centrally controlled by authorities of the exchange. Rather, integration will be achieved by sharing data and interfacing capabilities that are controlled in part by the brokerage houses and in part by the exchange. Thus integration involves coordinated systems design and adherence to mutually agreed-on standards and interfaces that support a global integrated system. Once such a view is accepted, the benefits accruing to all participants should be more than sufficient to enforce voluntary compliance with the standards. Thus we view the process of integration as the creation of voluntary, mutually beneficial arrangements that define and allocate interfaces and data management facilities among different subsystems. For presentation purposes, it is convenient to abstract at this stage from the existence of the interfaces between the brokerage houses and the exchange, and to describe the system as if it were centralized. The actual implementation, however, will involve integration by interfacing the brokerage houses' systems with the exchange's systems. We do argue that planning and design of the integrated system should be coordinated, and that the coordination role naturally belongs to the exchange.

Our system will allow traders' orders to be conditional on a combination of

1. Limit price qualifications, as in existing trading systems.
2. Their portfolio positions (for example, their cash positions or their positions in various securities).
3. Market data.

The system will be supported by the following data pools.

Portfolio Data

Each portfolio will be identified by a unique portfolio code. The corresponding data pool will contain investor's identification information, identification of securities for which the investor is an insider, identification of private information sources to which the investor subscribes, portfolio position in each traded security, cash position, margin data, and the times and details of recent transactions. This data pool will also contain a personal mailbox where various messages, pertaining to the investor, will be stored. Portfolio data will be updated in real time as transactions occur. The portfolio data pool is confidential and accessible only to the owning investor (or his authorized agent).

Securities Data

This data pool will contain relevant information on traded securities. It will contain financial data compiled from reports filed with the SEC as well as market information such as volume and price information, dividend data, price/earning ratios, beta, recent insiders' transactions, and recent announcements. This data pool contains public information that is available to all investors, and private information that is available to subscribers (for example, analysts' forecasts and evaluation, various ratings, and the like). Some of the data in this data pool will be updated in real time (for example, price information); some will be updated at each periodic clearing; and some will be updated daily. The public portion of the SECURITIES data pool will be updated by the exchange; the private portion will be the responsibility of the supplying vendors.

Order Data

This data pool is the heart of the trading system. It maintains all orders currently effective in the system. The order data consist of three logical subsets:

1. Enabled open auction orders: These are orders that are currently active on the open auction book.
2. Disabled open auction orders: These are potential orders that are currently inactive and would be activated (that is, enabled) as soon as a set of prespecified conditions are satisfied.
3. Clearing-house orders, submitted to the clearing-house trading procedure.

Enabled orders that have been submitted to the open auction procedure are secured at the individual level but public at the aggregate market level. In particular, each investor will be able to inquire the current bid and ask for each security, the quantities for which the current market quotes are applicable, and the overall quantity bid or asked at each possible price. Investors will also have access to a graphic representation of the prevailing demand and supply schedules. Disabled orders for the open auction procedure, as well as clearing-house orders, will be confidential at both the individual level and the aggregate level. The ORDER data pool is updated in real time.

Market Data

The MARKET data pool will contain real-time information on various market indicators and relevant information on the state of the economy. It will contain the values of various price indexes over time (as well as their current values, updated continuously), interest rates, money supply information, and so on. This information can be used for conditioning purposes and will be available to all investors. In addition, the MARKET data pool will contain a private portion that contains privately processed market information (for example, value line forecasts), available to subscribers. The MARKET data pool will be updated in real time.

The data pools maintained by the system will serve a number of purposes. First, they will be available for display as decision-support aids for investors. The system will facilitate the dissemination of public and private information throughout the market. Transactors will be able to use real-time market data when following the behavior of stock prices, various indexes, interest rates, and so forth, over time to support their investment decisions. Their ability to download a comprehensive set of relevant information into their own systems, which may then perform various analyses (depending on their investment strategies), will be very significantly increased. Arbitrageurs may use systems that continuously monitor prices as well as other relevant market data, and automatically create orders submitted to the exchange. Investors will be able to use the on-line statements of their securities accounts actively and in real time to support their investment decisions; they will be able to examine the implications of executing hypothetical orders on the value, risk, dividend yield, and expected return of their portfolios, using real-time market information (for example, sale at the current bid, purchase at the current ask).

In addition, the data pools will be necessary for the management of the system itself and, in particular, for order handling. A clearing-house order of the form "Buy IBM using 50% of my cash if the market index went up over the preceding hour and IBM price is below its level at 2 P.M. today" requires data from the PORTFOLIO data pool (to compute "50% of my cash" in real time), the SECURITIES data pool (to find IBM price at 2 P.M.) and the MARKET data pool (to check whether the index went up over the preceding hour). Similarly, all data pools may be used by the enable/disable procedures, as well as in functions such as checking the validity of orders submitted to the market, reporting insiders' transactions, and so forth.

Clearly, the ORDER data pool plays a central role in the management of the system. The management and handling of orders are described in the following section.

Order Handling

Our integrated trading system accepts orders to buy or sell securities that are listed for trade on the exchange. Orders are routed for execution either to the clearing-house or to the open auction procedure. Order quantities may be quoted either in cash or in shares. In the former case, the actual quantity purchased or sold will depend on the execution price; in the latter, quantity will be fixed, while the cash settlement will depend on price. Orders routed to the open auction market will be either market orders or limit orders. A market order routed to the open auction will be executed immediately at the currently best bid or offer; a limit order to sell below the current bid or buy above the current ask will also be executed instantaneously at the current bid or ask, respectively. All executions in the open auction market will follow price and time priority. When a limit order is submitted to the open auction market and does not qualify for immediate execution, it is stored on the Book and awaits crossing orders.

Orders routed to the open auction procedure may contain two types of conditions:

1. Execution conditions, which stipulate under what conditions the order should be executed: For an open auction order, the condition may involve only the price of the security under consideration, and must follow one of the following formats:

a. "Sell x shares at price y or better."
b. "Sell $\$x$ worth of shares at price y or better."
c. "Buy x shares at price y or better."
d. "Buy $\$x$ worth of shares at price y or better."

Clearly, prices and quantities may be quoted at any desired level of accuracy; in particular, price increments need not be limited to $\$1/8$ or $\$1/16$.

2. Enable/disable conditions, which specify an event or a combination of events that would render the order effective (in the case of enable conditions) or ineffective (in the case of disable conditions): Thus, an order may be viewed as a potential order that is activated as soon as the enable conditions are met, and is deactivated when the disable conditions are triggered. These conditions may involve any data in the data pools that are accessible to the investor who submitted the order—namely, his PORTFOLIO data pool, the SECURITIES and MARKET data pools, and orders submitted to the open auction procedure. For example, an order may be disabled as soon as a prespecified time interval has elapsed, or as soon as another order effecting the same portfolio has been executed, or as soon the price of the security under consideration has displayed some pattern specified in the order.

The Book will consist of two parts: the actual limit order Book, including all enabled limit orders; and a file of potential (or disabled) orders. As a matter of implementation, potential orders will be stored locally at the brokerage houses rather than at the exchange, and the monitoring of the enable/disable conditions will be performed by the brokerage houses' systems rather than by a centralized system. These systems will be fully integrated, however, so that the actual location where storage and processing take place will be transparent from a functional viewpoint. Although the Book itself is open (in the aggregate level), potential orders will be confidential and inaccessible to the public.

Orders submitted to the clearing-house procedure may be conditioned on any data that are accessible to the submitting trader (for example, his own PORTFOLIO data, or data from the SECURITIES or MARKET data pools) as well as on the price of the security to which the order applies. In principle, order execution may also be conditioned on the equilibrium prices of other securities as determined at clearing time.[2] Furthermore, the parameters of clearing-house orders, such as quantity (quoted in cash or shares) or limit price, may involve variable market information. This flexibility will enable transactors' orders to keep adjusting to market conditions without requiring constant monitoring. By quoting orders in terms of variable portfolio and market data, an investor can summarize a complex trading strategy by a few orders without requiring further monitoring or communications with the exchange.

The clearing-house procedure will be activated periodically at prespecified time intervals. The market will clear simultaneously for all securities participating in a given clearing; the clearing will include all orders submitted for execution through the clearing-house procedure, as well as all limit orders on the open auction Book that are enabled at clearing time but have not been executed by the open auction procedure. Partial execution (rationing of orders specifying the market clearing price as their limit price) may be required when there is excess demand or supply at the price where the two schedules intersect (see Mendelson 1984a, 1984b). In this event, orders submitted to the open auction procedure will be rationed first; if there is still excess demand or supply, limit orders may have to be rationed, and then market orders.

It is worth emphasizing the difference between the enable/disable options of the open auction procedure and the conditioning forms allowed in the clearing-house procedure. Once an order has been enabled for execution on the open auction Book, it remains static. This is required since traders will react to an order on the Book under the assumption that its terms are binding, fixed, and known. To make bids and offers binding, it is necessary to require them to remain effective for a minimal time interval. A trader may then withdraw his order from the Book but is not allowed continuously to alter the terms of his bids or offers. It will generally be significantly cheaper (in terms of direct trading costs) to leave a flexible order for the clearing-house trading procedure than to enable and disable orders every few minutes. Furthermore, since the information displayed to participants in the open auction market is some representation of the prevailing demand and supply schedules, only execution conditions that can be translated into a demand/supply schedule are legitimate in the open auction procedure. These constraints do not exist in the clearing-house trading procedure. Thus a clearing-house order may include parameters that change continuously prior to the clearing of the market, such as the trader's cash position, quantities in his portfolio, prior transactions, market indexes, financial stock information (such as dividends announced and p/e ratios), interest rates, and so on. Consequently, a single order (or pair of orders) submitted to the clearing-house procedure may represent a complex trading strategy.

An execution—either by the open auction procedure or by the clearing-house procedure—immediately updates all the relevant data pools: The PORTFOLIO data pool is updated to reflect the new portfolio and cash positions of the transactors involved, and to record the transaction; the SECURITIES data pool may be updated to reflect the possibly new price (which could also affect the MARKET data pool); the ORDERS data pool is updated to cancel fully executed orders or to adjust the quantities of partly executed orders.

In the following section we demonstrate how investors may interact with the system and take advantage of its capabilities.

Interacting with the System

There are two levels of access to the integrated trading system: The amateur level and the professional level. Access at the professional level, which takes full advantage of the available options, will be allowed only through members of the exchange. Access at the amateur level may be available to qualified transactors using terminals or home computers. All users will have access to all publicly available information, to private information sources to which they subscribe, and to their own ORDER and PORTFOLIO data; however, orders entered at the amateur level will include only market and simple limit orders (either to the open auction market or to the clearing-house). Amateur users will not be allowed to use either the enable/disable options or any form of compound conditioning (clearly, this rule may be modified to allow more options, intermediate levels, and the like).

A typical session with an amateur user will include performing a log-on procedure; displaying the contents of the user's mailbox on his CRT terminal (information on executed transactions, dividends received, newsletters to which the investor subscribes, and so forth); and browsing through the investor's portfolio to see if changes are necessary. Suppose the investor wishes to liquidate $2,000 worth of securities from his portfolio. He may invoke a graph showing the behavior of a market index as well as the prices of securities he owns over the last week. He may then focus on the behavior over the current day. Aided by these data as well as by fundamental information available through the system, he may decide to sell security XYZ. Next he observes that the current bid for XYZ is $32.74 with depth 200, the current ask is $33.23, and the last clearing-house price was $35.79. Given that there is a trend of decline throughout the market and in the price of XYZ, our investor has to choose between selling immediately at $32.74 or taking his chances at the next clearing in thirty minutes. Assuming he decides on immediate sale, he submits a market order to sell $2,000 worth of XYZ at the open auction, execution is confirmed, his cash position is immediately increased, and his position in XYZ is immediately reduced.

Now consider an investor who wishes to sell a block of XYZ shares. The sale is likely to be executed through a professional member according to one of a number of possible strategies. The investor may place the whole block for sale at the open auction. This will require a significant price concession, since the existence of the block will be evident. He may break the block into smaller pieces and enable the corresponding orders one at a time. This can be done automatically by specifying the execution of a previous order as the enabling condition for the next order. He may place an order in the clearing-house. Investors will not be aware of the existence of the block before clearing time; consequently, their limit prices will not reflect an anticipated price decline. If the block is relatively large, the clearing price may still go down, since the quantity demanded may not be significant and it may become necessary to travel down the demand schedule to execute the block sale. Another option is to send messages to the mailboxes of a select group of investors, effectively inviting them to bid on fractions of his block at the next clearing. Finally, a combination of these strategies is also possible; the ability to condition orders on the state of the portfolio can be applied to guarantee that the quantity ultimately sold will not exceed the planned quantity.

As another example, consider an investor who follows a trend-tracking strategy based on comparing the value of a market index to its fourteen-week moving average. If the index is higher than its fourteen-week moving average plus a fixed threshold, the investor invests 80 percent of his available cash in a given portfolio; if the index is lower than its fourteen-week moving average minus a fixed threshold, the investor liquidates his portfolio. Given the nature of this investment strategy, it is reasonable to assume that immediacy is not a major concern and to apply it using clearing-house orders. The ability to quote orders in cash, using data from the current state of the investor's portfolio, enables him to place fixed orders without ever having to monitor the state of the market (as long as he subscribes to this investment philosophy). He will place market buy orders (quoted in percentages of his cash position) conditional on the difference between the value of the market index and its moving average value (derived from historical data in the MARKET data pool) being above the threshold level; and sell orders for his full portfolio positions, conditional on the same difference being below the (negative) threshold. More complex investment strategies could similarly be translated into fixed orders.

Note that the extreme flexibility of our system may imply some risk to the over-smart investor. A trivial error in the submission of an order may be costly. This is one reason for distinguishing between the amateur and professional levels of access. By requiring traders to submit complex orders through members of the exchange, we add a layer of human intervention that will reduce the occurrence of such errors. Order handling by member firms will be restricted to well-trained professionals. The role of these professionals will be to get an idea about the preferences and beliefs of investors, and to translate their desires into investment strategies in the form of orders submitted to the market. Note that the extreme flexibility provided by the structure of orders submitted to the exchange may well imply a significant reduction in the required communications volume with the exchange, because of the high information content of each such order.

Some Implementation Considerations

The previous sections have presented the mode of operation of an integrated computerized trading system, while attempting to minimize the discussion of implementation issues. Many apparently arbitrary choices have been dictated by the issue of implementability. After all, the difference between fantasy and reality is essentially a question of implementation. In this section we discuss the question of system feasibility, and touch on some implementation problems.

Is our integrated system truly feasible? Let us reexamine the requirements of our system. First, we require on-line access to securities data, based on price information and on financial reports filed with the Securities and Exchange Commission. The provision of on-line price information is clearly feasible. As for financial data filed with the SEC, the commission is currently in the process of designing an Electronic Data Gathering and Retrieval system (EDGAR) which will provide the desired information online. We suggest that EDGAR will be more meaningful in the context of an integrated system, and its design should take this potential use into account. Second, we require the development of a subsystem to support an open auction procedure. Such systems are already in place in a number of securities exchanges, and there is little doubt about their technical feasibility. Third, we require the use of on-line portfolio management systems, which already exist in various formats. What will make our system so powerful is the integration of these capabilities with the trading process. The remaining major requirements are the enable/disable subsystem and the clearing-house subsystem.

First consider the enable/disable subsystem. It consists of two functional components: (1) a market monitoring function, and (2) an automatic order generation/cancellation function. Market monitoring involves a straightforward process of information retrieval from an on-line database system. Such monitoring is certainly feasible; in fact, the planned Merrill Lynch–IBM joint financial data venture will feature automatic tracking of selected securities, thus making automated market monitoring an industry standard for the second half of the 1980s. With a market monitoring system in place, there is no significant technical problem in reading the retrieved data by a computer program, processing it, and generating orders following a standardized format; in fact, this is already done in an ad hoc manner by some systems today. The possible difficulties lie in the sophisticated nature of the specifications leading to the generation of orders in our system; writing the software that accepts as inputs market data and transactors' specifications and generates orders (or cancellations) as its outputs is no trivial task. Yet this software development task is no more than a high-level, but still fairly standard, systems development project. The question is not whether the enable/disable options will be implemented in the future, but rather how and where: They may be implemented either in an ad hoc fashion—as independent input generators to the exchange's order handling processor—or as a well-designed, integral part of a unified trading system.

The hardware investment required to operate the open auction procedure as well as the enable/disable procedures is difficult to predict, but beyond a certain level it is almost linear in the number of orders submitted to the exchange. This implies that, using the open auction alone, the exchange will continuously have to upgrade its facilities to catch up with the anticipated volume increases. As has already been noticed in the context of the opening, a clearing-house operating procedure enjoys significant economies of scale, and its operation involves a high setup cost but a very low marginal cost. Consequently, adoption of this procedure could significantly relieve the hardware resources of the exchange and provide an answer to the anticipated surge in trading volumes. It is worth pointing out that central-processing-related costs (CPU costs) are an order of magnitude lower than data storage and retrieval costs, which in turn are an order of magnitude lower than communications costs. Further, prevailing cost trends guarantee that this discrepancy will grow in the future. The clearing-house procedure essentially substitutes increased CPU costs (since a large number of conditions and market clearing equations must be evaluated and solved in a short time interval) for decreased costs of access and communications, and the substitution is very significant because of the extreme flexibility of clearing-house orders. Combining these considerations, we suggest that the clearing-house is justifiable both on the grounds of its cost-saving potential and on the merits of the benefits it will provide for transactors. Clearly, detailed cost/benefit analysis is required to estimate the resulting net benefits.

A different implementation issue relates to the location of the various data pools. Clearly, the natural location of the SECURITIES and MARKET data pools is at the exchange, which will simply be a huge data-processing center (as it is already becoming today). Similarly, the PORTFOLIO data naturally belongs at the brokerage houses. The MARKET data pool, as well as select data from the SECURITIES pool, will be broadcast to the brokerage houses. Remaining SECURITIES data will be retrievable by explicit request. Prior to the periodic market clearing epochs, the brokerage houses' systems will be polled and relevant PORTFOLIO data will be communicated to the exchange. Enabled open auction orders and clearing-house orders will be stored in the exchange. Disabled open auction orders naturally belong at the brokerage houses.

We opened this chapter by arguing that at the current state of automation of the securities industry, there is no substitute for a long-run overall view that will enable planning with a sense of direction toward the final outcome. This chapter proposes such an outcome, which we believe is both technically feasible and economically desirable. Hopefully, this proposal will stimulate discussion that ultimately will lead to a clear conceptual view of the exchange of the future.

Notes

1. Proposed by Professor Avraham Beja of Tel Aviv University; see Hakansson, Beja, and Kale (1981).

2. Such conditioning, however, may give rise to a situation where prices are indeterminate; some limitations will be required to guarantee the attainability of market clearing prices. Since this issue is technical, we assume here that execution may be conditioned only on the price of the security in question (in addition to the aforementioned data pools). This is sufficient to guarantee orderly market clearing.

References

Amihud, Y., and Mendelson, H. 1980. Dealership market: Market-making with inventory. *Journal of Financial Economics* 8:31–53.

———. 1982. Asset price behavior in a dealership market. *Financial Analysts Journal* 38:50–59.

———. 1984a. Return-liquidity tradeoffs and investment policies, Working Paper, Graduate School of Business, New York University.

———. 1984b. Asset returns and the bid-ask spread, Working Paper, Graduate School of Mangement, University of Rochester.

Black, Fischer. 1971. Toward a fully automated stock exchange. *Financial Analysts Journal*, Part I: July–August 1971, pp. 29–44; Part II: November–December 1971, pp. 25–28, 86–87.

Cohen, K.J.; Maier, S.F.; Schwartz, R.A.; and Whitcomb, D.K. 1979. Market makers and the market spread: A review of recent literature. *Journal of Financial and Quantitative Analysis* 14:813–835.

Doron, S.P. 1960. *The Tel Aviv Stock Exchange—Its history and development*, Tel Aviv: Tel-Aviv Stock Exchange.

Hakansson, N.; Beja, A.; and Kale, J. 1981. On the feasibility of automated market-making by a programmed specialist. Working Paper No. 674/81, Tel Aviv University.

Ho, T.S.Y.; Schwartz, R.A.; and Whitcomb, D. 1985. The trading decision and market clearing under transactions and price uncertainty. *Journal of Finance*, March.

Mendelson, H. 1982. Market behavior in a clearing house. *Econometrica 50:* 1505–1524.

——— . 1983. Aggregation and the organization of exchange. Working Paper No. MERC 83-18, Graduate School of Management, University of Rochester.

——— . 1984a. Exchange with random quantities and discrete prices. Working Paper, Graduate School of Management, University of Rochester.

——— . 1984b. Consolidation, fragmentation and market liquidity. Working Paper, Graduate School of Management, University of Rochester.

Mendelson, M.; Peake, J.W.; and Williams, R.T. 1979. Toward a modern exchange: The Peake-Mendelson-Williams proposal for an electronically-assisted auction market. In E. Bloch and R.A. Schwartz, eds., *Impending changes for securities markets*, Greenwich, Conn.: JAI Press, pp. 53–74.

Noyes Data Corporation. 1973. *European Stock Exchange handbook.*

Smidt, S. 1971. Which road to an efficient stock market: Free competition or regulated monopoly? *Financial Analysts Journal* (September–October):18–20, 64–69.

Spray, D.E. 1964. *The principal stock exchanges of the world: Their operation, structure and development.* Washington, D.C.: International Economic Publishers.

Tinic, S.M., and West, R.R. 1979. *Investing in securities: An efficient market approach.* Reading, Mass.: Addison-Wesley.

US. Securities and Exchange Commission. 1971. *Institutional investor study report.* Washington, D.C.: U.S. Government Printing Office.

Whitcomb, D.K. 1985. An international comparison of stock exchange trading. (Chapter 16.)

16
An International Comparison of Stock Exchange Trading Structures

David K. Whitcomb

T he purpose of this chapter is to classify, contrast, and analyze the
fundamental trading structures found in stock exchanges around the
world. The information was gathered largely during visits (in 1980–
1981 and 1983) to sixteen stock exchanges on four continents.[1]

My focus is on the basic design of trading structures, because the way in
which orders are aggregated and price determined critically affects every
dimension of the services stock markets provide and is inextricably inter-
twined with the roles of the major market participants. For example, the
degree and quality of price and volume information disseminated vary widely
across stock exchanges in a way that is easily explained by the trading system
design, the relative importance of dealer versus public limit orders in "making
the market," and the degree of concentration among dealers. Similarly, the
kinds of stabilization offered depend directly (but of course not exclusively)
on trading system design.

The first part of the chapter presents a classification and analysis of the
fundamental types of exchange order handling and price determination systems. The next two parts examine two major categories of service provided by
stock exchanges: price (and volume) information and stabilization. Besides sur-
veying the extent and type of service provided, I explore the interaction between these services and the basic trading structure in an effort to explain some
of the differences that have been observed. Table 16–1 summarizes a good deal
of information concerning trading systems, hours of operation, various exchange services (including some I do not have space to consider here), and off-
exchange trading in the sixteen exchange markets. The final part is a brief conclusion that emphasizes the reasons for the existence of the various trading
structures and different levels of exchange service surveyed here.

Classification and Analysis of Trading Systems

There are several alternative ways to classify the tremendous variety of order
aggregation and price determination systems we observe. Perhaps the most

Table 16-1
Summary of Exchange Trading Systems and Services

	Trading System								Hours
	Batch				Continuous				
					Matching			Dealer	
	Criee	Written	at Opening	Number of Calls/d	Matching Order Book	Board	Crowd		
AMEX				1	Y				10:00–16:00
Amsterdam									
Bonds and Freq. Traded Stks.			Y+	2	Y				10:00–12:15 12:45–16:30
Infreq. Tr. Stks.		Y		2					11:30–12:15 12:45–13:30
Brussels									
Forward	Y+	Y+		1			Y*		12:30–IRR
Cash:Corbeille		Y+		1		Y	Y*		12:50–IRR
Cash: Parquet		Y		1		Y			13:10–IRR
Frankfurt									
Freq. Tr.			Y	1	Y				11:30–13:30
Infreq. Tr.		Y		1					12:00–12:15
Hong Kong						Y			9:30–12:30
London								Y	9:30–15:30 Phone: 15:30–17:30
Luxembourg	Y			1			Y		Stks: 12:00–13:00 Bonds: 11:00–13:00
Montreal			Y	1		Y			10:00–16:00
NYSE			Y	1	Y				10:00–16:00
Paris									
Forward	Y+			1			Y		12:30–14:30
Cash: par oppos.	Y	Y		1	Y		Y		16:00–17:00 U.S. Stocks 12:30–14:30
Cash: par cassier		Y		1	Y				Bonds: 11:30–12:30 Stks: 12:30–14:30
Unlisted		Y		1					12:30–14:30
Sydney	Y					Y			10:00–12:00 14:00–15:00
Tel-Aviv	Y	Y+		1					13:00–IRR
Tokyo									
Gekitaku	Y+			4					9:00–11:00 13:00–15:00
Other First and Second Section			Y+	2			Y		9:00–11:00 13:00–15:00 Foreign: 10:30–11:00 14:30–15:00
Toronto									
Floor Trading			Y	1		Y			10:00–16:00
CATS			Y+	1	Y				10:00–16:00
Vienna									
Freq. Tr.			Y	1	Y				10:30–12:45
Infreq. Tr.				1	Y				12:15–12:45
Zurich		Y+					Y		9:30–10:00 (unlisted) 10:00–IRR (listed)

	Stabilization			Oft. Mkt. Maker	Type of P, V Information Available	Cash v. Fwd.	Settlement		Off Exchange Trading	
	Max. P. Chg. Lim.	Indi-cation	Batch Trading				Period	Bk. Entry Transfer	In House	Blocks
AMEX	N	Y	N	AO	T, BA, NPV	C	5d.	N	Y, 19c.3	L
Amsterdam										
Bonds and Freq. Traded Stks.	10%	Y	N	Y	P, I, NPV	C	5d.	Y	N	PT
Infreq. Tr. Stks.	10%	Y	Y	Y	P, NPV	C	5d.	Y	N	PT
Brussels										
Forward	N	Y	N	N	T-, NPV	F	<2w.	Y	N	L
Cash: Corbeille	10%	Y	Y	Y	T-, NPV	C	1d.	Y	N	L
Cash: Parquet	2–5%	N	Y	Y	T-, NPV	C	1d.	Y	N	L
Frankfurt										
Freq. Tr.	N	Y	N	N	P, BA, NPV	C	2d.	Y	Y (bonds)	L (stocks)
Infreq. Tr.	N	Y	Y	N	P-, NPV	C	2d.	Y	Y (bonds)	Y (bonds)
Hong Kong	N	N	N	N	T, BA, NPV	C	1d.	N	N	L
London	N	N	N	Y	MS, NP	F	<2w.	N	Y	PT
Luxembourg	2–10%	Y	Y	N	NPV	C	1–6d.	Y	Y	Y
Montreal	N	N	N	Y	T, BA, NPV	C	5d.	N	N	L
NYSE	N	Y	N	AO	T, BA, NPV	C	5d.	N	Y, 19c.3	L
Paris										
Forward	5–10%	Y	Y	N	T-, NPV	F	<3w. +contango	Y, 80%	N	N
Cash: par oppos.	5–10%	N	Y	Y	T-, NPV	C	1d.	Y, 80%	N	N
Cash: par cassier	5–10%	N	Y	Y	T-, NPV	C	1d.	Y, 80%	N	N
Unlisted	5–10%	N	Y	Y	T-, NPV	C	1d.	Y, 80%	N	N
Sydney	N	N	N	N	T, BA, NPV	F	<2w.	N	N	L
Tel-Aviv	5–10%	Y	Y	N	T-, NPV	C	1d.	Y	NOB	L
Tokyo										
Gekitaku	N	Y	Y	N	T, I, NPV	C	3d.	N	N	PT
Other First and Second Section	20%	Y	N	N	T, O, NPV	C	3d.	N	N	PT
Toronto										
Floor Trading	N	N	N	AO	T, BA, NPV	C	5d.	N	N	L
CATS	N	Y	N	AO	T, I, O, NPV	C	5d.	N	N	L
Vienna										
Freq. Tr.	5%	Y	Y	N	P, I, BA, NP	F	<7d.	N.	Y	L
Infreq. Tr.	5%	Y	Y	N	P, I, BA, NP	F	<7d.	N	Y	L
Zurich	N	Y	N	N	P, BA, NPV	C	5d.	BSO	Y	Y
						F	<2m.	BSO		

Table 16–1 continued

Key

Y	=	Yes
Y+	=	Orders may be modified after trial P given
Y*	=	Orders may be labeled "opening only"
N	=	No
IRR	=	Closing hours irregular; closes when last issue called and no further orders received
AO	=	Mkt. makers with "affirmative obligation"
NA	=	Not available
T	=	On-line transaction record
T–	=	On-line transaction record, most volume at opening
P	=	On-line trans. prices
P–	=	On-line prices only, most volume at opening
BA	=	Bid-ask quotes available
I	=	Preopening "indication" P
NPV	=	Newspaper price and volume report
NP	=	Newspaper price report, no volume
MS	=	On-line midspread quotation
O	=	Open limit order book
C	=	Cash
F	=	Forward
BSO	=	Book entry transfer for bearer shares only
NOB	=	Netting orders before opening/call only
L	=	Limited off-exchange block trading (very large size or other special conditions)
PT	=	"Put-throughs"

useful for further analysis is to begin with a dichotomy between batch (or periodic call) trading and so-called continuous trading. I then further classify continuous systems according to whether they are primarily dealer systems or primarily matching systems. At a lower level of classification, I explore matters of trading technology that distinguish different types of batch and of continuous markets.

Batch (Periodic Call) Trading

In batch trading, orders are allowed to accumulate over time, rather than being transacted immediately, and are then *called* in a multilateral transaction at a single price. Calls are commonly made in rotation at prespecified times once a day, although several exchanges have more frequent calls,[2] and nothing in principle prevents less frequent calls or irregular intervals between calls.

Call markets exist for at least some securities, in all the exchanges we studied in continental Europe (except Zurich) Israel, and Japan (six heavily traded securities only). In addition, the opening transaction in the continuous trading systems in the United States, Canada, and Japan is a batch trade. All the call markets studied are primarily of the matching type; that is, public orders submitted through a broker or banker acting as agent make the market, and dealer or designated market maker orders are of secondary importance.[3]

Orders submitted to a call market state the quantity bid or offered and a limit price (unless they are designated as market orders).[4] Price is determined in the way described in elementary economics textbooks: The auctioneer aggregates demand and supply at each price and seeks a price that equates supply and demand. Because price is not a continuous variable (only integer or one-eighth and so forth prices are allowed and/or the number of separate orders is limited as a result of order cost), there may be no price that exactly equates supply and demand, and rules for the allocation of excess supply or demand must be stated. Most exchanges allocate by random selection of those heavy-side orders that are to be satisfied, although some specify that all market orders and those limit orders better than the batch price will be satisfied.[5] Nearly all exchanges set a minimum fulfillment proportion (for example, 25 percent) that must be met for a transaction to be permitted. Some disseminate information about excess demand or supply in order to encourage floor traders to enter additional orders on the light side before the batch transaction.[6]

The most important distinction in trading technology to be made among batch trading regimes is between verbal and written auctions. Paris, for example, has both, using a verbal auction (*a la criee*) for its more frequently traded issues and a written auction (*par cassiers*) for thinner issues. In a verbal auction, the auctioneer shouts out the name of the security and a price (for example, yesterday's call price), to which brokers and floor traders respond by crying out quantity bids and offers. If the number of shares bid exceeds the number of shares offered at this trial price, the auctioneer raises the price, and vice versa.[7] In a written auction, traders often are unable to respond to trial prices;[8] the auctioneer merely assembles written orders, sets the price that most nearly equates supply and demand, and reports executed trades to the parties.

Hence the distinction between verbal and written auctions is more one of behavior than one of mechanics.[9] It is no accident that the verbal auction is used for issues where relatively heavy volume is expected; for such issues, the cost of an iterative price discovery process is outweighed by the benefit to traders of being able to tailor their price, quantity orders precisely to the call price that will actually rule.[10]

Because information regarding stocks and the general market arrives throughout the day, many batch trading exchanges provide for call-backs (at least for their more heavily traded stocks) following the call. Generally, any floor trader may request a call-back for a stock that has already been called (by crying out its name in the ring where verbal calls are conducted or by approaching the order clerk in charge of the written call). If a crossing counterpart order is in the crowd or on the order book, a bilateral trade is effected and the regular call rotation continues.[11]

Continuous Trading

In a continuous trading system, transactions occur whenever a buy and a sell order cross (that is, the buy limit price equals or exceeds the sell price or one or more is a market order). All securities are traded continuously in the United Kingdom and its present and former colonies (notably the United States) and in Zurich; all but six are so traded in Japan; and many (relatively heavily traded stocks) are so traded in Amsterdam, Brussels, Frankfurt, and Vienna.

The main distinction within continuous markets is between *dealer* systems, where one or more intermediaries acting as principals make the market by servicing the ultimate investor's order from inventory, and *matching* systems, where intermediaries act as agents for the ultimate investors. Many matching systems allow for official market makers (specialists, dealers, and so on), but they are not solely or even primarily dealer markets because ordinary investors' limit orders can effectively compete with those of dealers.

Major examples of dealer stock markets are the London Stock Exchange and the U.S. over-the-counter market.[12] A London jobber (dealer—normally two or three to a stock) writes his midspread price (that is, he discloses publicly the price midway between his bid and offer price but does not disclose the size of the spread) for each stock he deals on a chalkboard above his post. Under London's single-capacity rule, jobbers must act only as principals and brokers only as agents. Floor brokers holding customer orders get bid and ask quotations (but without quantity offers) from competing jobbers without disclosing their specific trading intentions. The broker selects the best counterpart jobber quotation and must offer the entire order to that one jobber who will ordinarily take the full amount of the order at the quoted price as long as it involves no more than $250,000–$500,000. If the order is larger, the broker can ask how much the jobber will take at this quoted price and, if it is insufficient, either permit the jobber to take a portion and to put the rest on his book as a limit order,[13] or himself find a counterpart (for example, off-exchange) and put the arranged trade through the jobber.[14]

A long and expensive court case, in which the U.K. Office of Fair Trading (OFT) sought to void the London Stock Exchange's single capacity rule and fixed commission rates, was settled in August 1983. In addition to familiar arguments on fixed commissions, OFT briefs and draft testimony asserted that single capacity and the lack of a means of advertising public limit orders lead to insufficient competition in the dealership function. As a result of the settlement and of competitive pressure from foreign securities firms and British banks, fixed commission rates will be phased out by the end of 1986, member firms will be allowed to act in dual capacity, and an automated quotation system (SEAQ) explicitly patterned on NASDAQ will be installed. These structural changes will rapidly transform the London Stock Exchange into a market like the OTC National Market, with a number of competing (and heavily capitalized) dealers offering on-line firm quotes in large size. The implications for international trading are considerable.

Matching systems invariably have dealers (in the sense of professional traders who are usually willing to supply immediacy by trading to or from inventory), but public limit orders are given equal or preferred status. In some exchanges (notably Tokyo), dealers have no official status, whereas in the United States markets official dealers (specialists) compete with other dealers and with public limit orders. The specialist's role is complicated because it is multifaceted: order book clerk, sole owner of valuable demand information, and stabilizer. The important parts of the specialist's role will be discussed in the next two sections, but it should be noted here that when the role is limited to that of order book clerk (as it is for Tokyo's *saitori*), it becomes mechanical and can be performed by a computer.

Indeed, the entire operation of a so-called pure order-matching exchange can be automated, as Toronto's and Tokyo's Computer Assisted Trading Systems (CATS) demonstrate.[15] Both CATS are used for a large group of relatively less heavily traded stocks in each market (in Tokyo, Second Section stocks and, by mid-1985, all but 250 First Section stocks). Perhaps we can more easily understand the mechanics of the price determination process in a matching market and the behavioral impact of automation by considering these systems. CATS trading orders are entered on remote terminals (in brokers' offices) and relayed to the order book computer. The computer disseminates a display of the order book to remote terminals,[16] effects a transaction whenever counterpart orders cross, and prints transaction reports for brokers and the clearance system. Trading in non-CATS stocks on the Tokyo First Section operates in a structurally identical manner, although the order book clerk is human and the order book is only open to visual inspection by brokers on the floor.

Although the U.S. exchanges are also of the order-matching type, they differ behaviorally from the model described in several ways:

1. Computers assist (but do not literally effect) the execution of small orders.
2. As mentioned, the specialist has additional roles.
3. The order book is not open (although best bid and ask prices are disseminated electronically, and the specialist may give some depth information to floor traders).
4. There is occasional crowd trading, largely for some high-volume stocks on the NYSE.

By *crowd trading*, I mean bilateral bargains made by brokers and floor traders (agent or principal) who meet at the specialist's post but do not enter their orders on the book. Crowd trading is inconsistent with time priorities (which do not exist on the NYSE anyway); it appears to serve the needs of large traders and probably provides dealership competition to the specialist.[17] The Zurich Stock Exchange and most commodity and futures exchanges have a pure crowd trading system. In Zurich, brokers come to the trading ring (each stock is assigned to one of these) holding discretionary orders. The official clerk opens trading in an issue by crying its name, but does not call out prices or seek to reach a demand-supply balance. The traders call out bids and asks and reach essentially bilateral deals (hence there may be several prices in the first few minutes of trading, rather than the single price characterizing *a la criée* batch trading). The tendency to batch at the opening is reduced by the complete freedom to engage in off-exchange trading in Zurich. For the same reason, daily exchange volume is rather small in Zurich, but several commodity exchanges manage tremendous volume with a crowd trading system.[18]

A final variant on the matching system is *board trading,* found in Canada (except CATS), Hong Kong, Australia, and Singapore. In a board trading system, brokers or an exchange employee enter order prices on a chalk or electronic board. The essential features distinguishing board trading from order book trading are:

1. Traders do not reveal the sizes of their orders and are responsible for honoring only one board lot.

2. There is no special procedure for opening the market (brokers merely begin posting their bids and offers).

In the Hong Kong version, the exchange merely provides a room, telephones, and TV monitors (to scan the board); and it investigates complaints.

Price Information Systems

In this section I will survey the types (degree) of price information provided, discuss the need for such information and the types needed in different trading structures, and consider the interaction between price information systems and the basic trading structure.

Degree of Price/Volume Information Provided

Table 16–1 summarizes the types of price and volume information offered by the various exchanges, with an indication of how rapidly or broadly it is disseminated. Nearly every exchange reports price and volume at the end of the day via an exchange-published newspaper and/or the commercial press (keyed as NPV in table 16–1), while a few report only price (NP). Most now also provide an on-line transaction record (T) by entering prices and volumes collected from traders or auctioneers into a computer system that transmits the information to leased remote terminals or to commercial vendors such as Dow-Jones, Reuters, or Telekurs. An on-line record is less useful in a batch trading exchange (since once a price is recorded, the day's trading is mostly over), so that is marked (T −). Some exchanges report prices on-line, but not volume (P).

Price information can also be reported in advance of transactions. Most continuous auction exchanges (and the U.S. OTC market) report best bid and ask quotations (BA), although, as mentioned, the London Stock Exchange prior to 1986 reports only the midspread quote (MS).[19] This information is more valuable if it represents the entire order flow (as in exchanges that limit crowd trading), if the market's depth (average quantity offered) at the quotes is large, and if it is disseminated on line to remote terminals. In a batch market, or at the opening in a continuous market, the equivalent information is an *indicated* price (I), the price at which a transaction would occur were it allowed at the given moment. This is always available to floor traders in a verbal call (although it is unavailable or useless off the floor because of the rapidity of the price-making process) and is sometimes made available in a written call. A preopening indication is the only information discussed so far that is not available on line in the U.S. markets.

The most complete information is provided by opening the limit order book (in either call or continuous markets) to general inspection, concealing only the identities of traders so as to keep the market anonymous. At this writing, only Tokyo (both sections) and Toronto's CATS have completely open books, and only CATS makes feasible on-line dissemination to remote terminals.

Need for On-line Price/Volume Information

The value of instant price information may seem obvious to traders, but academics might wish to have conditions stated under which small (atomistic) traders care, since their orders may not affect price materially. Ho, Schwartz, and Whitcomb (1984) show that when transaction prices are uncertain and ordering costs prevent investors from transmitting their entire demand functions (for example, when you order by stating a simple price and quantity), investors cannot generally place optimal orders (in the individual or in the collective—Pareto—sense). The value of on-line limit order book information has been demonstrated in the simulation model of Cohen, Maier, Schwartz and Whitcomb (1983). This work shows that a trader can formulate profitable trading rules using order book information and at the same time reduce a security's overall price volatility.

Interaction between Price Information System and Trading System

A major point that emerged from the visits to stock exchanges and the discussions with exchange officials, brokers, and bankers was the extent to which the degree of price/volume information provided and the usefulness of that information depend on the basic structure of the trading system, and vice versa. An example, already mentioned, is the fact that an on-line transaction record is less useful when the basic structure is batch trading. There are other examples as well.

In an oligopolistic dealer market, there is a strong incentive not to disseminate much information on line. This is because, with few dealers, one dealer can estimate the others' inventory positions from a transaction record and can then devise trading strategies.[20] The resulting trading behavior may harm all dealers (in a manner akin to introducing price competition in a classical duopoly) and lead them collectively to oppose information dissemination. Such an incentive is eliminated as the number of dealers per stock increases. This observation may provide an economic explanation for the fact that on-line bid-ask and transaction information is available in the U.S. OTC market (and in most nondealer markets) but not (until 1986) on the London Stock Exchange, where the number of dealers per stock is small. It is also clear that in any market where dealers receive the order flow and are in control of information dissemination, there is incentive not to facilitate competition by exposing the limit orders of public traders. On the other hand, when brokers (as agents) control information dissemination, the incentive is to expand trading by exposing all orders.

Floor traders also have an incentive to oppose on-line dissemination of information. The less information is available off the floor, the more important is the role of the floor trader as agent for discretionary orders and the greater are his potential trading profits as principal. Since fully automated trading systems disseminate information with equal rapidity to all locations, it is not surprising that floor traders are unenthusiastic. They are rational, not backward.[21] It is also not surprising that the automated trading systems that exist at present serve mainly low-volume securities (where discretionary orders are uncommon) and small transaction sizes.[22] On the other hand, Instinet has for a long time been able to attract block orders in major stocks to its automated institutional trading system. Now that it also offers automated execution of small orders (up to 1000 shares) at the inside spread, its institutional order book gets first crack at the considerable flow of small orders passing through and is likely to attract substantially more volume.

Stabilization Mechanisms

This section will examine the types of stabilization mechanism used in the various stock exchanges, consider how the design of the trading system affects the sort of stabilization offered and the role of official market makers as stabilizers, and finally turn to the unresolved issue of whether stabilization (beyond what is provided automatically by limit orders and speculation) is desirable.

Types of Stabilization Mechanism

The most common and perhaps the most primitive type of stabilization is by maximum price change limits. Under this mechanism, no transaction that would cause a price change exceeding a specified percentage of the previous day's closing or batch price is allowed (see table 16–1 for the percentage or ranges in those exchanges using price limits). If no trade is allowed under these rules on one day, the previous day's price plus or minus the specified percentage becomes the base for the next day's allowed price change. In this way, regardless of the size of the change in equilibrium prices, a day must come when trading is allowed.[23] Although the rationale for maximum price change limits may be elusive to those of us schooled in the efficient-market hypothesis, price limits do ensure the widest dissemination of information relating to a stock's value before a major price change is allowed. It is debatable whether the equity gains from this outweigh the efficiency losses. Closing the market also creates an incentive for off-exchange trading, which may make it costly for an exchange to offer this stabilization method.

A few exchanges halt trading temporarily when an "excessive" price would otherwise occur, "indicate" a price, accumulate orders for 10 or 20 minutes, and then resume trading with no price limit. This has a purpose similar to that of the preopening price indication mentioned earlier: to publicize "bargains," so as to let stabilizing orders come in if they will.

A number of exchanges (see table 16–1) have official market makers (Specialists in the U.S., Professional Traders in Toronto, Hoekmen in Amsterdam, and so on) who are given some sort of special position (for example, lower transaction costs, favored access to information regarding the order flow, lesser restrictions on short selling). All markets have professional traders, of course, but presumably the purpose of those exchanges that create a special position is to encourage this activity in the hope that it will lead to greater liquidity or more stable prices. One mechanism by which this might occur is what Cohen, Maier, Schwartz and Whitcomb (1983) call "stabilizing speculation" by market makers with knowledge of the limit order book. As mentioned earlier, our simulation shows that such traders can formulate mechanical trading rules that earn them profits (thereby giving incentive for their trading) and simultaneously reduce the security's price volatility.[24]

U.S. exchanges go further and give specialists an "affirmative obligation" to stabilize by holding them responsible if transaction-to-transaction price changes or price changes over each 1,000 shares traded exceed certain limits.[25] Since it is difficult to measure the separate stabilization outputs of multiple specialists, affirmative obligation stabilization, unlike market making, would appear to be a natural monopoly. It is necessary to compensate the specialist for stabilization losses (which U.S. exchanges do by commissions and by granting sole access to order book information) unless some means can be found to charge directly for the service.

A final stabilization method is unique to Tel Aviv. There, banks have traditionally stabilized their own shares by making purchases and sales in the market. This is generally illegal elsewhere (imagine this tool in the hands of an Alan Bond or a T. Boone Pickens!). It came to grief in Israel in fall 1983 because the banks tried to peg instead of merely to stabilize, nearly bankrupting themselves in the process, and a government bailout ensued.

Interaction between Stabilization and Trading Systems

The fundamental design of the trading and price information system affects the need for supplementary stabilization as well as the type of stabilization offered. For example, batch trading systems provide temporal concentration of the order flow, which ought to reduce trade-to-trade and daily price volatility, all else being equal. By using public limit orders to provide counterpart liquidity, batch trading should also reduce the possible role of professional market making, and it appears to do just that. On the other hand, existing batch trading systems do not generally provide price information that is timely enough to be of use in trading decisions made off the floor. This is why it is mainly those exchanges that use batch trading for at least some stocks that impose daily maximum price change limits.

Among continuous trading systems, the role of the market maker in stabilization also depends on the structure of the trading system. In markets with official market makers, there is an affirmative obligation to stabilize only when market makers have an exclusive franchise on the stocks they handle because only then can the stabilization output be assessed. Similarly, affirmative obligation stabilization cannot be maintained in the face of off-exchange trading (which reduces the traditional compensation offered stabilizers).[26] In addition, proponents of pure dealer markets would maintain that well-financed dealers can easily provide all the stabilization needed to prevent runs caused by liquidity-motivated trades, and proponents of pure order book markets would assert that their limit order books are thicker, *ceteris paribus,* than those of mixed exchanges.

What Type(s) and Mechanism(s) of Stabilization Are Desirable?

Many academicians, in keeping with their general belief that competitive market prices are Fama efficient and Pareto optimal, would argue that only the so-called automatic stabilization that comes as a by-product of the existence of the limit order book and the profit-motivated trading of professional traders (who may be either selling immediacy or speculating) is desirable. All, I think, would agree that maximum price change limits with full-day trading halts are undesirable; with current information transmission technology, preopening indications and occasional brief trading halts with indicated prices are sufficient to ensure efficient and equitable responses to major news.

My own opinion is that affirmative obligation stabilization may be desirable because it is a public-good externality that may be undersupplied in a competitive market.[27] Stabilization reduces systematic risk, which would be desirable to present shareholders if it could be done at a cost less than the aggregate gain in value. In addition, a reduction in clearing price uncertainty leads to more nearly optimal orders. Because stabilization is indivisible, however, individual shareholders cannot effectively be charged via the price system that works for ordinary private goods. The U.S. specialist system seeks to solve the problem by imposing stabilization as a joint product of exchange listing, but there is no reason to believe the pricing system is optimal.

In my opinion, the solution to determining via the marketplace whether the benefits of stabilization exceed the costs and, if so, to charging for it appropriately, would be to let the decision concerning whether and how much to stabilize be made and the cost paid by the issuer of the stock. As with other corporate expenditures, all those who expect to benefit will be forced to pay. The role of the stock exchange would be to prevent fear of possible manipulation by interposing itself between the issuer and the stabilizer.

Conclusion

This chapter has focused on the fundamental structure of exchange trading systems and their interaction with the price information and stabilization services exchanges offer. Such a focus makes it possible to go beyond merely describing the various structures and services and to explain why features exist in the combinations they do.

The most pervasive structural difference among exchanges is between batch and continuous trading systems. Batch trading seems to exist (at least for the relatively thin securities to which it is best adapted) in markets where the brokerage sector is fairly concentrated, as is the case in continental Europe, where the major banks do most of the broking. A possible reason for this lies in the fact that accumulating orders for batch trading gives the broker expected-price information of value to his own-account trading if the broker is large enough to see a meaningful sample of the order flow.[28]

The choice between a verbal and a written batch auction reflects a trade-off between the greater personnel cost of the former and the superior price information it provides floor traders. For frequently traded stocks, the benefits normally exceed the costs, which explains the distribution across stocks of verbal versus written auctions. Technological change is rapidly eroding this trade-off, however; with automated trading, it is possible to provide indicated prices to all traders. Thus professional floor traders in either batch or continuous markets are likely to accept automated trading most readily for thin securities where their loss of the informational advantage from conventional trading may be balanced by cost savings.

In continuous markets, the dealer-matching distinction largely determines the extent of price and volume information made available. Where a few dealers get the entire public order flow for a stock, there is a powerful competitive incentive to avoid on-line transmission of quotation and transaction price information, whereas in competitive dealer or matching markets such information can only increase the public order flow, with gains to dealers and brokers. Where a matching system also incorporates an official market maker, however, there is an incentive for that market maker to retain possession of order book density information; hence an open limit order book is offered only in pure matching systems.

Stabilization mechanisms are also strongly affected by market structure. Batch trading provides some automatic stabilization and reduces the potential role of market makers in stabilization. Because batch trading (absent electronic dissemination of indicated prices) provides poor price information, batch trading exchanges frequently use price change limits to stabilize by equalizing the information flow following a major event. Markets where dealers or market makers have an important role (even if it is only to supplement the public limit order flow) do not use daily price change limits. Instead, such markets encourage market makers to engage in so-called stabilizing speculation and, in the U.S., in affirmative obligation stabilization.

Although I suggested a design for effective stabilization and commented on the nature and extent of information dissemination needed, I did not state a preferred type of fundamental trading structure. There may be no single trading structure that is ideal for all situations, but I believe some of the trading mechanisms we have observed abroad, combined with available technology, can have important applications in U.S. exchanges. Developing these applications, however, is far beyond the scope of this chapter.

Notes

1. The visits were funded by a grant from the New York Stock Exchange to Thomas Ho, Robert Schwartz, and me. We are grateful to Dr. William Freund of the NYSE for introductions and to the senior executives and staffs of the exchanges for spending substantial amounts of time with us. I am grateful to my two coinvestigators for their major insights into the processes we studied together. This chapter is part of a larger body of work we have been doing together (see Ho, Schwartz, and Whitcomb 1981, 1985), although I take responsibility for any errors of fact or interpretation in this chapter.

2. Twice-a-day calls are held in Amsterdam, and Tokyo's *Gekitaku* market calls the six major stocks it handles four times a day (see table 16–1 for call frequencies by market). Paris, which now has once-a-day calls, may someday have an automated system with very frequent calls, under a Perouse Commission proposal.

3. A few call markets (for example, Amsterdam and the Paris *par cassier* market) have designated market makers, but their roles vary from modest intervention down to purely clerical.

4. Before the call there may not have been a transaction for a full trading day, and there are not standing bid and asked quotations to respond to. Hence market orders might seem to be quite risky, because the transaction price could be very different from what the order's maker expects. However, the practice of many exchanges of stating maximum price change limits reduces that risk and encourages market orders.

5. The latter allocation rule would appear superior because it would reduce (costly) recontracting by giving stock in the intial trade to those who want it most. According to the analysis of Ho, Schwartz, and Whitcomb (1985), *initial*-round behavior is unaffected by the allocation rule, since in batch trading under transaction price

uncertainty investors determine their order prices from their reservation price demand curves, using their predictions of the actual transaction price as an input. There is no reason to believe the allocation rule will affect the predicted price.

6. Frankfurt, Vienna, and Tokyo's *Gekitaku* (batch trading in six large issues) do not permit a batched trade unless supply exactly equals demand. Although this pressures traders to enter balancing orders, it does not always lead to a trade.

7. Economists will recognize this price-discovery process as a Walrasian tatonnement. A large body of literature (see, for example, Arrow and Hurwicz 1958; Davis and Whinston 1966; and Whitcomb 1972, chap. 5) explores conditions under which a tatonnement attains Pareto-efficient prices in an informationally decentralized manner (you do not have to submit your entire demand curve to Big Brother, just respond to his trial prices). Another large body of economic literature explores the very different price setting process in one-sided auctions (exemplified by the sealed-bid auction for Treasury bills) (see Vickrey 1962, Wilson 1967, and Milgrom 1979).

8. A few exchanges permit traders in certain written-auction stocks to modify their orders in response to trial prices; these are indicated in table 16–1 by a Y + symbol.

9. The fact that the distinction is behavioral is emphasized by considering the batched opening procedure in Toronto's automated CATS (Computer Assisted Trading System). Entering orders on a terminal is technically equivalent to writing; but because trial prices are displayed and orders can be changed up to the time of the opening batch transaction, the procedure is behaviorally equivalent to a verbal auction.

10. Another way of putting it would be to say that the iterative (tatonnement) price-discovery process eliminates transaction price uncertainty (although of course it does not change uncertainty about future value). That this is of value to traders (including atomistic investors) and that its absence leads to Pareto inefficiency in the sense of a demand for costly recontracting is demonstrated formally by Ho, Schwartz, and Whitcomb (1985).

11. Table 16–1 identifies those sections of exchanges offering batch trading and call backs with a Y in *both* the appropriate batch trading column and the "Continuous:Crowd" column.

12. The OTC market is studied by Thomas Ho in chapter 3 of this book, and is of course not a stock exchange (in the sense of a marketplace), since it is a geographically dispersed telephone market with a computer information linkage. For these reasons, I mention it only as it is relevant to contrast its design and behavior with that of the London Stock Exchange.

13. Only orders large enough to exceed a jobber's inventory capacity are accorded *displayed limit order* (my phrase) status. A customer may always give his broker a limit price, but jobbers will not advertise the existence of limit prices better than their own by posting them on their boards, and no other effective means exists for displaying such orders in the London market. Hence ordinary investors cannot compete on equal terms with jobbers. Whether it is much easier to advertise a small (investor) limit order through the U.S. OTC NASDAQ system is unclear to me. There is clearly greater competition among OTC dealers, however, and a better price information system.

14. Put-through rules (in force in several exchanges; see table 16–1) serve a dual purpose: They tie the on- and off-exchange markets together, and they provide revenue to official market makers. It can, of course, be argued that one party to an

off-exchange block transaction always has an incentive to offer part of the block to anyone on the exchange who can give a better price than the block counterpart, and is prevented from doing this only by diseconomies of small-scale transactions. Put-throughs would then be seen as an uneconomical linkage of the on- and off-exchange markets. This argument ascribes no public-goods value to the information provided by forcing the transaction onto the exchange.

15. The Toronto and Tokyo systems are similar, but Tokyo provides continued employment for its saitori by letting them override computer-arranged trades that violate the exchange's maximum allowable price change rules. However, they can place the system on "automatic pilot."

16. The display shows the price and size of each order with the broker's iden-tification (but not the customer's). A Toronto trader may elect to conceal any part of his order beyond a board lot (100 shares) at the cost that the undisclosed part of the order goes to the end of the time priority trading queue at that price. At the opening, the prices on buy orders above and sell orders below the indicated crossing price are not identified, and time priorities are not observed.

17. Crowd trading is limited (and the book is made thicker) in Tokyo by a rule that allows interbroker floor trading only for orders that are between the book quotes.

18. See Smidt (1984) for comparative volume figures and more detail on com-modity and futures trading.

19. The on-line bid and ask quotations represent prices at which small traders can sell and buy, respectively, with perfect certainty via market order (although one may occasionally do better in the U.S. markets if the specialist executes the order against a simultaneous counterpart market order or against his own account). Limit order traders can also use the quotes in stating their own prices; one can increase his probability of transacting by setting a limit price inside the quotes. See Cohen, Maier, Schwartz and Whitcomb (1981) for an analysis of the trader's pricing strategy decision and its implications for the bid-ask spread in a matching market, and Ho and Stoll (1983) for a dealer-market analysis.

20. The competing dealer model of Ho and Stoll (1983) shows how one dealer uses his competitors' "reservation fees" in setting his own quotes. Ho and Stoll note (their footnote 4) that these so-called reservation fees can be calculated from knowledge of dealer inventory positions, which in turn can be inferred from observed transactions.

21. Floor traders with experience on Toronto's CATS report that its somewhat complicated edit procedures make it slower than trading would be on the floor, although it is faster to use CATS than to phone orders in from remote locations. Thus CATS neutralizes an advantage floor traders have over others.

22. There are other reasons as well for automation's concentration on small securities and small orders. When order sizes are large, trading is typically done by quiet negotiation rather than public advertising of order prices. This fact appears to account in part for the failure of the EUREX automated Eurobond trading system and the small size of the NYSE's Automated Bond System. In addition, when a security has frequent heavy volume, crowd trading is common. A person interacting with crowd trading from a remote terminal may be at a speed disadvantage (see note 21).

23. The reaction on the Bourse de Paris following the election of Socialist Presi-dent Mitterand on Sunday, May 10, 1981, makes an interesting example. Hardly any stocks traded on Monday or Tuesday, so most were marked down at least 20 percent

before trading at their new equilibrium level on Wednesday. Their subsequent price behavior suggests that the two- to three-day trading delay allowed the market to reach a consensus without as much movement of price around the new equilibrium as seems to characterize markets without price-change limits. (I am not aware of a careful test of this hypothesis, however.)

24. Of course, professional traders may use fundamental analysis or other forms of technical analysis than the one we simulated. Some but not necessarily all of these trading strategies may be stabilizing. In a market without barriers to entry by such traders, an economist would expect that the last (or least talented) one to enter would make a normal risk-adjusted return on his investment of time and capital, and hence that the market would be efficient.

25. The limits vary from stock to stock according to its size, measured by price and transaction volume, hence relating the objective to what is feasible to attain.

26. Off-exchange trading has the further effect of making price more volatile if there is imperfect arbitrage among the satellite markets. (For a formal proof, see Mendelson 1984).

27. This line of reasoning is developed in more detail in Cohen, Maier, Schwartz and Whitcomb (1977).

28. This explanation was advanced during an interchange with Professor Seymour Smidt at the conference on "Trading Mechanisms in Securities Exchanges: Towards the Era of Sophisticated Automation" at Tel-Aviv University, January 1984. Zurich, which I did not classify as a batch trading exchange because it uses a crowd system of bilateral bargains, might appear to be an exception, since it has a concentrated brokerage sector. However, Zurich still fits the rule, since stocks are called once a day, so banks get to accumulate orders. The call-backs that most call markets allow for frequently traded stocks are simply a necessary response to the potential off-exchange competition created by batching.

References

Arrow, K.J., and Hurwicz, L. 1958. On the stability of competitive equilibrium: I. *Econometrica* 26 (October):522–552.

Cohen, K.J.; Maier, S.F.; Schwartz, R.A.; and Whitcomb, D.K. 1977. The impact of designated market makers on security prices: II. Policy Proposals. *Journal of Banking and Finance* 1:219–235.

——— . 1981. Transaction costs, order placement strategy and the existence of the bid-ask spread. *Journal of Political Economy* 89:287–305.

——— . 1983. A simulation model of stock exchange trading. *Simulation 41* (November):181–190.

Davis, O., and Whinston, A. 1966. On externalities, information and the government-assisted invisible hand. *Economica* (August).

Ho, T.; Schwartz, R.A.; and Whitcomb, D.K. 1981. *A comparative analysis of alternative security market trading arrangements,* Vols. I and II. New York: New York Stock Exchange.

——— . 1985. The trading decision and market clearing under transaction price uncertainty. Forthcoming, *Journal of Finance.* (March)

Ho, T. and H.R. Stoll. 1983. "The dynamics of dealer markets under competition," *Journal of Finance,* 38.

Mendelson, H. 1984. Consolidation, fragmentation and market liquidity. Working Paper, Tel-Aviv University.

Milgrom, P.R. 1979. *The structure of information in competitive bidding.* New York: Garland.

Smidt, S. 1984. The micro-ecology of floor trading on futures exchanges. Working Paper, Cornell University, January.

Vickrey, W. 1961. "Counterspeculation, auctions and competitive sealed tenders," *Journal of Finance,* 16:8–37.

Whitcomb, D.K. 1972. *Externalities and welfare.* New York: Columbia University Press.

Wilson, R. 1967. Competitive bidding with asymmetric information. *Management Science* 13:A816–A820.

17
The Evolving National Market System

Stephen L. Williams

T he *national market system* (NMS) has been developing for more than ten years. This chapter briefly traces the history of the NMS and some of the important forces that have shaped its development. The extent to which the NMS has met its objectives and the hopes held for it are evaluated. Finally, the future course of NMS development is discussed from the standpoint of the economic forces now at work, and the likely application of new (or, more precisely, newly deliverable) technology to securities trading.

Before discussing the future of the emerging NMS, it is worthwhile to review briefly how we got to where we are: where the concept of NMS came from, what were the goals of the 1975 Securities Act Amendments that made NMS a national objective, what steps have been taken to realize those goals, and to what extent the goals (and hopes) for an NMS have been fulfilled by developments to date.[1]

Origins of NMS

As far as I know, the first published reference to a *central market system* by the SEC came in a letter to Congress in 1971. The letter, which accompanied a report by the Commission on its then recently completed study of institutional investors,[2] stated, in part: "A major goal and ideal of the securities markets and the securities industry has been the creation of a strong central market system. . . ."

In retrospect, this is an extraordinarily casual first mention of a subject that would become a major preoccupation for the next decade and more. The report itself did not mention an NMS but did point out the Commission's concern with fragmented markets related to increasing institutional trading on regional exchanges, and in the third market. In particular, the Commission expressed a belief that individual investors should be able to participate in the institutional trades that often took place at prices significantly different from those prevailing in the primary markets. In addition the study concluded that the NYSE specialist system was unable to meet the demand for market-making capital in an increasingly institutionalized market, and pointed out that market makers' (including specialists') ability to participate could be inhibited by off-board trading and other rules that restricted their exposure to orders. The report alluded to an NMS by noting that "modern communications and data processing facilities [make it] possible to preserve geographically separated trading markets while at the same time tying them together on a national basis."[3]

Presumably, the SEC saw a "central market system" as the ideal solution to its concerns with fragmented markets, divergent prices, and inadequate market-making capital. The linking of all markets in a stock in some undefined but fair manner would, the Commission believed, prevent the ill effects of fragmentation while encouraging competition among market makers and increasing aggregate market-making capacity.

Once proposed, the concept of an NMS was widely supported, notwithstanding significant differences in interpretation. In 1972 the SEC began taking steps to create an NMS. By 1974 agreement was reached on the first component, the Consolidated Transaction System (CTS), which provides a facility for public dissemination of reports of completed transactions in listed securities, and implementation had begun.

Congressional Goals

In 1975 Congress passed the Securities Act Amendments of 1975, which established an NMS as an important national objective and charged the SEC with responsibility to bring it about. Congress did not, however, go as far as to actually define what the NMS would be. Instead, it set forth five goals, which it said would be achieved by linking markets:

1. Economically efficient execution of transactions.
2. Fair competition among brokers, dealers, and markets.
3. Broad availability of information with respect to quotations and transactions.
4. Practicability of executing investors' orders in the best market.
5. An opportunity for investors' orders to meet without participation of a dealer.

Economically Efficient Execution of Transactions

Congress evidently meant that transaction costs would be determined in a freely competitive environment, which would not permit uneconomically high charges. In other words, Congress was addressing cost efficiency rather than the efficiency of prices determined in the NMS. Presumably Congress assumed that appropriate prices were, and would continue to be, established in the securities markets and therefore did not see any need to address price efficiency. Efficient prices are not necessarily discovered, however, even when the markets are competitive; for further discussion, see chapter 2 by Schreiber and Schwartz.

Fair Competition among Brokers, Dealers, and Markets

Congress believed that an NMS would make it possible for regional exchange specialists and OTC market makers to provide meaningful competition to primary market specialists.

Broad Availability of Information with Respect to Quotations and Transactions

At the time the 1975 act was adopted, a consolidated transaction system was in the process of being implemented, which would provide for prompt reporting (within 90 seconds) and wide public dissemination of information regarding completed trades. Congress evidently desired that information with respect to bids and offers should be similarly available. In 1975 such bids and offers in the primary exchanges were commonly made available only to members of those exchanges.

Practicability of Executing Investors' Orders in the Best Market

Congress envisioned a number of markets or market makers engaging in price competition to attract orders. A fundamental goal of the NMS, therefore, was to provide "the ability to determine, at any given time, when a particular transaction can be effected at the most favorable price. . . ."[4]

An Opportunity for Investors' Orders to Meet Without Participation of a Dealer

The SEC had earlier proposed that the NMS should incorporate two principles: (1) protection of public limit orders (that is, every public limit order must be filled before any execution is permitted at an inferior price), and (2) priority of public orders over dealer bids and offers at the same price. Congress was apparently in general agreement, but chose to express its goals in terms of "best execution" and the opportunity for investor's orders to meet each other.[5] In any case, it is clear that Congress did not envision an NMS based on the dealer-market model of OTC markets.

Components of an NMS

The SEC has identified five components that, together with certain regulatory changes, would in its view constitute an NMS. These five components are: (1) a consolidated transaction reporting system, (2) a consolidated quotation reporting system, (3) a market linkage system (or systems), (4) a limit order protection facility, and (5) a national clearance and settlement system. Related regulatory changes would include (1) elimination of off-board trading rules, and (2) a definition of "qualifying securities." The SEC, which had already begun to press for the development of an NMS, was given additional authority in the 1975 act and a mandate to continue. Progress in implementing the various facilities was not rapid and was accompanied by controversy, but systems have been built that arguably provide most, if not all, of the features envisioned for the SEC's NMS components.

The definition of *qualifying securities*—those that are to be included in the NMS—has turned out to be inseparable from the definitions of the NMS facilities. As a result, the effective definition of qualifying securities has come to be those securities that qualify for inclusion in one or more of the NMS reporting facilities or linkage systems. As a practical matter, this turns out to be basically those securities that are listed on the New York or American Exchange, plus a few others that are listed only on a regional exchange. In addition, the SEC has designated certain OTC securities that are subject to last-sale reporting and are often referred to as NASDAQ/NMS securities.

Consolidated Transaction System (CTS)

The CTS was first proposed by the SEC in 1972. A negotiated agreement was reached in 1974, and the CTS was fully implemented in 1976. It was established by the exchanges and the NASD acting jointly through the Consolidated Tape Association (CTA) pursuant to a written plan and agreement (the CTA plan) that was filed with and approved by the SEC. This method established a pattern for subsequent development of other NMS facilities. As previously noted, CTS provides for prompt reporting and broad dissemination of transaction reports.

Consolidated Quotation System (CQS)

The CQS was developed jointly by the exchanges and the NASD in 1978, and is also operated under a formal plan (the CQ plan) approved by the SEC. CQS provides for joint, uniform dissemination of the bid and offer, together with size, for each market in each security. In addition, CQS calculates and disseminates the best bid and best offer (BBO) for each security from all the bids and offers that are available. Although there continue to be doubts about the value of some quotes disseminated by regional exchanges and third market makers, it is generally true that quotes relating to securities and markets included in the Intermarket Trading System (discussed later) have proved reliable enough to be used regularly by trading professionals for execution of orders. During periods of extremely active trading, however, quotes may become nonfirm and are then not used as a basis for intermarket trading.

Market Linkage Systems

The Intermarket Trading System (ITS) was implemented in 1978 by a group of exchanges,[6] pursuant to a formal plan (the ITS Plan) approved by the SEC. ITS began as an experimental linkage of five exchanges providing two services for a limited number of securities. First, ITS enables public agency orders and specialist proprietary interest represented at any participant exchange to take part in the opening at any other linked exchange (the preopening application); second, ITS provides a means for a broker or specialist to reach a bid or offer distributed through the CQS by any other participant market during regular trading (the general application). Originally there was no requirement that a broker try to obtain a better bid or offer shown away; instead, the choice of whether or not to do so was left to each broker's judgment.[7] With more experience, the number of securities in ITS has now been expanded to include virtually all listed securities that have specialists on more than one exchange (approximately 1,200). Moreover, a uniform rule (the trade-through rule) has been adopted by all ITS participant exchanges and requires that better bids or offers displayed away must be filled before any execution can take place at an inferior price.

The SEC has also approved the National Securities Trading System (NSTS) as a market linkage system. NSTS is a fully automated trading system operated under the auspices of the Cincinnati Stock Exchange. NSTS supports terminals located in the offices of various broker/dealers and connects them to a central computer facility in Jersey City, New Jersey. At one stage in its development, NSTS terminals were offered to specialists on regional exchanges, and a few terminals were actually installed on regional exchange floors. At present, however, NSTS is an automated marketplace, separate and distinct from the other exchanges but linked to them through ITS. With the recent withdrawal from NSTS of a major integrated securities firm, the future of NSTS appears clouded.

Limit Order Protection Facility

In the Institutional Investor Study the SEC expressed concern about the inability of individual investors to participate in executions of institutional orders (away from the primary markets) at significant discounts or premiums from prevailing prices. It seems reasonable to conclude that this concern was the genesis of the SEC's desire to provide protection to public limit orders. In 1978 the SEC proposed the construction of a consolidated limit order book (CLOB), which would have provided not only price protection to limit orders but also priority based on time of entry to the CLOB. Faced with overwhelming adverse commentary from the industry, the SEC quickly retreated to its first priority of nationwide price protection.

At present there is no facility capable of guaranteeing protection for limit orders. However, limit orders present on exchanges are incorporated in the published bids and offers that are distributed through CQS, and are protected by the operation of ITS and the ITS trade-through rule described earlier. Of course, the published quotation includes only the highest bid price and lowest offer price from each market, so that limit orders to buy at lower prices and sell at higher prices (that is, away-from-the-market limit orders) are not included in the quote. Nevertheless, as long as trading takes place with 1/8 point changes, and there is time to refresh quotes before trades at successively divergent prices are executed, it can be said that CQS and ITS provide effective protection for limit orders.[8] As a practical matter, limit orders are left unprotected only when large transactions take place at prices significantly away from the current quoted markets. It should come as no surprise that this is precisely the problem that first made limit order protection a priority of the SEC. What may be surprising, however, is that this problem appears to be substantially less prevalent than has been generally thought. In 1982 the American Stock Exchange conducted a survey to determine the number of limit orders on its floor that remained unexecuted as a result of such transactions. Approximately 20,000 to 25,000 orders per day come to the AMEX floor, of which a majority are limit orders. At any given time there may be about 15,000 to 20,000 limit orders awaiting execution. By contrast, the number of limit orders left unexecuted when transactions took place at inferior prices on other exchanges was estimated to be fewer than two per day. It is reasonable to guess that the magnitude of the problem at regional exchanges is also minimal. Even at the NYSE, the proportions are probably similar, although the absolute numbers are certainly much larger. These numbers suggest little economic motivation to pursue increased protection for limit orders beyond that which now exists.

National Clearance and Settlement System

Not always recognized as a component of the NMS, a unified national clearance and settlement system was actually a prerequisite for successful linkage of geographically disparate markets. To see that this is true, imagine a similar linkage of commodity markets—for example, wheat. Any market participant buying wheat in one city and requiring delivery in another must consider transportation costs. A buyer or seller in such a market cannot be indifferent to the geographic location. Arbitrage between such markets will take place only when price differentials exceed the cost of transportation.

In securities markets, the clearance and settlement system has evolved to the point that traders can virtually ignore any differences in delivery costs associated with particular markets. This was achieved in part by the formation in 1976 of the National Securities Clearing Corporation (NSCC) from the associated clearing agencies of the AMEX, NYSE, and NASD, and by the subsequent development of interfaces between NSCC and the regional clearing agencies. These developments were a prerequisite for the implementation of ITS which permits an order represented in one market to be executed in a second market. The member representing the order in the first market may not even be a member of the second market, so he(she) must be able to clear the trade as if he(she) had dealt with another member in his(her) own market.[9] Otherwise there would be a significant incentive to avoid intermarket trades. Of course, it would be absurd to maintain that the primary purpose of national clearing and settlement was to permit intermarket trading. Nevertheless, it is true that, without it, an NMS based on linked markets would be impossible.

Off-Board Trading Rules

One of the hoped-for results of creating an NMS was an increase in overall market-making capacity. In order to achieve this, both Congress and the SEC thought that the rules of exchanges prohibiting their members from trading OTC in listed stocks should be reviewed and probably removed. This, it was thought, would encourage well-capitalized broker-dealers to commit capital to making markets and relieve the shortage of market-making capital noted by the SEC in the Institutional Investor Study. Although this logic is certainly clear, it ignores some obvious facts. Since the need for extra market-making capacity derived from the fact that large institutional trades exceeded the specialists' ability to offset temporary imbalances in supply and demand, and therefore were taking place at substantial discounts or premiums from true value, a first-year economics student would suspect, correctly, that there was an economic incentive to commit capital *in such situations*. However, there is no such obvious reason for a well-capitalized dealer to make a long-term commitment of capital to an ongoing obligation to make markets for transactions of all sizes and under all circumstances.

Not surprisingly, large broker-dealers have, in fact, come to act as dealers (or *block positioners*) when needed to facilitate large trades by their customers. The capital used for this purpose is available for block positioning in a large number of stocks and is not committed to an ongoing obligation to make markets in particular stocks. If asked, most block positioners would likely say that the bids and offers they make for blocks are for the purpose of attracting orders of institutional customers and not because of the profitability of opportunistic market making. Of course, such statements may not be entirely true; but to the extent that they are true, it indicates that additional market-making capital has been made available insofar as it is economically sound to do so.[10]

Further changes in off-board trading rules will not change this fact and are therefore unlikely to result in more competition among market makers or increased market-making capital on a regular basis. (Structural changes that have the effect of increasing the overall profits of market makers would, of course, attract more capital. Such profits would most likely be at the direct expense of investors.)

The SEC, pursuing its vision of attracting market-making capital by removing barriers to competition, has in a series of steps (1) caused the removal of those aspects of off-board trading rules limiting agency orders to exchanges, and (2) prohibited the application of off-board trading rules to securities first listed on a national securities exchange after April 26, 1979 (Rule 19c.3). Although there are now nearly 600 listed securities subject to Rule 19c.3, there has been no dramatic effect on the way such securities trade in comparison with previously listed securities not subject to Rule 19c.3. Nor is there any evidence that Rule 19c.3 has done anything to encourage effective competition with the primary exchanges or to attract additional capital to regular market making in Rule 19c.3 securities.

At first the SEC apparently attributed the failure of Rule 19c.3 to provide the expected benefits to the absence of linkage between the exchanges and OTC markets. In April 1981 the SEC ordered the ITS participating exchanges and the National Association of Securities Dealers (NASD) to act jointly in planning, developing, and operating an interface between ITS and NASD's Computer Assisted Execution System (CAES). After difficult and inconclusive negotiations, the ITS/NASD linkage was finally implemented on a pilot basis in May 1982.[11] The ITS/NASD at first provided a means through which several major securities firms experimented with market making in listed securities. However, these experiments were largely abandoned by mid-1983, and have not been resumed. As a result, there is little evidence of increased competition with the primary exchanges or increased market-making capacity that can be attributed to the removal of off-board trading rules (by Rule 19c.3) and the linkage between exchange and OTC markets.

Likely Future Developments

One might argue with considerable justification that the NMS contemplated by Congress and the SEC is now largely in existence. Substantially all the NMS components described by the SEC now exist and are functioning. The only substantial exceptions are:

1. Nationwide limit order protection has not been achieved in all cases.
2. The OTC markets in listed securities have not been fully integrated with the exchange markets.
3. Some off-board trading rules remain in force, though of declining importance.

In all these areas there are likely to be significant developments over the next several years. It is not the purpose of this chapter to forecast what regulatory initiatives are likely to be undertaken but, rather, to discuss the more foreseeable effects of technological changes and economic forces. These are likely to be of greater importance than regulatory changes for some time to come.

Significant changes are likely to come in three areas. First, technical improvements to existing components of the NMS and the day-to-day functioning of stock exchanges will substantially improve the services provided by the exchanges and will cause dramatic improvement in the overall functioning of the NMS. Second, technical improvements in the means of handling limit orders will again significantly improve the operations of existing exchanges and may within a few years make possible nationwide limit order protection for the first time, at least in some securities. Third, economic forces will lead to competition across an ever-broader front between listed and OTC markets with far-reaching—and as yet unforeseeable—consequences.

Technical Improvements in NMS Components

In recent years new so-called user-friendly technology has become increasingly available for applications in securities trading. This will help to overcome what has always been the greatest problem in trading automation: capturing the judgments of trading professionals (and the results of negotiations between professionals) in an accurate and timely way. The solutions will build on two approaches: First, sophisticated programming will guess what the trading professional will choose to do in a given situation. Second, new devices will be used to put powerful computer assistance almost literally in the hands of the traders. These devices will incorporate both the user-friendly technologies and the sophisticated guesses. In order to make use of the powerful computer aids for their own benefit, traders will begin to relate directly to an automated environment—perhaps for the first time. The result will be direct human-machine interface in a trading environment.

These changes, which have already begun, will not be completed quickly. Perhaps they will never be carried to a logical conclusion in which all interface between traders is through automated equipment. Still, it is already foreseeable that within a few years such new technology as touch sensitive CRTs, voice recognition equipment, and the programming techniques of expert systems will improve the operations of most marketplaces dramatically, and will enable existing NMS facilities to fulfill their functions more completely. Quotations and last-sale reports will be more nearly current and accurate; bids and offers will be accepted through ITS more quickly and with fewer failed attempts; routine orders will be handled quickly and efficiently, untouched by human hands. The clearing of transactions will be faster and nearly error-free. At least in a mechanical sense, the NMS will function more smoothly than its critics would have thought possible a few years ago.

Forerunners of these systems can already be seen on the floors of the American and New York Stock Exchanges, and elsewhere in the industry.[12] On the American Stock Exchange, with which I am most familiar, most small orders are no longer printed in any form. The orders come to the floor from member firm order-routing systems, to an Exchange routing system where each order is directed to a touch-sensitive display terminal at the location of the appropriate specialist. The system guesses the most likely price at which the order will be executed. With a few touches of the terminal, requiring only a few seconds, the specialist can confirm, or correct, the execution price and match the order against the other side of the transaction, whether it is in the crowd, on the book, or from the specialist's own account.

Within the next few years, this system and others using similar techniques will be developed to much higher levels of sophistication, giving specialists (and other market makers) vastly improved capability to manage the orders that come to them and to control their own trading accounts, with no loss of their ability to exercise market judgment. Indeed, the availability of more accurate and more current information, better analysis of that information, and less busy work, should improve the quality of judgments made in the heat of trading.

In a somewhat longer period, we are likely to see brokers on exchange trading floors armed with very small but powerful microcomputers, in continuous two-way communication with exchange and member firm routing systems. Although it is too early to foresee exactly how these capabilities will develop and how they will be used, it may be that the time is approaching when nearly all the clerical functions of stock exchange trading can be automated, and even the results of oral negotiations between two professionals can be promptly and accurately captured by machine.

Improved Handling of Limit Orders

For many years, there has been a lot of talk—and little effective action—regarding the so-called *electronic book*. Within the next few years, the electronic book will finally become a functioning reality. A working prototype called a *display book* already exists at the NYSE.

The display book has been used for several months as a pilot on the NYSE for a small number of actively traded stocks. The pilot has shown that not only can a fully automated book be made to work in an active auction market, but also the automation can be dramatically beneficial to the specialist's operation and to the smooth functioning of the market. Indeed, it has been said that it would have been impossible to conduct trading in the new Bell operating companies without the display book pilot. Even if that is somewhat exaggerated, it is an indication of the success of this experiment. There still remain a few questions and problems to work out before automated books will be in general use, and before the precise application of automated books becomes clear.[13]

In any case, within the context of NMS, it is clear that the existence and growing prevalence of automated limit order books may well become the basis of nationwide limit order protection in a practical way, and that this could occur within the next several years.

Competition between Listed and OTC Markets

One thing that seems clear about the next few years is that there will be increasing competition between exchange and OTC markets. This will occur first of all through the continuing action of Rule 19c.3, which prevents the application of off-board trading restrictions to any securities not already subject to such restrictions. The current number of about 600 19c.3 securities can only increase and the number of securities subject to off-board trading rules will decline due to mergers, acquisitions, and delistings for other causes. Thus off-board trading rules will have steadily declining importance.

However, exchanges (including regional exchanges) have been very successful in competing with OTC markets in Rule 19c.3 securities. These facts may well encourage at least some of the exchanges to consider unlisted trading privileges for certain OTC securities. It is too early to foresee how, if at all, such unlisted trading would be structured. Exchanges have not extended unlisted trading privileges since the 1930s and will not do so now without controversy. However, it is not the purpose of this chapter to explore the regulatory framework in which the debate will take place. For this discussion it suffices to observe that the operational capability exists for exchanges to trade unlisted securities, and that the economic incentives to do so are both significant and growing.

Notes

1. The author is a senior officer of the American Stock Exchange, Inc. The views and opinions expressed herein are those of the author and do not necessarily represent the position of the American Stock Exchange.

2. SEC Institutional Investor Study Report (1971).

3. Institutional Investor Study, summary volume. The Commission seems to have concluded in 1971 that the problems it found in securities markets were susceptible to solutions based on modern technology. It isn't altogether clear how it reached this conclusion. A priori, there would seem to be little precedent or intuitive argument that suggests mechanical solutions to such problems as encouraging risk taking, and facilitating price discovery in a traditionally complex, negotiated market environment. In retrospect, it seems likely that the Commission, or its expert advisors, may have extrapolated from the obvious potential to automate the clerical handling of orders without giving a lot of thought to how the professional judgment of market makers and brokers would be incorporated.

4. Senate Report No. 75, 94th Congress, 1st Session.

5. It is perhaps worth noting in passing that each exchange provides for protection of public limit orders within its marketplace, but a specialist's bid or offer may have *parity* (equal priority) with a public limit order under certain circumstances.

6. The American, Boston, New York, Pacific, and Philadelphia Stock Exchanges were the original participants. The Midwest Stock Exchange joined a short time later. Subsequently, the Cincinnati Stock Exchange and the NASD have also become participants.

7. Although no rules of the exchanges required a broker to try to obtain a better price away, his responsibility as a fiduciary may have had the same effect in most cases.

8. An example will make this statement clearer: If market center A quotes a bid of 40 for 1,000 shares, no transaction in any linked market can take place at 39 7/8 until the bid in market center A for 1,000 shares at 40 has been filled. Market center A may also have orders at 39 7/8, but these will not be left unprotected ("traded through") unless a trade takes place at 39 3/4 or lower in another market after the bid at 40 is filled, but before a new bid at 39 7/8 is distributed by market center A.

9. Intermarket trades actually result in three clearing transactions being created: In each market a trade is created between the exchange and its member; a third transaction is created between the two exchanges.

10. The reasoning for this statement is simply that if the excess profits of opportunistic market making have already been competed away, there is no longer an incentive to commit additional risk capital to this purpose.

11. A discussion of the problems inherent in linking exchange and OTC markets is outside the scope of this chapter. However, these problems are difficult and intractable, ranging from narrow technical problems relating to different business practices that have developed in separate markets (for example, reported transaction prices do not always have the same meaning) to significant questions of market structure and economic efficiency (for example, the threat that permitting major firms to internalize their orders would significantly affect the central pricing mechanism and lead to inappropriate prices of securities).

12. For further discussion, see chapter 19 by Marshall and Carlson.

13. A detailed discussion is not appropriate here, but in general the questions that remain to be explored have to do with such things as how to get all limit orders on the book in an efficient, timely way; and how to synchronize the book with the oral auction in a security that is both active and volatile in price.

18

The Intermarket Trading System and The Cincinnati Experiment

Jeffry L. Davis

I n 1975 Congress directed the Securities and Exchange Commission (SEC) to ". . . facilitate the establishment of a national market system for securities."[1] This action was based on Congress's perception that the nation's securities markets were in urgent need of restructuring. The anticompetitive rules and practices (particularly fixed commission rates) so central to the structure and operation of the industry no longer meshed with economic reality, and hadn't for some time. The growing importance of institutional customers—customers that, for example, demanded evasion of the fixed commission rate schedule—clashed with the old way of doing business. That clash, along with operational problems attributable to archaic processing and record-keeping practices, brought the securities industry under Congressional scrutiny.

Having focused on the industry and its problems, Congress concluded that a national market system (NMS) linking the diverse markets throughout the country was a necessary and desirable objective, which the SEC should seek to achieve. Congress did not, however, impose any deadlines on the SEC, nor did it clearly define the tasks to be accomplished. Instead, it established certain general principles to guide the SEC's facilitation, and left it to the agency to flesh out this skeletal outline. This kind of assignment is common of course; indeed, independent agencies are designed and created precisely to perform such assignments.[2]

This particular assignment called for the SEC to bring about (or facilitate) the development of a more perfect securities market. Congress's instructions to the SEC were vague enough to be consistent with (or equally inconsistent with) a number of quite different market designs.[3] Seizing on Congress's endorsement of "new data processing and communications techniques" and

Director of Economic and Policy Analysis, Securities and Exchange Commission. The SEC, as a matter of policy, disclaims responsibility for any private publication by any of its employees. The views expressed herein are solely those of the author and do not necessarily reflect the views of the Commission or the author's colleagues on the staff of the Commission. Terry Chuppe, William Atkinson, William Dale, and Richard Ketchum provided valuable comments and suggestions, some of which were heeded.

the criteria of efficiency and best execution for customers,[4] some have argued that the SEC should turn the national market system concept into a totally computerized trading system.[5] In this ideal market there would be no place for the antiquated exchanges; there would be but a single marketplace, consisting of a central computer and a network of terminals through which brokers and dealers would carry on their business. A prototype of this computerized market exists in the National Securities Trading System (NSTS), also known as the Cincinnati experiment.

A much more modest approach, embodied in the Intermarket Trading System (ITS), is based primarily on Congress's call for "the linking of all markets for qualified securities through communication and data processing facilities."[6] This approach preserves all the existing marketplaces but seeks to improve their collective efficiency by providing a mechanism for trades to take place between brokers and dealers in physically separate marketplaces.

These two approaches to NMS design do not exhaust the possibilities; but there has been some experience with them, and, I think, something can be learned from this experience.[7] This chapter describes these alternative system designs, discusses our experience with them, examines the key concerns associated with each, and identifies what I think is the key difference in terms of system design—namely, the absence of time priority in the ITS. The chapter concludes that the continued existence of competing marketplaces is incompatible with time priority in the ITS.

The Intermarket Trading System

The ITS was created by the exchanges as their joint response to Congress' and the SEC's calls for linkage of competing marketplaces.[8] It is unlikely that, left to themselves, the exchanges would have come up with any linkage at all. Rather, it is probably better to view the ITS as the product of the exchanges' efforts to stave off what they saw as more disruptive versions of linkage. From this viewpoint, it is not surprising that the ITS is really very modest in its design and operation. It is simply a communications system that uses a computer to receive, process, and route messages from one marketplace to another. Messages are entered into and received from computer terminals located on the floors of the exchanges.[9]

The messages routed by the ITS are called *commitments to trade*. A commitment, as its name implies, commits the originator in one marketplace (usually on the floor of an exchange) to buy or sell a stated number of round lots at a stated price. The originator is expected to—and generally does—assign a price to correspond to the current quotation advertised by the marketplace to which he is sending his commitment.[10] Occasionally, however, the originator will try to improve on the advertised quotation by assigning a price better (for him) than the quoted price—and sometimes he succeeds.

In addition to number of shares and price (and, of course, the stock identification, necessary clearing information, and whether the commitment is to buy or to sell), the commitment also includes an expiration time—either one minute or two minutes. If the receiving marketplace does not act on the commitment before it expires, the system will cancel the commitment and send notification of the cancellation to the originator. Before the commitment expires, the receiving marketplace may cancel it if, for example, the quotation was being changed while the commitment was in transit. If the commitment is accepted, an execution report will be sent to the originator.

The ITS is best understood by a simple illustration. Suppose a broker on the floor of the New York Stock Exchange (NYSE) has gone to the specialist's post where XYZ stock is traded. He has in hand a market order to buy 100 shares of XYZ. He asks the specialist what the market is in XYZ stock, and he also looks at the electronic display of the quotes from the other marketplaces. Let's say the NYSE quote is 30, the quote on the Philadelphia Stock Exchange (PHLX) is 29 7/8, and the quotes from the other marketplaces are above 30. In order to get the best price for his order, then, he sends a commitment to the PHLX via the ITS. If the commitment is accepted on the PHLX (usually by the specialist), the NYSE broker will be sent an execution report. The commitment may be rejected, however, or may expire by lapse of time (usually one minute).

The ITS began operating on April 17, 1978. At first it linked only the NYSE and the PHLX, and trading was limited to eleven stocks. By the end of 1978 the American Stock Exchange (AMEX) and four of the five regional exchanges were linked. In February 1981 the Cincinnati Stock Exchange (CSE) entered the system. Finally, in May 1982, the National Association of Securities Dealers (NASD) became a participant by means of a pilot automated interface known as the CAES (Computer Assisted Execution System) linkage.[11]

From the initial 11 stocks, the number of ITS stocks grew rapidly to 300 by the end of 1978. At the end of 1983 there were 1,120 ITS stocks. The volume of shares traded through the ITS also grew, of course, as more and more stocks were added. Relative to composite share volume in ITS stocks, ITS volume grew slightly for the first couple of years. By 1981, however, it had stabilized at about 4 percent of composite volume, and it remains at that level today (see table 18–1 for more detail on the growth of the ITS). Although the NYSE participates in transactions accounting for about 90 percent of total ITS volume, the share volume of ITS trades completed on the NYSE is less than 3 percent of total NYSE share volume. As shown in table 18–2, ITS volume as a percentage of total volume is about 13 percent for the Midwest Stock Exchange (MSE), 19 percent for the PHLX, 25 percent for the Pacific Stock Exchange (PSE), 28 percent for the Boston Stock Exchange (BSE), and about 44 percent for the CSE. The regional exchanges—especially the PSE, the BSE, and the CSE—therefore, derive a sizable portion of their volume

Table 18–1
Growth of the ITS

Year	Number of Eligible Stocks (End of Year)	ITS Share Volume (Millions)	ITS Volume as a Percentage of Composite Volume in ITS Stocks
1978	300	42.3	5.0
1979	688	209.4	3.5
1980	884	396.2	3.6
1981	947	542.6	4.0
1982	1,039	825.8	4.3
1983	1,120	1,038.3	4.1

from the ITS. As shown in table 18–3, most of the regionals' ITS volume is transacted with the NYSE, and most of this volume results from commitments sent to the NYSE from the regional exchanges.

It is significant that some of the regional exchanges have shown a dependence on the ITS for a large portion of their trading. This development has several possible interpretations. First, it could mean simply that the ITS is a success. Second, it could mean that the regional exchanges have ceased to exist as separate marketplaces (or never were truly independent). Third, it could mean that the NYSE is supporting nominal competitors to forestall a more serious competitive threat—such as off-board trading by upstairs firms. Undoubtedly there are several other possible interpretations.

A critical question whose answer might help to sort out these interpretations is: What is the measure of success for the ITS? That depends, of course, on what is expected of the ITS. If linkage is desirable solely for its own sake, the measure of success in this case is simply how much the ITS has been used. Since it has been used a lot, it can be said to have been a success.

If the linkage was expected to improve the quality of the markets or otherwise benefit investors, then mere use is not enough. In one sense, however, use of the ITS implies benefit because it is generally used only to obtain a better price than that available in the originating marketplace. Thus every time the ITS is used, the originating order should obtain a benefit of at least one-eighth on each share purchased or sold. The current ITS volume of about 4 million shares per day, then, implies an aggregate daily benefit of $500,000. It is not clear, however, how much of this supposed benefit goes to customers and how much is simply transferred between market makers.

If the benefit is largely a transfer between market makers, it appears that it is mostly a transfer from the NYSE specialists to the regional specialists, since the commitment flow is mostly from the regional exchanges toward the NYSE. Even if this is the case, however, it does not mean that customers do not derive an indirect benefit. In fact, whether or not customers receive the immediate benefit, we would expect the price competition implied by the use

Table 18-2
ITS Share Volume by Marketplace, 1983

Exchange	ITS Share Volume (millions)[a]			ITS Share Volume as a Percentage of Total Marketplace Volume		
	As Originating Marketplace	As Executing Marketplace	Total	As Originating Marketplace	As Executing Marketplace	Total
AMEX	8.1	11.4	19.5	1.1	1.5	2.6
BSE	31.0	20.0	51.0	16.9	10.9	27.8
CSE	9.1	16.0	25.1	15.8	27.8	43.6
MSE	123.8	74.7	198.5	8.0	4.8	12.8
NYSE	177.4	287.5	464.9	0.9	1.5	2.4
PSE	112.6	93.2	205.8	13.7	11.3	25.0
PHLX	56.2	13.8	70.0	15.1	3.7	18.8
NASD	1.2	2.4	3.6	0.3	0.6	0.9

[a]Since two marketplaces participate in each ITS trade, there would be double counting of ITS share volume if both participating marketplaces are credited with the volume. To avoid this double counting, this table gives one-half of the volume to the originating marketplace and the other half to the executing marketplace.

Table 18–3
NYSE Participation in ITS Transactions, 1983

Exchange	Percentage of Marketplace's ITS Share Volume Received from NYSE	Percentage of Marketplace's ITS Share Volume Sent to NYSE	Total
AMEX	0.1	0.0	0.1
BSE	29.7	48.0	77.7
CSE	48.3	30.2	78.5
MSE	31.2	55.8	87.0
PSE	36.5	45.9	82.4
PHLX	15.7	70.8	86.5
NASD	53.5	23.0	76.5

of the ITS to result in narrower spreads, which would clearly benefit customers. There is no evidence yet that this has happened, however. Consequently, it is not clear that investors have benefited from—or that the market has been improved by—the ITS. Some regional specialists may have tighter spreads as a result of their direct access to the NYSE for laying off positions they have accumulated.[12] But I am skeptical of claims that the ITS has saved investors millions of dollars when I cannot find evidence of narrower spreads on the NYSE, where about 85 percent of all the trading continues to take place.[13]

The Cincinnati Experiment

The Cincinnati experiment (hereafter NSTS) was officially launched in June 1978 with 38 stocks eligible for trading and authorization from the SEC to expand to 200.[14] Compared with the ITS, the NSTS offered (and continues to offer) a radically new market mechanism. Participating dealers and brokers can enter bids and offers for themselves or for their customers through a computer terminal.[15] The market is managed, so to speak, by a central computer, which keeps track of all bids and offers, orders them by price and time of entry, and executes trades between matching bids and offers.[16] In short, the NSTS embodies all of the elements of the ideal black-box market promoted by the more adventurous would-be NMS engineers.

Although the NSTS is sponsored by—and is treated as a part of—the CSE, it is, or could be, an independent marketplace. It requires no exchange floor; all it needs is a network of dealers to make markets and, of course, a flow of retail orders. A participating dealer enters and updates his bids and offers through his computer terminal. On his terminal he can display a ranked list of the current bids and offers (including priced orders for retail customers) stored in the central computer. He can trigger an execution simply by entering, for example, a bid (or altering his current bid) to match the best offer appearing on his screen. Or he can simply maintain competitive bids and offers and wait for another participant to hit his quote. When a trade occurs, the system reports the trade and updates its ranking of bids and offers.

Terminals for the entry of customer orders are distinct from those used by dealers, but the entry and alteration of customer orders is analogous to the entry and alteration of dealer quotes. Both types of terminals display the ranked list of quotes and orders. A broker-dealer using the system both to make markets and to execute customer orders must have both types of terminals.

Prior to the linkage of the NSTS with the ITS, the upstairs dealers (especially Merrill Lynch and Moseley Hallgarten) accounted for well over 90 percent of the system's trading volume. Since then—and particularly since Merrill Lynch withdrew as a participant in April 1983—the ITS has become a dominant participant accounting for about 40 percent of volume in the NSTS. As of December 31, 1983, however, there were still seven market makers and thirteen agency-only participants.

Table 18–4 provides some basic data on activity in the NSTS. The number of stocks eligible for trading in the NSTS had grown from the initial 38 to only 49 by the end of 1980, but stood at 188 by the end of 1983. Trading volume has not kept pace with the growth in number of stocks, however. In 1979 NSTS volume was about 2 percent of composite volume in eligible stocks, but even this small percentage has fallen off over the years, to only 0.6 percent in 1983.

The failure of the NSTS to capture more than a tiny portion of trading volume has undoubtedly been a profound disappointment to black-box advocates. Of course, they may claim that the experiment was not properly designed, lacked the necessary support of the SEC, was inhibited by SEC caution in authorizing it, was undermined by powerful anticompetitive interests, or was simply a victim of industry inertia.

It may be that at some uncertain date in the future the black box will have established itself as the dominant trading mechanism. Certainly the trend in

Table 18–4
NSTS Experience

Exchange	Number of Eligible Stocks (End of Year)	Number of Upstairs Participants	Share Volume (Millions)	Share Volume as a Percentage of Composite Volume in NSTS Stocks
1978	38	4	7.1	2.0
1979	41	5	23.0	1.9
1980	49	5	32.5	1.8
1981	73	9	40.9	1.8
1982	117	10	48.8	1.1
1983	188	7	57.3	0.6

securities trading is toward greater automation. It is not at all clear, however, that this trend will extend all the way to totally automated trading. The NSTS experience has shown us that broker-dealers are not yet prepared to abandon the exchanges for the black box.

Concerns Arising from System Design

The differences between the ITS and the NSTS in terms of system design have given rise to quite different concerns. From its inception, the NSTS was criticized by some as contributing to fragmentation and making it possible for integrated firms (such as Merrill Lynch) to internalize their order flow. Neither fragmentation nor internalization was of concern with the ITS, but in the early stages of its development there was some concern over trade-throughs, and there may be some lingering concern that the ITS linkage could be made ineffective through quote matching.

Fragmentation and Internalization

What is *fragmentation?* If we ignore the evil sound of this term, we can define it very simply. A market for a good or service is said to be fragmented if any of the transactions involving that good or service take place anywhere other than a single marketplace. The market for NYSE-listed securities is fragmented, therefore, because not all the trades in these securities take place on the NYSE or in any other single marketplace.

Whether fragmentation is good or bad depends on how it affects the cost of transacting. If fragmentation is nothing more than the manifestation of effective competition, and if that competition results in lower transaction costs for investors, then it is good. If, however, fragmentation so reduces the efficiency of the primary marketplace that transaction costs are increased, then fragmentation would be bad.[17]

In the NSTS the effect of fragmentation may be especially difficult to evaluate because it is complicated by internalization. *Internalization* is actually a particular type of fragmentation. A broker-dealer is said to internalize its order flow when, instead of sending its customer orders to an exchange for execution, it executes the orders independently, either by crossing buys and sells or by executing the orders against its own account. Since the NSTS permits its participants both to make markets and to enter customer orders, there has been some concern that the system permits—and has been used for—internalization.

In theory, internalization is not possible in the NSTS. Transactions take place only when orders and quotes are matched in the system, which is *external* to each participant. That is, customer orders are exposed to outside dealer interests and to customer orders entered by other participants.

In practice, however, the broker-dealers that enter customer orders and also make markets in the NSTS (so-called integrated firms) have executed a large percentage (well over half) of their customer orders on an intrafirm basis—either by crossing them or by executing them against their own accounts. Effectively, then, these broker-dealers have achieved indirect internalization; but this indirect internalization would undoubtedly diminish if the NSTS were to attract substantially more participants and more volume. If the NSTS were to become the dominant marketplace, it might even disappear. Thus internalization in the NSTS might be viewed as self-correcting if, indeed, it is considered a problem in the first place.

Although greater success in attracting volume to the NSTS would tend to eliminate internalization, it would clearly increase fragmentation (of the non-internalized variety). Of course, if the success was so great that the NSTS became the dominant marketplace and continued to attract more market share, then the fragmentation concern would be transitory, or at least its focus would shift to the NYSE as the nondominant marketplace and, therefore, the source of the fragmentation.

At the volume levels attracted by the NSTS, there has never been enough fragmentation, in my view, even to suggest a concern. If the NSTS had really caught on and started to grow, then the SEC would have been forced to deal with the fragmentation concern. It would have had to decide (1) that the fragmentation caused by the NSTS was too harmful to be tolerated, or (2) that it was on balance beneficial as a result of its competitive effects, or (3) that it might be a transitory condition to be tolerated en route to a more efficient market mechanism. I do not know what the decision would have been, but I'm sure it would not have been an easy one to make.

Trade-Throughs and Quote Matching

The occurrence of trade-throughs is best viewed as a minor, but aggravating, bug in the ITS. A trade-through occurs when a trade takes place on one exchange at a price that is inferior, for either the buyer or the seller, to a current bid or offer published by another exchange. For example, suppose the current PHLX quotation for XYZ stock is 40–40 1/2. Now suppose a trade takes place on the NYSE at a price of 39 7/8. The seller in this trade, instead of selling his shares for 39 7/8 on the NYSE, could have sold them for 40 on the PHLX, via the ITS. In this example, there has been a trade-through: The NYSE seller traded-through the PHLX quotation.

Obviously, trade-throughs frustrate the by-passed bidders. More important, if left unremedied, they could represent a major system design failure of the ITS. The designers of the ITS, therefore, remedied the failure by adopting rules against trade-throughs and procedures for satisfying the frustrated bidder whenever a trade-through occurs.

I have never really understood why any trade-throughs occur. But since they have never amounted to more than a tiny fraction of trades in ITS stocks, I suspect they were generally nothing more than the results of errors or oversights and perhaps some resentment of the linkage. Had they occurred more frequently, they could have been a sign of gross inefficiency (or slowness) of the ITS for communicating trading interests.

A potentially much more serious system design flaw of the ITS is its susceptibility to quote-matching. To explain what quote-matching is I refer to another example. First, assume the NYSE quotation in XYZ stock is 39 7/8–40 3/8 and the PHLX quotation is 40–40 1/2. Now assume a floor broker on the PHLX has an order to buy XYZ. He could execute it immediately against the best PHLX offer for 40 1/2, but he notices that he could get a better price (40 3/8) from the NYSE, via the ITS. Instead of using the ITS, however, he asks the PHLX specialist to match the NYSE offer. If the latter does so and the trade takes place at 40 3/8, then we have witnessed a case of quote-matching.

For my immediate purpose it is irrelevant whether anyone is harmed by this particular (or any other) instance of quote-matching. Nevertheless, although quote-matching is a common and presumably healthy occurrence in our everyday dealings with merchants involving all sorts of consumer goods, quote-matching in the ITS does represent a very serious failure of the system to achieve true linkage. Like the broker or specialist whose quotation is traded through, the broker or specialist whose quotation is matched has good reason to feel frustrated and even cheated.

Of course, even without the ITS, a broker or specialist on the floor of one exchange might well feel frustrated by an occurrence of quote-matching on another exchange. With the ITS, however, this frustration rises to the level of a system concern. Why? Because the ITS, based on the concept of linkage, is supposed to create a new plane of intermarket competition. On this new plane the exchanges are supposed to compete with one another for executions on the basis of published quotations, without regard to where an order seeking execution is initially sent.

In our quote-matching example, this is not the case. The exchange where the order was sent (the PHLX) has a definite advantage; it has, in a sense, the right of first refusal. Only if the PHLX specialist in the example is unwilling to match the NYSE offer will the order be sent to the NYSE for execution.

Although I am not aware of any grave concern over this potential for quote-matching, it seems to me that this potential represents a clear conflict between the design of the ITS and the concept of linkage. In my opinion, true linkage eliminates the geographic distinctions between the various marketplaces. In a linked system of marketplaces, it should be irrelevant which marketplace brings an order into the system; this is a mere conduit function. Once an order has entered this linked system, then each marketplace should have an equal opportunity to compete for its execution. Of course, this view of linkage goes far beyond what we find in the ITS. It would require systemwide time priority for quotations (including limit orders) to eliminate the potential for quote-matching.

Thus, at least in my view, the ITS offers only partial linkage. It represents a compromise between linkage and the preservation of the geographically distinct marketplaces. In the ITS it still matters which marketplace attracts orders in the first place. The marketplace that brings an order into the system retains a clear advantage—the right of first refusal. Without that advantage—that is, if we had systemwide time priority—there would be no incentive whatsoever to seeking initial order flow. A linked marketplace could simply compete for orders brought into the system by other marketplaces. It could, that is, cast off its conduit function and simply compete on the new plane of intermarket competition.

The problem with this linkage concept should now be clear. There would be no incentive for any marketplace to bring orders into the system. The existing market structure, consisting of geographically distinct marketplaces competing primarily for initial order flow, is inconsistent with time priority and, therefore, with true linkage. The only market structure, it seems to me, that could accommodate time priority is one consisting of a single marketplace—either a single exchange or a black box.[18] As I understand the history of the national market system concept, it appears that the single exchange model has been rejected.[19] So we are left with a black box if we insist on time priority.

Conclusion

Both the ITS and the NSTS were designed to achieve the goals set by Congress for a national market system. As I have said, the NSTS, if successful, would have achieved this by replacing the existing marketplaces. In doing so, it would have guaranteed price and time priority to all customer orders and dealer quotations. The cost of this achievement, however, would have been the demise of the existing marketplaces and the loss of the benefits of their competition with one another.

On the other hand, the ITS has been designed to preserve the separate marketplaces, or at least to preserve their incentives to compete for initial order flow. Because of this, the ITS must tolerate a significant system flaw—its potential for quote-matching.[20] The cost of eliminating this flaw (by imposing time priority) would be, I think, the demise of intermarket competition. Time priority in the ITS would destroy the incentive for the different marketplaces to compete for the initial flow of orders seeking execution. This competition, however, is the basis for the separate existence of the different marketplaces. I must conclude, then, that time priority in the ITS would lead to the consolidation of marketplaces into a single entity—possibly one of the existing marketplaces, but more likely a black box with all the characteristics of the NSTS.

The ITS, therefore, can remain a modest communications system for resolving the order-flow imbalances of the participating marketplaces; or it can adopt time priority, in which case we cannot expect the separate marketplaces to continue their separate identities. Whether the ITS should be improved to incorporate time priority is for others to decide. It is important, however, that the effect of such a change should be clearly understood. In my view, time priority is the critical difference between the ITS design and that of the NSTS.[21] Adding it to the ITS would bridge this difference and, consequently, push the ITS toward the black-box model of the NSTS.

Notes

1. Securities Exchange Act of 1934, Section 11A(a)(2), as added by the Securities Acts Amendments of 1975, P.L. No. 94-29 (June 4, 1975).
2. Some students of regulation have criticized Congress for its lack of restraint in creating agencies and delegating broad authority to them. See, for example, Mashaw, "Regulation, Logic, and Ideology," 3 *Regulation* 44 (November–December 1979) and Davis, "Regulatory Reform and Congressional Control of Regulation," 17 *New England Law Review* 1199 (1981–1982).
3. Section 11A(a)(1) of the Securities Exchange Act states:

The Congress finds that—

(A) The securities markets are an important national asset which must be preserved and strengthened.

(B) New data processing and communications techniques create the opportunity for more efficient and effective market operations.

(C) It is in the public interest and appropriate for the protection of investors and the maintenance of fair and orderly markets to assure—

(i) economically efficient execution of securities transactions;

(ii) fair competition among brokers and dealers, among exchange markets, and between exchange markets and markets other than exchange markets;

(iii) the availability to brokers, dealers, and investors of information with respect to quotations for and transactions in securities;

(iv) the practicability of brokers executing investors' orders in the best market; and

(v) an opportunity, consistent with the provisions of clauses (i) and (iv) of this subparagraph, for investors' orders to be executed without the participation of a dealer.

(D) The linking of all markets for qualified securities through communication and data processing facilities will foster efficiency, enhance competition, increase information available to brokers, dealers, and investors, facilitate the offsetting of investors' orders, and contribute to best execution of such orders.

4. See Section 11A(a)(1)(B), (C)(i) and C(iv) of the Securities Exchange Act, quoted in note 3.

5. Three particularly outspoken advocates of a totally automated securities market describe their proposal in Mendelson, Peake, and Williams, "Toward a Modern Exchange: The Peake-Mendelson-Williams Proposal for an Electronically Assisted Auction Market," in Bloch and Schwartz, eds., *Impending Changes for Securities Markets: What Role for the Exchanges?* (1979), chapter III.

6. See Section 11A(a)(1)(D) of the Securities Exchange Act, quoted in note 3.

7. I can think of at least two other national market system designs. One would emphasize Congress's endorsement of enhanced competition. This would require nothing more than eliminating all impediments to competition between and among marketplaces (in particular, Rule 390 of the New York Stock Exchange). A second design would restrict all trading in a given security to a single marketplace, but permit marketplaces to compete for exclusive listings.

8. For a more detailed description and analysis of the ITS, see SEC (Directorate of Economic and Policy Analysis), *A Monitoring Report on the Operation of the Intermarket Trading System: 1978–1981* (June 1982).

On January 26, 1978, the SEC states that it expected the exchanges and the National Association of Securities Dealers (NASD) to act jointly to establish, among other things, market linkage facilities within eight months. Securities Exchange Act Release No. 14416 (January 26, 1978). On March 9, 1978, five exchanges filed with the SEC a plan to establish and operate the ITS. The SEC approved the operation of the ITS for four months. Securities Exchange Act Release No. 14661 (April 14, 1978). The SEC extended its approval for an additional year in August 1978 and again for an additional 40 months in September 1979. Securities Exchange Act Release Nos. 15058 (August 11, 1978) and 16214 (September 21, 1979). Finally, in January 1983 the SEC approved continued operation of the ITS for an indefinite period. Securities Exchange Act Release No. 19456 (January 27, 1983).

9. Since NSTS participants need not be on the floor of the Cincinnati Stock Exchange (CSE), their access to an ITS terminal is indirect. A CSE employee on the floor relays ITS commitments between other marketplaces and NSTS participants. The linkage with the over-the-counter market, where obviously there is no exchange floor, is limited. See note 11.

10. The ITS also allows a commitment to be sent with no price assigned and to be executed "at the market" at the receiving marketplace.

11. The pilot phase of the CAES linkage was limited to thirty Rule 19c.3 stocks. The pilot phase (and the limitation on the number of stocks) was extended by the SEC pending action on a proposed order exposure rule. When the SEC decided to defer action on an order exposure rule, it permitted the expansion of the CAES linkage to include all Rule 19c.3 stocks effective September 15, 1983. Securities Exchange Act Release No. 20074 (August 12, 1983). Rule 19c.3 is beyond the scope of this chapter. Essentially, it permits exchange members to trade exchange-listed stocks over the counter—a practice that is otherwise prohibited by exchange rules. For more information, see Securities Exchange Act Release No. 18062 (August 25, 1981).

12. By making it easier and less costly for regional specialists to lay off imbalances, the ITS may also have contributed to the success of the small order execution systems of the regional exchanges. This success, in turn, may have stimulated the NYSE's development of its Registered Representative Rapid Response (R4) service.

13. The SEC has attempted to discern the effect of the ITS on primary market (NYSE and AMEX) bid-ask spreads by means of multiple regression analysis. No statistically significant effect has been found. See the report cited in note 8 and SEC (Directorate of Economic and Policy Analysis), *Analysis of Spreads on the New York Stock Exchange* (March 1981).

14. For a more detailed description and analysis of the NSTS, see SEC (Directorate of Economic and Policy Analysis), *A Monitoring Report on the Operation of the Cincinnati Stock Exchange National Securities Trading System: 1978–1982* (September 1982).

The SEC approved a nine-month pilot test of the NSTS in April 1978. Securities Exchange Act Release No. 14674 (April 18, 1978). The SEC extended its approval for one year in December 1978, and again in September 1979 extended it until January 31, 1983. Securities Exchange Act Release Nos. 15413 (December 15, 1978) and 16216 (September 21, 1979). In December 1982 the SEC gave the NSTS an indefinite extension. Securities Exchange Act Release No. 19315 (December 9, 1982).

15. Only "approved dealers" may enter both agency orders and dealer quotes. An approved dealer may be either a CSE member, in which case he participates from upstairs (in his own offices) via computer terminal, or a regional exchange specialist, in which case he uses a terminal located on his own floor (but no regional exchange currently has an NSTS terminal). Any CSE member may enter agency orders, either directly by means of an upstairs terminal or indirectly through a CSE employee.

16. The NSTS ensures price and time priority, but an agency order is always given priority over a dealer quote at the same price.

17. Researchers have not reached a consensus as to whether fragmentation is good or bad. Hamilton, for example, has concluded that the beneficial competitive effects of fragmentation exceed any detrimental effects. Hamilton, "Marketplace Fragmentation, Competition, and the Efficiency of the Stock Exchange," 34 *Journal of Finance* 171 (1979). On the other hand, Cohen et al. have concluded that fragmentation has a negative effect on the quality of securities markets. Cohen, Maier, Schwartz, and Whitcomb, "An Analysis of the Economic Justification for Consolidation in a Secondary Security Market," 6 *Journal of Banking and Finance* 117 (1982).

18. The conclusions of Cohen et al. are, I think, consistent with this. Cohen et al. recognize the practical inability of the ITS to provide time priority. They state, ". . . by its very nature an ITS linkage cannot preserve secondary trading priority rules (such as arrival time or size priority) that are used within an exchange." Ibid., p. 120. Thus Cohen et al. are saying that the ITS would not work, practically speaking, to provide time priority, whereas I am saying that if the ITS did work, the separate marketplaces (as sources of order flow) would ultimately merge into a single marketplace—either an exchange or a black box.

19. The SEC first endorsed the idea of a national market system (then referred to as a central market system) in the transmittal letter accompanying its *Institutional Investor Study Report* to Congress. H.R. doc. No. 92-64, 92nd Congress, 1st Session (March 10, 1971). In response to this endorsement, William McChesney Martin, Jr., produced a report, commissioned by the NYSE, in which he recommended the establishment of a "national exchange system." In this system all trading in a given stock would be confined to a single exchange. Martin, *The Securities Market: A Report with Recommendations* (August 5, 1971). Three weeks after the Martin Report was

published, the SEC announced that it would conduct hearings to examine, among other things, ". . . the desirability, structure and means of developing a national system of securities exchanges and the relationship of such a system to other securities markets." Securities Exchange Act Release No. 9315 (Aug. 26, 1971). At the conclusion of the hearings the SEC issued its *Statement of the Securities and Exchange Commission on the Future Structure of the Securities Markets* (February 2, 1972). Although the national market system remained a somewhat hazy concept, this statement clearly rejected Martin's recommendations. It called instead for ". . . a system of communications by which the various elements of the marketplace, be they exchanges or over-the-counter markets, are tied together," (p. 8). For a full discussion of the Martin Report, see Mendelson, "The Martin Report and Its Aftermath," *Bell Journal of Economics and Management Science* (Spring 1973), p. 250.

20. The potential for quote-matching in the ITS is a flaw only in the sense that it is inconsistent with true linkage. If viewed simply as a system to help smooth imbalances across marketplaces, the ITS, in my view, has no serious flaws.

21. Another obvious difference is the lack of an immediate execution capability in the ITS. I think, however, that time priority in the ITS would necessarily bring with it immediate execution. Without an immediate execution capability time priority would be unworkable. If an order were required to seek execution in the marketplace with time priority, there would have to be assurance that a commitment would not be rejected by that marketplace. Only immediate (or guaranteed) execution could provide that assurance. It is possible, of course, for the ITS to have an immediate execution capability without time priority. To be successful, however, a market-maker guaranteeing immediate execution through the ITS would need assurance that his quotes were not simply being matched by the other market makers. Only time priority could provide that assurance. I think, therefore, that time priority and immediate execution are inseparable.

19
Electronic Trading Systems: The User's Point of View

Roger W. Marshall
Severin C. Carlson

T here have been numerous attempts over the last twenty-five years to introduce innovative electronic trading technology to the security trading markets. In the first stage technology introduced by Quotron Inc. in 1957 provided subscribers with timely transmissions of stock prices, bond prices, news reports, and interrogative capabilities. In the next stage, technology progressed beyond the basic reporting of past information to the provision of bid and offer price information prior to executing a trade. Finally, technology now available allows electronic trade execution without intervention by a broker or market maker. Some of these attempts have succeeded and are currently in use; others have clearly failed.

Since the early years of organized trading in equity securities, a number of forces have affected the methods of trading equity securities. The relatively recent flurry of changes and proposed changes in the way equity securities are traded should be considered both evolutionary and revolutionary. The interaction between the actual participants in market trading and the suppliers of market-trading technology results in an evolution of the trading process. On the other hand, government regulations can initiate, interrupt, or stop the evolutionary process by proposing revolutionary changes. These major participants and the innovation process itself will determine the future of electronic trading.

Evaluating the evolutionary advancement of electronic trading systems requires an understanding of innovation as a process and the interaction of participants in the trading industry. Kamien and Schwartz provide an extensive survey of the market conditions most conducive to innovation;[1] their findings show that innovation within an industry requires more than the development of new technology. The employment of available technology to provide a new product or service is unlikely to occur unless there is an expected economic gain. Once the economic gain is present, it is inconclusive whether innovation is advanced more rapidly by suppliers or users of technology.

The views presented in this chapter are those of the authors and are not to be interpreted in any way as the views of Smith Barney, Harris Upham & Co., Inc.

The second catalyst of innovation results from government regulation. Therefore, a significant participant in electronic trading innovation is the federal government and its agencies. In its March 10, 1971, Letter of Transmittal to Congress regarding its Institutional Investor Study Report,[2] the Securities and Exchange Commission (SEC) wrote:

> A major goal and ideal of the securities markets and the securities industry has been the creation of a strong central market system for securities of national importance, in which all buying and selling interests in these securities could participate and be represented under a competitive regime. Until comparatively recently there were serious technological limitations on creating a system where all interests of investors could be represented in a central market. This is no longer the case.

In 1975 Congress amended the Securities Exchange Act of 1934 and directed the SEC to establish a national market system (NMS). The NMS concept requires technological innovation with uncertain economic consequence. The intent of the NMS is the creation of the most efficient market possible. In the absence of economic innovation, however, an NMS may result in a trading system that is marginally more efficient but less economical.

Although the purpose of this chapter is to review successful technology transfers of electronic trading in order to provide a clearer picture of the future trading arena, the discussion will focus on examples of electronic trading systems. The next section will review the evolving nature of electronic trading fostered by the suppliers and users of the technology. The final section will examine the efforts to develop and regulate a national market system. A listing of additional systems is presented at the end of this chapter to illustrate the extent to which innovation is occurring.

Evolution of Electronic Trading

The necessary climate for evolutionary innovation in electronic trading includes the availability of technology and economic gains from adoption. Although the development of electronic technology is exogenous to the securities industry, the suppliers of electronic trading technology must provide state-of-the-art electronics tailored to industry needs, and they must receive economic gain. These gains may result from increases in revenues and/or decreases in costs in excess of the technology adoption costs. We will review various electronic trading innovations and the potential sources of economic gain to evaluate possible motives of the innovation adopter.

Examples of early innovation in electronic trading include: Quotron (1957), AutEx (1969), INSTINET (1969), and the National Association of

Securities Dealers' automated quotation system (NASDAQ) 1971. Each of these services provided state-of-the-art delivery of information to users. Each service introduced up-to-the-minute quotations on recent stock and bond prices, as well as world news information. A review of the basic role of each service will provide insight into the motivation behind user adoption.

Quotron terminals initially provided bond and stock prices to all segments of the trading community. The technology involved the electronic transmission of current stock prices, bond prices, and news information. Quotron's ability to provide information faster, along with its ability to recall specific securities latest prices, represented a significant advance over the ticker tape. The central role of speed of information in security trading is the primary motive for adopting this technology. Fast access to the latest information presumably allows better investment advice and potential profit to broker-dealers. In addition, a broker advertising the latest information can gain through increased sales.

AutEx began as a computer network for large block traders. As an electronic link between block traders, AutEx claims to provide a comprehensive view of the block trading market. The system is interactive, permitting traders to inform the institutional community of their desire to execute a large trade. The messages may express general interest or more specific information on price and quantity. The users include broker-dealers and institutional investors interested in block trades. AutEx was initiated at the time the third market was expanding as a significant market for large block orders of NYSE securities. More efficient third markets offered an alternative to trading on the NYSE, with both traders and institutions receiving economic gains from lower transaction costs.

NASDAQ provides market-making information on nationally traded over-the-counter (OTC) securities. Unlike AutEx, which specializes in block transactions, NASDAQ developed the first electronic trading markets for individual securities where market makers could enter their latest bid and offer prices on securities. Users of NASDAQ Level III now have access to the complete range of bid and offer prices and can trade by telephone with the market-maker offering the best price. The potential for a more efficient market in OTC securities provided the best motive for adopting this new technology. The users of the technology could be profit-motivated dealers or brokers intent on advertising the availability of the best price information. Increased business for those brokers would provide economic gain, justifying the adoption of the technology.

The third stage in the evolution of electronic trading moves beyond the timely delivery of information toward improving the actual security transaction. The absence of fixed commission rate, combined with adopted first-stage innovations providing fast, accurate information to all participants, introduced the securities industry to the world of price competition. The primary motive to innovate continues to be economic gain, but the innovative systems reflect the new environment; here cost reduction has replaced timely information as the primary motive modifying the trading environment.

AUTOPER (1983), SCOREX (1979), MAX (1980), and CAES (1979) are examples of national, regional, and OTC market attempts to provide cost-saving electronic trading to brokers. The economic gain for the sponsoring market is increased trading attracted by low-cost electronic systems available on their market. Cost savings to brokers include reduced paperwork and labor savings from reduced time spent on each transaction. Additional factors affecting adoption of electronic trading include the following: system reliability, turnaround time, the cost of integrating into present systems, and the quality of execution.

The development and implementation of the AUTOPER system at the American Stock Exchange (AMEX) is an example of an electronic trading system on a national exchange. Before AUTOPER was available, small orders were automatically routed to the specialist and printed as they arrived. After printing, a clerk would tear off the order and hand it to the specialist. Once in the specialist's hand, the order would be held until executed. Upon execution, numerous pieces of information required for tape reporting, clearing, and confirmation were entered on a mark-sense card and fed into a card reader.

AUTOPER was implemented to replace the need for hard copy, thereby saving time and reducing the potential for human error. As an order coming in on AUTOPER is displayed on a touch screen, the specialist is alerted to the order by a tone from the system. If the trade is acceptable, the simplest option available to the specialist is to touch the screen and thereby execute the trade. Another touch will provide clearing information. AUTOPER then sends confirmation electronically to the brokerage firm that has entered the order. At present, reporting the trade to the tape is completed manually; future automation of this task is likely. AUTOPER provides economic gain by reducing paperwork, bookkeeping, and labor. In addition, AUTOPER uses existing facilities to minimize integration costs.

SCOREX is a successful electronic trading system sponsored by the Pacific Stock Exchange (PSE). SCOREX offers the actual execution of trades without benefit of a dealer. The motivation for the development and implementation of SCOREX include the cost-saving motives underlying the development of AUTOPER, plus the desire to compete with national markets. Since many securities listed on the New York Stock Exchange (NYSE) are also traded on the PSE, the design of SCOREX guarantees that orders will be executed at a price at least equal to the best quote available on any of five regional and two national exchanges. The system claims to execute trades within 30 seconds. Further, it automatically reports the trade to the tape, sends confirmation to the broker, and transmits clearing information to the Clearing

ing technology that has been developed or adapted exogenous to the industry has provided economic gain by solving or reducing an existing problem. Quotron and AutEx are prime examples of technical developments that benefit investors by improving the timeliness of information. Changes in the competitive environment have also acted as catalysts for technological advances. The relatively recent emphasis on price competition between retail brokerage houses intent on providing lowest cost trading has fostered innovations. Electronic trading systems such as AUTOPER and SCOREX provide high-quality executions for traders while reducing costs. The future evolution of trading is expected to follow the past pattern of adoption when accompanied by economic gain. In a competitive industry, innovation spurred by economic gain will benefit consumers through lower prices. Alternatively, innovations mandated by regulatory constraints generally result in economic costs that are passed on to the consumer in the form of higher prices.

Regulatory pressure is the prime force behind the adoption of technology that is unlikely to produce economic gains for the ultimate users. The development of the national market system's Consolidated Quotation System presents a clear example of new technology that not only automates information, but also alters the structure of the trading market. Unless the users of the technology agree on the benefits, implementation of a usable system is not feasible. Even though the motives behind rule changes may be virtually faultless, the absence of economic gain necessitates costly and in some cases impossible enforcement.

If the SEC were to adopt an evolutionary rather than a revolutionary approach to developing a national market system, success would be more likely. As we have noted, rule changes generally result in costs to brokerage firms or specialists, but in little observable gain. Perhaps less costly solutions would be developed if the affected parties were included in the design and implementation of future changes. Further, those responsible for regulating the trading industry must understand the full impact that adoption of a particular technology has on the actual working structure of the market. A program of on-the-job training for SEC staff at exchanges, the NASD, or brokerage firms would provide valuable insight. Finally, the SEC should acknowledge the role of economic gain in the innovation process, and should encourage profit-making ventures by firms outside the trading industry.

Chronology of Electronic Innovations

1867 Stock tickers first introduced.[8]

1878 First telephones introduced in the NYSE.

1881 Annunciator board installed for paging members.

1919 Separate ticker system for bonds installed.

1930 Faster ticker (500 characters a minute) installed.

1957 Quotron Systems, Inc., begins disseminating information on last sale.

1964 New ticker (900 characters a minute) put in service.

1966 Transmission of trade and quote data from floor fully automated.

1969 Autex Systems, a subsidiary of Xerox Corporation, offers block traders a means of seeking out interests.

Instinet, a trading system developed by Institutional Networks Corp., begins operation.

COMEX, an order-routing system of the Pacific Stock Exchange (later known as SCOREX) begins accepting order flow.

1971 NASDAQ begins operation in OTC securities.

1974 Consolidated tape pilot initiated.

1976 New high-speed data line at the NYSE transmitting up to 36,000 characters a minute.

The NYSE's Designated Order Turnaround (DOT) system inaugurated.

The Philadelphia Stock Exchange's PACE system begins operation.

1977 The NYSE's Automated Bond System begins.

The American Stock Exchange begins its PER system.

1978 The Intermarket Trading System begins.

The Cincinnati Stock Exchange's National Securities Trading System (NTS) begins.

AutoQuote is initiated.

1979 The COMEX system on the Pacific Stock Exchange is upgraded and renamed SCOREX.

The NASD adds an automatic execution capability to the NASDAQ system (CAES).

1980 The NYSE begins its OARS system.

The Midwest Stock Exchange introduces its automated execution system (MAX).

The NYSE begins its Registered Representative Rapid Response experiment (R4).

1982 Experimental linkage between ITS and CAES begins.

1983 The American Stock Exchange introduces AUTOPER.

Instinet adds automatic execution capabilities.

1984 The American Stock Exchange experiments with AUTO AMOS, adaptation of AUTOPER to options.

Herzog, Heine, and Geduld introduce their COLT system for executing orders automatically.

The Midwest Stock Exchange introduces MAX OTC, an automated trading system for OTC securities.

The NASD plans to introduce a Small Order Execution System (SOES) allowing automated executions.

The NYSE introduces super-DOT, which allows automated execution in certain stocks when the bid-ask spread equals one-eighth.

Notes

1. M. Kamien and N. Schwartz, "Market Structure and Innovation: A Survey," *Journal of Economic Literature* 13(1975):1–37.

2. SEC, Institutional Investor Study Report, H.R. Doc. #92-64, 92nd Congress, 1st Session.

3. Securities and Exchange Act of 1934, 11a, 15 U.S.C. 78k-1(a)(1)(A) (1976).

4. Id.

5. N.S. Posner, "Restructuring the Stock Markets: A Critical Look at the SEC's National Market System," *New York University Law Review* 56, no. 883 (November–December 1981):916.

6. The American, Cincinnati, Boston, Midwest, New York, Pacific, and Philadelphia Stock Exchanges are members of ITS.

7. U.S. Securities and Exchange Commission, Directorate of Economic and Policy Analysis, "A Monitoring Report on the Operation of the Intermarket Trading System" (February 1981), Appendix B.

8. The principal source for this chronology is NYSE, *1983 Fact Book,* New York Stock Exchange, Inc., June 1983.

20
Can You Get There from Here?

Seymour Smidt

This chapter focuses on the process of achieving change in the structure of the securities markets. My comments concerning this issue might be viewed in relation to four chapters of this book. Amihud and Mendelson (chapter 15) provide a vision of what an ideal trading system might look like; to focus on this objective, they wisely avoid dealing with the issue of how you get there from here. Marshall and Carlson (chapter 19) focus our attention on the issue of how change can be brought about; to accomplish *their* objective, they wisely avoid the issue of where we are going (arguing about the ultimate objective is almost always guaranteed to prevent agreement about the next step). Davis (chapter 18) focuses on whether or not the last step was in the right direction; this is a useful way of deciding the right direction for the next step. Williams (chapter 17) summarizes the recent steps that have been taken by the industry to satisfy the Congressional mandate that there be a national market system.

As for where and how we might want to proceed, consider the following statement by Amihud and Mendelson: ". . . a computerized exchange is likely to benefit from potential competition among these three forms of exchange. Even if some of the mechanisms may ultimately be eliminated for some securities, this should occur through natural forces, rather than by design." As I read that I thought it sounded familiar; I wondered where I had heard it before. Then I found the following sentence: "Our objective is to see a strong central market system created, to which all investors have access, in which all may participate in accordance with their respective capabilities, and which is controlled not only by regulation, but also by the forces of competition."

This second sentence comes from the letter of transmittal of the Institutional Investor Study.[1] It is a key sentence for our purposes. It can be read in at least two different ways. It can be read to emphasize that a strong central market system be created, or to emphasize ". . . which is controlled by the forces of competition." I have a point of view about how it should be read, and about how at least some of us who had a role in it *thought* it should be read. My feeling is that the key part of the sentence is ". . . controlled by the forces of competition. . . ." That is, the idea of a central or national market system was advanced as a means to achieve that competition. I will explain how this came about and why I think that is the right interpretation. More details concerning the history are given in chapter 17 by Williams.

In the late 1960s Congress and others were worried that the increasing role of financial institutions in the equity markets might be creating various undesirable consequences for those markets. Accordingly, they asked the SEC to do a study on that subject. This study concluded, essentially, that institutions were a benign influence in the market—that they were not creating the kinds of problems that people had feared. Rather, it was believed that the markets were suffering from a lack of competition in the market-making function.

Both the conclusion with respect to institutions and the conclusion with respect to competition were based on solid factual grounds. Facts, of course, are seldom 100 percent decisive about any issue. But these conclusions, however controversial, did have a solid basis in fact.

An implication one might draw from these factual conclusions is that more competition would be better. That, however, is a policy judgment. There is not the same factual basis for comparing a system in which market makers do not compete with one in which market makers do compete. It could, in fact, turn out that the problems with competing market makers are even worse that those created by noncompeting market makers. In that case, one certainly would not want to proceed to strengthen competition between the market makers. Nonetheless, the authors of the sentence wanted more competition; they wanted it among the market makers in particular; and they believed the national market system was one of the opening wedges that might lead to that increased competition.

Congress also, at the same time, eliminated fixed minimum commissions. Or, more accurately, Congress ratified the elimination of fixed minimum commissions among institutional investors (because the market had already done that), and extended the elimination to individual investors (which the market had not done, and probably would not do today).

One might well question what the proper role of government is in these areas. My own feeling is that there is substantial evidence that market making in itself is *not* a natural monopoly, that economies of scale are minimal, and that in certain circumstances it is very easy to develop competition among market makers. If that is the case, the role of government could be minimal.

On the other hand, I think there is substantial evidence that there are sizable economies of scale in providing a marketplace (that is, an exchange), so in this area there is a problem of potential monopoly. It is here that we continue to recognize a possible role for government. Although we may, of course, still do best to let the forces of competition do the work, the competitive forces will have a harder struggle, they will not work as effectively, and they will not work as fast.

For example, one might interpret the existence and the popularity of stock options as a way of competing. Buying and selling stock options of various kinds is a substitute for buying and selling stocks, and the transaction costs may be considerably lower. Thus the stock exchange may indeed have lost potential business because the new options market developed. The futures market also has developed products that are to some extent substitutes for owning stock. These are not exact substitutes, and they have limitations; but this form of competition can be very effective in providing competition to the traditional equity marketplace.

In my view, the SEC and Congress wanted to introduce more competition and were using the mechanism of a national market system to do so. Rather than making a heavy-handed, frontal attack (in a way that would be much more dramatic than the examples given by Marshall and Carlson), the regulators made a flank attack, saying, "Maybe we can get these exchanges to compete."

With hindsight, this does not look like a totally successful strategy. However, I think that to evaluate it, you ought to put yourself back in time seven or eight years and try to say, "Well, successful compared to what? What else might they have done? Do nothing? Try even more direct ways of breaking up the monopoly? Adjust to the monopoly?" Perhaps the end result will turn out to be successful, perhaps not. In any event, I do not think we ought to judge progress by how well we have succeeded in developing a national market system. On that score, we have not done well, but I do not think that is where we were trying to go.

In some respects I am reasonably optimistic; the system has been opened up to some extent. The economies of scale in providing a marketplace are still very substantial, however, and one could imagine the technological changes that are taking place right now simply grinding to a halt. Or else change might just slow down dramatically until at some point it is forced to occur in a revolutionary rather than an evolutionary way. The problem of continuing the kind of progress we have been experiencing is real; so too is the problem of deciding what, if anything, the role of government ought to be in relation to the issue.

There are dramatically different systems of trading around the world (a point well illustrated by Whitcomb in chapter 16). It may be hard to explain some of them in terms of the demands of the trading community. Sometimes the markets have moved in a direction one would not at all expect from the nature of trading. The most important thing is that the systems that exist are the ones people are accustomed to. For example, do we have a typewriter keyboard that is optimal for its use? The important fact is that there are millions of people who have learned to type on that keyboard, and they are most reluctant to change. The simple fact that we are used to it, that people are adjusted to it, is a big part of the economies of scale we are referring to in the marketplace. An immense sort of inertia keeps us in the existing situation. Only if the system gets obsolete *enough* will some change eventually occur.

Before 1965 (to be safe), the New York Stock Exchange operated in essentially the same way it did in 1875. Nothing much had happened. Now, by comparison, we are in a period of somewhat rapid change, but it is still slow when compared to other activities. I do not think there is anything in the system that will guarantee that it will ever evolve to a competitive optimum; at least, I do not think so when I consider how the marketplace actually operates in reality.

Note

1. See U.S. Securities and Exchange Commission, *Institutional Investor Study Report* (Washington, D.C.: U.S. Government Printing Office, 1971).

21
Star Wars Technology in Trading

William A. Lupien

I have spent seventeen years as a specialist on the Pacific Exchange, one of those regionals that has been trying to get more than a 15 percent share of the market. Through that experience, and from representing the Pacific Exchange at both Congressional and SEC hearings on market structure, I have had the opportunity over the years to hear a lot of the debate, both official and informal. In addition, I spent over two years working on the ITS system.

Around 1976, after hearing about Instinet (Institutional Networks, Inc.) for five years, I became the first specialist in the country to subscribe to that system. It was a big step. Instinet was a so-called fourth-market system that was considered anathema to the specialist system. Why would a specialist be interested in such a system? There are several reasons. It was a far superior information system; it told me a lot about what my competitors were doing and what the markets were. It was an efficient way of having that information delivered to me. There were orders within the system with which I did want to trade. There were customer orders I represented in the specialist book that matched up with the orders in the Instinet system. Thus we began trading on the Pacific Exchange with Instinet. Then Instinet became a member of the exchange. And so the evolution continued; it still is continuing in 1984.

During the last five years I personally participated in four private financings of Instinet. A year and a half ago, the industry was ready for a new type of technology; Instinet had what we were looking for. Last year, I moved to New York and joined Instinet.

The securities industry, unfortunately, is still fragmented. So far there has been no cohesive way of integrating the various strong points the different markets have to offer. Instinet, as it evolves and improves, goes into the various markets—the over-the-counter market, the national and regional exchanges, the primary market, the international market—and pulls out of those markets the best they have to offer. Instinet then provides the information.

A big change has occurred in the securities industry. Ten years ago we used to fight fiercely over our own turf because everyone was afraid of being gored economically. Today, people have adjusted to the changes and are willing to look at new ideas. For instance, many people who fought the concept of automated trading are now strong advocates of it. Ten years ago we had tremendous debates. Now the problem we all face is simply adjusting fast enough to the various technological and structural changes that are taking place, regardless of the debates.

Instinet demonstrates the important role of electronic trading in the securities industries. At present the electronic systems are mostly providers of information on quotes and prices from the various markets, and a few of them allow automated trading. They save time and money in execution and, by providing a link between the markets that already exist, increase market efficiency. It is possible, however, that there will be an electronic trading system that will become a marketplace by itself, which will replace rather than serve the existing securities market. This marketplace will allow for open or concealed bids, direct execution against quoted prices or entering orders on open limit order books, block trading as well as small-order executions, price negotiations, and so on. That is, the electronic trading system will serve as a market by itself, not as an auxiliary to the existing market.

I also see a big opportunity for the securities industry. There is a latent demand in our markets that would far exceed the current volume records we think of as being so high today. If you opened up the opportunity, and had access and information freely exchanged across the potential universe of investors, we might be looking at not 100 million but perhaps 500 million share days. Of course, the systems would have to be in place to handle it. They will be, however, for today we are experiencing rapid technological change. Not only has technology changed, but the cost of using that technology has come down appreciably. Now costs are at a level where suddenly there are clear economic advantages for the industry to take advantage of the new high-tech systems. Consequently, our industry and the United States are not only the leaders but the envy of the world in terms of markets. I hope we continue to stay out in front, and continue to innovate.

To date, we have argued about the national market system; I think we should forget that and get on with a much bigger issue. This is happening anyway, even without our talking about it: Internationalization of the securities markets is occurring rapidly. Today technology allows people in distant places to interact and actually to trade, almost as if they were on the floor of an exchange.

In February 1984 I personally did some trades (for both listed and over-the-counter securities) on an IBM PC in Johannesburg, South Africa. Even though I knew that technologically it was supposed to work, it still excited me when I pushed the button and, in 22 seconds, had a 4,400 share execution for an over-the-counter stock—right on an IBM PC in Johannesburg, South Africa. It challenged a lot of people who were observing my demonstration. "Well, that's obviously a canned program you've got in that PC," someone said. "No," I replied, "that was real live trading in the United States." One person challenged me to such an extent that he made me buy 100 shares of a stock I did not even know; after that, he agreed that the system did indeed work.

In Johannesburg it takes 10 to 30 minutes to get an international phone line; but you can consummate a trade on an IBM PC in 22 seconds. Opportunities of this kind are going to broaden what we think of as a great market today. They can bring in tremendous liquidity, for there is much latent demand out there. Still, there is a great gulf between what technology can do today and what is available. In the not-too-distant future, trading will be far more technologically advanced than it is today. Furthermore, as part of that development, markets from around the world will be far more closely linked together. Let us hope that we will become the focal point of that international system.

Index

Glossary

ADR   American Depository Receipt

Agency Market   A system where market professionals act as agents for public orders

AMEX   American Stock Exchange

Arbitrage   Buying and selling the same (or similar) securities to take advantage of price differentials

Ask Price   A quoted price at which a trader is willing to sell, also called offer price

Auction Market   A system where agents participate in a centralized location, the trading floor

Autex   An electronic system that enables block traders to seek out interest

Autoper   The American Stock Exchange's automated small order handling system

Bid Price   A quoted price at which a trader is willing to buy

Block Trades   Trades involving more than 10,000 shares

CAES   NASD's automated execution system for NASDAQ-NMS issues

Call Market   A trading system where orders are batched for simultaneous execution at the same price

CATS   Computer Assisted Trading System

CBOE   Chicago Board of Options Exchange

CFTC   Commodity Futures Trading Commission

Chess Strategy   When you are in trouble, push the pawns

CLOB   Consolidated limit order book

Consolidated Tape   A consolidated display of transaction prices and volume on a real time basis

Continuous Market   A trading system where orders are executed any time they cross during the trading day

CQS   Consolidated Quotations System

Dealer Market   A system in which dealers negotiate and participate in transactions generally in geographically dispersed locations

DOT   The New York Stock Exchange's automated small order handling system

Externalities   The costs/benefits of a trade that are not realized by the participants of that trade

Instinet   An electronic system that provides a fourth market and brokerage services

ITS   Intermarket Trading System

Limit Order   An order to buy (sell) which specifies a maximum (minimum) price at which a buyer (seller) is willing to transact

Limit Order Book   The book in which specialists record limit orders

Market Maker   A professional trader who provides quotes to the market

Market Order   An order to buy or to sell at the prevailing market quotes

MAX   The Midwest Stock Exchange's automated execution system

NASD   National Association of Securities Dealers Inc.

NASDAQ   National Association of Securities Dealers Automated Quotations

NASDAQ-NMS   NASDAQ stocks that are traded in ITS

NMS   National Market System, a national integration of securities markets according to the Congressional mandate of 1975

19c-3 Stocks   Listed stocks that can be traded off-board by member firms

NSTS   The Cincinnati Stock Exchange's National Securities Trading System

NYSE   New York Stock Exchange

NYSE Rule 390   NYSE's trading rule that prohibits off-board trading by member firms

OARS   Opening Automated Reporting System, an NYSE order handling system

Offer Price   See *ask price*

OTC   Over-the-Counter

Pareto Optimal   A market result is pareto optimal if no one participant can benefit without making at least one other participant worse off

Price Priority   A trading rule which specifies that best priced orders (highest bids and lowest asks) execute first

Quotron System   A system that provides on line dissemination of quotations, news, and other trading information for stocks and bonds

R4   The NYSE's Registered Representative Rapid Response service

Reservation Price   The highest (lowest) price at which a buyer (seller) is willing to transact

SCOREX   An order routing system of the Pacific Stock Exchange

Securities Acts Amendments of 1975   Congressional amendments of the Securities Acts of 1933 and 1934; the amendments introduced negotiated commissions and mandated development of the National Market System

SEC   Securities & Exchange Commission

SEC Rule 19c-3   SEC rule that overrides off-board trading rules for listed stocks

SEC Rule 415   SEC rule that permits shelf registration of new issues

Short Sell   The sale of borrowed shares

SIAC   Securities Industry Automation Corporation

SOES   NASD's automated small order execution system

Spread   The difference between the bid and the ask prices

SRO   Self-regulatory organization (e.g., NYSE, AMEX, NASD)

Super DOT   The New York Stock Exchange's automated small order execution system

Surveillance System   An SRO system for monitoring trades and the quality of the market

TARS   Trade Acceptance and Reconciliation Service

The Crowd   Floor traders who gather at the specialist's post to trade shares

Tick Test Rule   An exchange rule prohibiting the specialist from buying (selling) at a price higher (lower) than the last transaction price

Time Priority   A trading rule which specifies that, when orders are at the same price, they execute according to their time of arrival, with those which were placed first executing first

Upstairs Trading   Generally refers to trades that are negotiated off the exchange

About the Contributors

William M. Batten is the former chairman and chief executive officer of the New York Stock Exchange. Previously, he had served as chairman and CEO of J.C. Penney Co. He is currently a member of the White House Preservation Fund and the President's Commission on Executive Exchange. He is a graduate of Ohio State University, Columbus.

Ernest Bloch is the C.W. Gerstenberg Professor of Finance, Graduate School of Business Administration, New York University. Previously, he was an economist and special assistant with the Federal Reserve Bank of New York. His current research interests are in the areas of investment banking and the regulation of financial institutions. He is currently completing a textbook, *Investment Banking*. He received a B.S.S. degree (City College), an M.A. (Columbia University), and a Ph.D. (The New School).

Severin Carlson is an assistant professor of finance, University of Rhode Island. He holds a BS degree (Northeastern University), and MBA and DBA degrees (Indiana University).

Kalman J. Cohen is the Distinguished Bank Research Professor at the Fuqua School of Business, Duke University. He is the author of six books and numerous articles in banking, finance, and securities markets. He holds a B.A. degree (Reed College), and M. Litt. (Oxford University), and M.S. and Ph.D. degrees (Carnegie Institute of Technology).

Robert M. Conroy is an assistant professor of finance, University of North Carolina—Chapel Hill. He has published a number of articles in the microstructure literature. He received his doctorate in finance from Indiana University.

Jeffry L. Davis is the director of Directorate of Economic and Policy Analysis at the Securities and Exchange Commission. He holds a B.A. degree (University of California, Riverside), an M.A. (University of California, Los Angeles), and a J.D. (George Washington University).

Richard S. Falk is executive vice president and manager of the Equity Division, Paine Webber Capital Markets. Previously he was executive vice president at Paine Webber Mitchell Hutchins. He is a member of the Securities Industry Association's Institutional Committee and the New York Stock Exchange's Upstairs Traders Advisory Committee. He is a graduate of Stanford University.

Samuel E. Hunter is a senior vice president and director of Merrill Lynch, Pierce, Fenner & Smith Inc., and director of the Securities Trading Division. Previously, he has been chairman of the NYSE's Upstairs Traders Advisory Committee, governor of the AMEX, and director of the Security Traders Association of New York. He holds a B.A. degree (Yale University) and an MBA degree (New York University).

William A. Lupien is president and chairman of the board of the Institutional Networks Corporation. Previously he was a specialist at the Pacific Stock Exchange, and served on that exchange's Board of Governors. He is a graduate of San Diego State College.

Richard G. Macris is a research analyst with the First Boston Corporation in the financial futures/options area. Previously he held a position as an option strategist with Smith Barney, Harris Upham & Co., Inc. and has published articles on trading strategies. He received both his B.A. and M.B.A. from New York University.

Steven F. Maier is president and CEO of UAI Technology, Inc., and adjunct professor of business administration at the Fuqua School of Business, Duke University. He has authored two books and many articles in the areas of security market structure and cash management. He holds a B.A. degree (Cornell University) and M.S. and Ph.D. degrees (Stanford University).

Roger W. Marshall is Second Vice President, Strategic Planning, Smith Barney Harris Upham & Co. Previously he was a financial economist at the Directorate of Economic and Policy Analysis of the Securities and Exchange Commission, and was the Assistant Director of Marketing Research and Planning of the American Stock Exchange. He holds B.A. and M.A. degrees (the State University of New York, Binghamton).

Haim Mendelson is an associate professor of business administration at the University of Rochester. His research interests include the study of exchange mechanisms, the economics of computer management, and database management systems. He is currently working on a book on the economics of information systems management. He holds B.Sc. and M.Sc. degrees (Hebrew University) and a Ph.D. (Tel Aviv University).

John J. Phelan, Jr. is chairman and chief executive officer of the New York Stock Exchange and of the New York Futures Exchange. Previous to his current position, he was a member on the NYSE's trading floor, a vice chairman, and then president and chief operating officer of the Exchange. He is a graduate of Adelphi University.

Susan M. Phillips is chairman of the Commodity Futures Trading Commission. Currently, she is on leave from a faculty position at the Business School of the University of Iowa. Previously she was a Brookings Economic Policy Fellow and an Economic Fellow with the Securities and Exchange Commission. Along with numerous articles, she has coauthored *The SEC and the Public Interest*. She holds a B.A. degree (Agnes Scott College) and M.A. and Ph.D. degrees (Louisiana State University).

Douglas Scarff is a partner of Lane and Edison, and adjunct professor at Georgetown University Law Center. Previously he served on the staff of the Division of Market Regulation of the Securities and Exchange Commission. He received a B.A. (Dartmouth College) and a J.D. (Michigan Law School).

Paul S. Schreiber is a partner at Kramer, Levin, Nessen, Kamin & Frankel. An active practitioner of securities and commodities law, he has represented brokerage firms, investment companies, and other institutions in the financial services industry, has written on the investment activities and fiduciary responsibility of institutional investors, and is a member of the New York Bar Association's committee on commodities regulation. He received a B.S. degree (City University of New York), and LL.B. and LL.M. degrees (New York University).

Seymour Smidt is the Nicholas H. Noyes Professor of Economics and Finance, Graduate School of Management, Cornell University. Previously, he served as associate director of the Securities and Exchange Commission's Institutional Investor Study. He has published two books and many articles in the areas of security market structure and capital budgeting. He recently completed a report comparing trading floor practices on futures exchanges and stock exchanges for the American Enterprise Institute. He received a Ph.D. degree from the University of Chicago.

Hans R. Stoll is the Anne Marie and Thomas B. Walker, Jr. Professor of Finance at the Owen Graduate School of Management, Vanderbilt University. Previously, he had been on the staff of the Institutional Investor Study of the Securities and Exchange Commission. He has published numerous articles in the areas of securities markets, commodity and option markets, and foreign exchange rates. He received a B.A. degree (Swarthmore College), and MBA and Ph.D. degrees (the University of Chicago).

Donald Stone is a senior partner of Lasker, Stone, and Stern. Previously, he held the position of vice chairman of the New York Stock Exchange, was a member of the board of directors of the New York Stock Exchange and of the New York Futures Exchange, and served as a member of the Securities and Exchange Commission's Institutional Investor Study. He is a graduate of New York University.

John T. Wall is executive vice president, Member and Market Services of the National Association of Securities Dealers. He is responsible for the overall development of the market for NASDAQ securities, through NASD services to NASDAQ issuers, market makers and securities salesmen. He is a graduate of the University of Notre Dame.

David K. Whitcomb is professor of finance, Graduate School of Management, Rutgers University. He is the author of two books and numerous articles in the areas of security market microstructure, industrial organization, and welfare economics. He holds a B.S.B.A. degree (Babson College) and a Ph.D. (Columbia University).

Lawrence J. White is professor of economics at the Graduate School of Business Administration, New York University. He has held the position of director of Economic Policy Office, Antitrust Division, U.S. Department of Justice, and served on the senior staff of the President's Council of Economic Advisors. He has published seven books and numerous articles in the areas of industrial organization and regulation. He holds a B.A. degree (Harvard University), an M.Sc. (London School of Economics) and a Ph.D. (Harvard University).

Stephen L. Williams is senior vice president, Planning Division, the American Stock Exchange. He is responsible for the development of new automation and communications services, including the long-range planning of trading systems and operations. He serves as president of the American Stock Exchange Clearing Corporation and as a director of the National Securities Clearing Corporation. He received a Ph.D. degree from the Massachusetts Institute of Technology.

About the Editors

Yakov Amihud is associate professor of finance at the Graduate School of Business Administration, New York University, visiting from the Faculty of Management, Tel Aviv University. He holds a B.Sc. from the Hebrew University and M.Sc. and Ph.D. from New York University. He has published extensively in leading journals. His research interests include the microstructure of securities markets, capital markets, corporate finance policies, industrial organization, and monetary economics.

Thomas S.Y. Ho is associate professor of finance at New York University. He received his B.Sc. from Warwick University, M.Sc. and Ph.D. from the University of Pennsylvania. He has written papers on optimal dealer pricing strategies and designs of securities markets. Beyond microstructure research, he also studies the pricing of fixed-income securities and contingent claims.

Robert A. Schwartz is professor of economics and finance at the Graduate School of Business Administration, New York University. He has been a member of the faculty of New York University's Graduate Business School since 1965. He received a Ph.D. in economics from Columbia University, an MBA degree from the Graduate School of Business of Columbia University, and a B.A. from New York University. His recent research has been in the area of financial economics, with a primary focus on the microstructure and architecture of security markets. He has also made contributions in the areas of credit market theory, industrial organization, and philanthropic contributions. He has published numerous journal papers, is co-editor of *Impending Changes for Securities Markets: What Role for the Exchanges?*, JAI Press, is co-author of *The Microstructure of Security Markets: Theory and Implications,* Prentice-Hall, forthcoming, and is currently working with Thomas S.Y. Ho on *Security Markets: Structure, Market Making, and Trading*, a textbook to be published by Harper & Row. For the past two years, he has been an associate editor of *The Journal of Finance.*